The V. Sorrowful Mystery.
The Brazen Serpent in the Wilderness.

LEGE ☩ ET ☩ IN ☩ PROPHETIS

ƆEUM ☩ ET ☩ FILIUM ☩ TUUM

THE SIGN OF SALVATION ON WHICH ALL WHO LOOKED WERE HEALED.

See p. 91.

The Old Testament Types of
The Prayer of Moses on the Mount.

ROSA ☩ MYSTICA ☩ PASSIM ☩ IN

ᴀᴄUMBRA ☩ ᴀ ☩ ORA ☩ PRO ☩ NOBIS

THE VICTORY GAINED BY THE OUTSTRETCHED HANDS OF THE LEADER OF THE PEOPLE.

Frontispiece.

THE BOOK OF THE HOLY ROSARY

A

POPULAR DOCTRINAL EXPOSITION

OF ITS

FIFTEEN MYSTERIES,

MAINLY CONVEYED IN

SELECT EXTRACTS FROM THE FATHERS AND DOCTORS OF THE CHURCH.

WITH AN EXPLANATION OF THEIR

CORRESPONDING TYPES IN THE OLD TESTAMENT.

A PRESERVATIVE AGAINST UNBELIEF.

BY THE

REV. HENRY FORMBY,

OF THE THIRD ORDER OF ST DOMINIC.

Embellished with 36 full-page Illustrations,

DESIGNED BY C. CLASEN, D. MOSLER, AND J. H. POWELL.

"Intellectum da mihi et vivam."—Ps. CXVIII. 144.

LONDON:
BURNS, OATES, & COMPANY,
17 PORTMAN STREET, W., AND 63 PATERNOSTER ROW, E.C.
1872.

This scarce antiquarian book is included in our special *Legacy Reprint Series*. In the interest of creating a more extensive selection of rare historical book reprints, we have chosen to reproduce this title even though it may possibly have occasional imperfections such as missing and blurred pages, missing text, poor pictures, markings, dark backgrounds and other reproduction issues beyond our control. Because this work is culturally important, we have made it available as a part of our commitment to protecting, preserving and promoting the world's literature.

The Book of the Holy Rosary.

LONDON
BURNS & OATES: Portman Sq:

DEDICATION

TO THE MEMBERS OF THE CONFRATERNITY OF THE HOLY ROSARY.

St Paul says, "*I will pray with the spirit, and I will pray with the understanding also*" (1 Cor. xiv. 15). It cannot but be the greatest joy to us to know that the Devotion of the Holy Rosary which St Dominic received from the most Blessed Virgin Mother of God, and of which the great Dominican Order has ever been the chief and foremost preacher, is now spread over the earth as the waters cover the sea. May it be our earnest and persevering purpose to bend every effort of ours, however small they may be, to bring about not only that the Devotion of the Holy Rosary be even still more widely extended over the earth, but that the knowledge of God's Holy Incarnation, Passion, Death, and Resurrection, and of the glories of His most Blessed Virgin Mother and His Saints, may always go hand in hand with the devotion; so that the knowledge of God may also come to cover the earth as the waters cover the sea (Isa. xi. 9).

To you, then, dear fellow-members of the Confraternity, I hasten to offer the ensuing pages, the fruits of such humble efforts towards attaining this great and holy end, as could be made by your attached servant in Christ,

H. FORMBY.

SANCTA MARIA IMMACULATA ORA PRO POPULO.

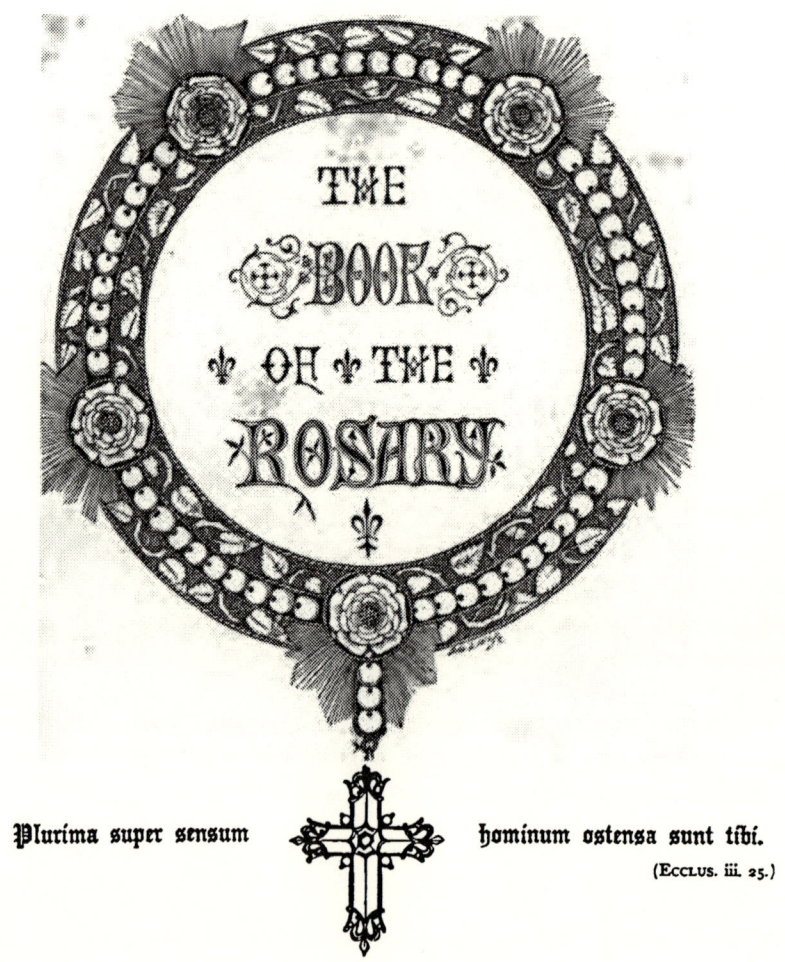

Plurima super sensum hominum ostensa sunt tibi.
(Ecclus. iii. 25.)

THE

BOOK OF THE HOLY ROSARY.

TO THE CHRISTIAN READER.

BRIEF ADMONITION ON THE BENEFIT OF ASSOCIATING KNOWLEDGE WITH PRAYER.

ST PAUL, in so many places, and so urgently, exhorts all "to walk worthy of God, pleasing Him in all things," by bearing fruit in every good work, and by "*increasing in knowledge*" (Col. i. 10); that a priest possessed of leisure could not but seek to employ his time in trying to offer, if possible, an acceptable help to his fellow-Christians in their efforts to please God "*by increasing in knowledge.*"

Taking a lesson from the wisdom of the Church (who, in prescribing to her Clergy and Religious Communities a system of prayer in common, uses especial care that the Breviary employed for this end shall be the richest possible repertory of knowledge ranging through the Sacred Scriptures, Patristic Theology, and Biographies of Saints), and the conclusion could not but plainly appear, that the knowledge of God and the spirit of prayer were always intended to be yoked together, and that the happiest fruits were to be looked for from their union. Knowledge by itself alone, St Paul says, puffeth up (1 Cor. viii. 1), and ignorant piety borders on superstition; it is their union that tends to make the Christian.

But if knowledge and prayer are always intended to be yoked together, there certainly will be found in use in the great body of the faithful, at least some one well beloved and universally accepted form of prayer, to whose nature it would likewise belong to be in a similar manner associated with knowledge, and which in consequence could not fail to possess capacities for conferring upon the general body of the faithful benefits similar in kind to those which accrue to the Clergy from the use of their Breviary. And what other can this be than the Devotion of the Holy Rosary, with the beautiful system of popular Theology contained in its fifteen mysteries? Again, like the Breviary, the Rosary enjoys the privilege of being either the joyous social prayer of a multitude or the pious exercise of complete solitude. And in either case, the use of the Devotion makes the same demand upon the mind of the pious reciter, for a knowledge of the particular mystery which at the moment happens to be under contemplation.

It remained, then, but to endeavour to collect together a volume of such doctrinal explanatory matter, relating to each of the fifteen mysteries, as would suffice to store the mind with the knowledge requisite to enable the act of the intelligence easily and pleasantly to accompany the words of the prayer; and thereby to offer the valuable twofold benefit of bringing a perceptible access of continually growing relish for the practice of the devotion, as also a pleasant and acceptable aid, in what St Paul declares to be the very necessary labour of endeavouring to please God "*by growing in knowledge.*"

The book will be seen to consist in substance of a selection of extracts chiefly taken from the writings of the great Saints and Doctors of the Church, nearly all of them probably now for the first time accessible in the English language. Great care, however, has also been taken to point out the several stages or steps in the progress of the Divine work of human redemption, to which each of the fifteen mysteries bears its respective and most instructive testimony. To the above has likewise been added a somewhat new feature, in the careful comparison of each mystery with its corresponding types in the Old Testament. This has been done as well for the sake of the general preservative efficacy against unbelief, which such an insight into the marvellous methods by which Divine Wisdom, long ages ago, has prepared the way for the Christian mysteries, could not but be calculated to have on the mind; as also for the sake of the new and beautiful light which the comparison with the type is frequently found to reflect upon the mystery itself.

That it may then please God, the Giver of all good, to bless a labour continued through many years, in order, dear Reader, to assist you to please God by "increasing in knowledge," is the earnest prayer in your behalf of your very humble servant in Christ,

THE AUTHOR.

ST PETER'S PRIORY, HINCKLEY,
   Easter Monday, 1872.

TABLE OF CONTENTS.

	PAGE
GENERAL INTRODUCTION—	1

    I. The Duty of Taking Pains to acquire the Knowledge of God.
    II. The Benefit of studying the Sacred Scriptures.
    III. The Testimony of the Types and Figures of the Old Testament.

PART I.—THE FIVE JOYFUL MYSTERIES.

CHAP.
I.—Introduction to the Joyful Mysteries typified in the Ark of the Covenant brought by King David to Mount Sion 6
II.—THE ANNUNCIATION 12
III.—Scripture Types. 1. The Comparison between Eve and Mary. 2. Anna the Mother of Samuel 17
IV.—THE VISITATION OF ST ELIZABETH 23
V.—Scripture Types. 1. The Ark of the Covenant in the House of Obededom. 2. The Bush burning with Fire but not consumed 26
VI.—THE NATIVITY 30
VII.—Scripture Types. 1. The Fleece of Gideon. 2. The Manna that came down from Heaven 35
VIII.—THE PRESENTATION OF JESUS IN THE TEMPLE 38
IX.—Scripture Types. 1. Samuel presented to the High Priest. 2. Moses allowed to see the Promised Land 41
X.—THE FINDING OF JESUS IN THE TEMPLE 44
XI.—Scripture Types. 1. The Sorrow of his Parents for the Absence of Tobias. 2. The Joyful Meeting on his Return 47

PART II.—THE FIVE SORROWFUL MYSTERIES.

I.—Introduction to the Sorrowful Mysteries typified by the Hostility shown to the Rebuilding of Jerusalem 49
II.—THE AGONY AND PRAYER OF JESUS IN THE GARDEN . . . 55

CHAP.		PAGE
III.—SCRIPTURE TYPES. 1. THE PRAYER OF ELIAS FOR THE DEAD CHILD. 2. THE WEARINESS OF ELIAS FOR THE SINS OF THE PEOPLE		59
IV.—JESUS IS SCOURGED AT THE PILLAR		62
V.—SCRIPTURE TYPES. 1. JOB SMITTEN BY SATAN. 2. THE RAINBOW THE SIGN OF MERCY IN THE HEAVENS		66
VI.—JESUS IS CROWNED WITH THORNS.		70
VII.—SCRIPTURE TYPES. 1. THE VICTIM OF SACRIFICE CAUGHT IN THE THORNS. 2. THE PROPHET WHOM HIS FRIEND EXPOSED TO THE LIONS		73
VIII.—JESUS CARRIES HIS CROSS		76
IX.—SCRIPTURE TYPES. 1. ISAAC CARRYING THE WOOD OF THE SACRIFICE. 2. DAVID GOING FORTH WITH HIS SHEPHERD'S STAFF AGAINST GOLIATH		79
X.—JESUS DIES ON THE CROSS		82
XI.—SCRIPTURE TYPES. 1. THE FOUNTAIN OF THE RIVER IN PARADISE. 2. THE PASCHAL LAMB. 3. THE PASSAGE OF THE RED SEA. 4. THE PRAYER OF MOSES ON THE MOUNT. 5. THE BRAZEN SERPENT IN THE WILDERNESS. 6. THE ROCK WHICH YIELDED SWEET WATER		90

PART III.—THE FIVE GLORIOUS MYSTERIES.

I.—INTRODUCTION TO THE GLORIOUS MYSTERIES TYPIFIED BY THE SONG OF TRIUMPH OF THE THREE CHILDREN IN THE FURNACE		94
II.—THE RESURRECTION OF JESUS FROM THE DEAD		99
III.—SCRIPTURE TYPES. 1. JONAS IS CAST OUT FROM THE WHALE'S BELLY. 2. SAMSON BURSTS HIS BANDS		105
IV.—THE ASCENSION OF JESUS INTO HEAVEN		110
V.—SCRIPTURE TYPES. 1. THE HIGH PRIEST ENTERS THE HOLY OF HOLIES. 2. ELIAS IS TAKEN UP INTO HEAVEN		114
VI.—THE MISSION OF THE HOLY GHOST		116
VII.—SCRIPTURE TYPES. 1. THE LAW GIVEN ON THE HOLY MOUNT. 2. THE SACRIFICE CONSUMED WITH FIRE FROM HEAVEN		121
VIII.—THE ASSUMPTION OF THE BLESSED VIRGIN		125
IX.—SCRIPTURE TYPES. 1. THE QUEEN OF SABA GOES UP TO JERUSALEM TO SEE THE GLORY OF SOLOMON. 2. JUDITH RETURNS WITH THE HEAD OF HOLOFERNES		128
X.—THE CORONATION OF THE BLESSED VIRGIN		132
XI.—SCRIPTURE TYPES. 1. THE RAISING OF THE JEWESS ESTHER TO THE ROYAL THRONE OF PERSIA. 2. THE INTERCESSION OF QUEEN ESTHER FOR HER PEOPLE		137

LIST OF ILLUSTRATIONS.

FRONTISPIECE—"Types of the Crucifixion" . J. H. Powell.
Ornamental Title Page . . . R. Buckler.

PART I.—THE JOYFUL MYSTERIES.

		Drawn by	Opposite to page
INTRODUCTION.—THE ARK OF THE COVENANT BROUGHT BY KING DAVID TO THE MOUNT SION		C. Clasen	6
I.—THE ANNUNCIATION		D. Mosler	12
SCRIPTURE TYPES	Eve and Adam banished from Paradise / The Prayer of Anna	J. H. Powell	17
II.—THE VISITATION		D. Mosler	23
SCRIPTURE TYPES	The Ark in the house of Obededom. / The Bush which burned with Fire and was not consumed	J. H. Powell	26
III.—THE NATIVITY		D. Mosler	30
SCRIPTURE TYPES	The Fleece of Gideon / The Manna that came from Heaven	J. H. Powell	35
IV.—THE PRESENTATION		D. Mosler	38
SCRIPTURE TYPES	The Infant Samuel presented to Eli / Moses sees the Promised Land	J. H. Powell	41
V.—THE FINDING OF JESUS IN THE TEMPLE		D. Mosler	44
SCRIPTURE TYPES	The Sorrow of Anna for the Absence of Tobias / The Joy for the Return of Tobias	J. H. Powell	47

PART II.—THE SORROWFUL MYSTERIES.

		Drawn by	Opposite to page
INTRODUCTION.—THE REBUILDING OF JERUSALEM IN STRAITNESS OF TIMES		C. Clasen	49
I.—THE AGONY IN THE GARDEN		D. Mosler	55
SCRIPTURE TYPES	The Prayer of Elias for the Dead Child / The Weariness of Elias for the Sins of the People	J. H. Powell	59
II.—THE SCOURGING AT THE PILLAR		D. Mosler	61
SCRIPTURE TYPES	Job smitten by Satan / The Rainbow of many Colours	J. H. Powell	65

		Drawn by	Opposite to page
III.—THE CROWNING WITH THORNS		D. Mosler	69
SCRIPTURE TYPES	The Ram caught in the Thorns Daniel in the Den of Lions	J. H. Powell	73
IV.—THE CARRIAGE OF THE CROSS		D. Mosler	75
SCRIPTURE TYPES	Isaac carries the Wood of the Sacrifice David goes forth against Goliath	J. H. Powell	79
V.—THE CRUCIFIXION		C. Clasen	81
SCRIPTURE TYPES	The Fountain in Paradise The Paschal Lamb	J. H. Powell	89
	The Passage of the Red Sea The Rock in the Wilderness	J. H. Powell	91

PART III.—THE GLORIOUS MYSTERIES.

		Drawn by	Opposite to page
INTRODUCTION.—The Song of Triumph in the Flames of the Furnace		C. Clasen	93
I.—THE RESURRECTION		D. Mosler	98
SCRIPTURE TYPES	The Sign of the Prophet Jonas Samson bursts the Bands of the Philistines	J. H. Powell	104
II.—THE ASCENSION		D. Mosler	109
SCRIPTURE TYPES	The High Priest enters into the Holy of Holies Elias taken up from Earth	J. H. Powell	114
III.—THE MISSION OF THE HOLY GHOST		D. Mosler	115
SCRIPTURE TYPES	The Law given on the Holy Mount The Sacrifice consumed by Fire from Heaven	J. H. Powell	122
IV.—THE ASSUMPTION		J. H. Powell	125
SCRIPTURE TYPES	The Visit of the Queen of Saba to King Solomon Judith returns with the Head of Holofernes	J. H. Powell	129
V.—THE CORONATION		J. H. Powell	133
SCRIPTURE TYPES	Esther raised to the Royal Throne Queen Esther intercedes for her People	J. H. Powell	136

SHORT BIOGRAPHICAL NOTICES

OF THE
PRINCIPAL FATHERS AND OTHERS, EXTRACTS FROM WHOSE WRITINGS OCCUR IN THE ENSUING PAGES.

D. AMEDEUS CASTRO COSTA was born of noble parents near Vienne, in Gaul, and surpassed the nobility of his birth in the blamelessness of his life, and in his virtues and erudition. He became a professed monk of the Cistercian Order, in the Monastery of Altecumba, and was made Bishop of Lausanne, about the year A.D. 1144.

ST ALPHONSUS LIGUORI was born of noble parentage in the kingdom of Naples, A.D. 1696; and was ordained priest A.D. 1725. In A.D. 1732 he commenced the work of founding the Congregation of the Most Holy Redeemer. At the command of Pope Clement XIII. he became Bishop of St Agatha of the Goths, and died full of merits 2d August 1789, in his 90th year. He was canonised A.D. 1839, and further distinguished by being pronounced Doctor of the Universal Church, A.D. 1871.

ST ANDREW OF CRETE was born at Damascus, or, as some Greek authorities say, at Triodium, and passed a large portion of his life as a monk in Jerusalem, on which account he has often been quoted as St Andrew of Jerusalem. He was present by command of Theodore, Patriarch of Jerusalem, at the sixth Œcumenical Council, in the year A.D. 680. His writings have a place in the 13th volume of the Bibliotheca Patrum.

ST ANSELM, Doctor of the Universal Church, was born in Piedmont, A.D. 1033. In his 27th year he entered the Monastery of Bec in Normandy as novice, of which he rose to become Prior and subsequently Abbot. In A.D. 1093 he was consecrated Archbishop of Canterbury, and took possession of his See in the December of that year. He passed some years in forced exile, and died at Canterbury, aged 76, A.D. 1109. Though his writings have unhappily ceased to be generally studied, St Anselm will always remain known as one of the great lights of Christendom.

ST ATHANASIUS, Doctor of the Universal Church, was born A.D. 300, and brought up at Alexandria, under its Bishop, Alexander, with whom he went to the Council of Nice. He took a leading part in resisting the false doctrines of Arius, and became an object of great hatred to the Arian party. He succeeded Alexander in the See of Alexandria, from which he was frequently driven into exile by the persecution of the Arians, but died there in peace A.D. 373.

ST AUGUSTINE OF AFRICA, Doctor of the Universal Church, was born A.D. 354, at Tagaste, in Numidia, kept a school of rhetoric in Milan, and was baptized in the year 388 by St Ambrose. In A.D. 392 he was ordained priest by Valerius, Bishop of Hippo, and shortly afterwards was made Bishop. His writings, in which he has interpreted the Sacred Scripture, defended and brought out the doctrine of the Church, and refuted the heresies of his time, are almost countless. He died A.D. 430, and his life belongs to the history of the Church at that time.

ST BERNARD, Doctor of the Universal Church, was born in the year A.D. 1091. His parents were of noble family, his father being Jocelyn, a Burgundian Count, owner of the Castle of Fontaines, and his mother a daughter of Count Bernard of Montbar. He was brought up at a school attached to the Collegiate Church of Chatillon, on the Seine, and in his 22d year entered as novice into the Cistercian Monastery of Citeaux. Two years afterwards, he became Abbot of Clairvaux, in the diocese of Langres. He died A.D. 1153, and his life may be said to belong to that of the Universal Church, as well in consequence of his writings as through his eloquence as a preacher.

ST BUONAVENTURE, Doctor of the Universal Church, was attracted early in life to the Franciscan Order, from having owed his life while a child of four years to the prayers of St Francis. He taught publicly at the University of Paris, was created Cardinal by Pope Gregory X., and made Bishop of Albano. He is famous for his writings and for being a master of the spiritual life.

F. CAMPHAUSEN, a learned Jesuit, author of "Passio Christi Adumbrata" and other works.

ST CYRIL OF ALEXANDRIA was born in Alexandria, and was nephew to Theophilus of Alexandria. He succeeded to the Patriarchal See of Alexandria in the year A.D. 412, a time when heresies, and particularly that of Nestorius, were breaking out on all sides, to all of which he strenuously opposed himself. He presided at the Council of Ephesus as the Legate of Pope Celestine.

ST EPHREM THE SYRIAN was brought up under monastic discipline from a very early age. Becoming a deacon of the Church of Edessa, he would not receive any higher order. St Ephrem's writings are much admired for their eloquence. He died in the year 378, at a very advanced age.

ST EPIPHANIUS was born in Palestine, from whence he journeyed to Egypt; returning thence to Palestine, he built the monastery called the Old AD. (Vetus AD.) of which he became the head. About the year A.D. 368 he was made Bishop of Salamis in Cyprus.

GEORGE OF NICOMEDIA flourished about the year A.D. 880. He commenced his career as archive keeper for the chief church of Constantinople, and afterwards became Metropolitan of Nicomedia.

ST GERMANUS was born at Constantinople,

and at an early age attached to the metropolitan Church. He was made Bishop of Cyzicum, from which See he was promoted to become Patriarch of Constantinople. Unable to restrain the Emperor Leo, the Isaurian, and to bring him to a better mind, he abdicated his dignity in the year A.D. 730, and died in retirement in the year A D. 733.

ST HESYCHIUS, the Presbyter of Jerusalem. Nothing is known with certainty of his life, but he has gained great repute as a writer of homilies. Cave thinks that he died A.D. 609.

ST ILDEPHONSUS OF TOLEDO was born of a noble family in Toledo, and found in Eugenius, the then Archbishop of Toledo, the patron of his early studies. He went to study at Hispalis under St Isidore, and became a professed monk in the Monastery of Agalia, of which he was chosen as the head. He was in great repute for his learning and piety, and in the year 657 succeeded to the See of Toledo.

ST PETER CHRYSOLOGUS, Doctor of the Universal Church, was promoted to the Archiepiscopal See of Ravenna by St Sixtus III. Pope. He was famous for his learning, and died A.D. 450.

ST JOHN CHRYSOSTOM, Doctor of the Universal Church, was born about A.D. 344, at Antioch, and promoted to the priesthood in that city. He was raised to the Patriarchal See of Constantinople A.D. 398. He became an object of dislike to the Imperial family from his apostolic liberty of speech, and was more than once driven from his See into exile. He died in exile in the year A.D. 407.

ST JOHN DAMASCENE was born at Damascus, and brought up in his father's house under the tutorship of one Cosmas. On the death of his father, he entered into the service of the reigning Chaliph as his private secretary. Afterwards he went to Jerusalem, where he was ordained priest, and afterwards became a professed monk in the Convent of St Saba. He distinguished himself as a defender of orthodoxy against both Nestorians, Eutychians, and Iconoclasts. He died about the year A.D. 750. His writings are held in great esteem.

LEO THE EMPEROR—He succeeded his father Basilius on the throne of Constantinople in the year 886, and from his proficiency in both theological and other learning, he is commonly called the Wise Man or Philosopher. He was more renowned for his writings, of which a great number are extant, than for his military feats. He died A.D. 961.

LUDOLPH OF SAXONY, a pious and exemplary Carthusian monk of the fourteenth century, famous for his learned "Life of Christ."

ORIGEN was born A.D. 186, in Alexandria, his father's name being Leontius; he is sometimes called "Adamantine," on account of his incredible application to studious pursuits in the cause of religion. He studied under St Clement of Alexandria, and on the death of St Clement, succeeded him as public teacher in the School of Catechists, where he had many celebrated scholars. Origen caused great disturbance by many of his writings, and St Jerome bears this testimony of him, that where he wrote well, no one wrote better, and no one worse when he wrote ill.

ST PETER DAMIAN, Doctor of the Universal Church, was born in Ravenna, and obtained the name of Damian from an elder brother who was his guardian. He became a professed monk in the monastery built near Fons Avellanus, rising to the office of Prior, and later on to the post of Abbot. He was made a Cardinal of the Roman Church by Pope Stephen, A.D. 1057, and was an intimate friend of St Gregory VII., and a great preacher of voluntary penances, to satisfy Divine justice for the sins and scandal of the time. He died peaceably at Florence, A.D. 1072, in his 66th year.

ST PROCLUS was in early life private secretary to St John Chrysostom. In the year A.D. 427, he was made Bishop of Cyzicum by Pope Sisinnius. Proclus afterwards retired to Constantinople, on his See being seized by the monk Dalmatius, and took part in the Council of Ephesus, where he boldly opposed the Nestorian doctrines. In A.D. 434, he yielded to the repeated solicitations of the people, and was elevated to the See of Constantinople, where he died, A.D. 447.

THEODOTUS OF ANCYRA became Bishop of Ancyra, in Galatia, between the years A.D. 430 and 440. He assisted St Cyril of Alexandria in combating the Nestorian heresy, and was present at the Council of Ephesus.

THOMAS À KEMPIS was born at Kempen, a little town of the diocese of Cologne, A.D. 1380. His father's name was John, and his mother's Gertrude, both being in very humble life. He received an ecclesiastical education through the aid of an elder brother, and at the age of nineteen was admitted as novice into the Augustinian house of Mount St Agnes. He remained five years in the noviciate, and was then professed. He lived to the great age of ninety-two, and died in peace at his monastery, A.D. 1471. The celebrated book of the "Imitation" has been attributed by some few to John Gerson, but Cardinal Bellarmine, besides other great authorities, declare themselves perfectly satisfied that it is the work of Thomas à Kempis.

ST THOMAS OF AQUIN, Doctor of the Universal Church, was born of noble parentage in the kingdom of Naples. Early in life he joined the Dominican Order, and having studied under Albertus Magnus at Cologne, was removed to Paris, in whose University he became a Professor. St Thomas ranks, together with St Augustine, as one of the greatest of the masters of Theological Science who have been raised up to the Church.

TIMOTHY OF JERUSALEM—no certain details of his life have been preserved.

TITUS, Bishop of Bostri, in Arabia, flourished about A.D. 362. His writings are highly commended by St Jerome.

GENERAL INTRODUCTION.

§ 1. *The Christian duty of taking pains to acquire the knowledge of God.*

§ 2. *The benefit of acquiring the knowledge of God from the Sacred Scriptures.*

§ 3. *The testimony of the types and figures of the Old Testament to the mysteries of the New.*

§ 1. *The duty of acquiring the knowledge of God.*

NOTHING can more nearly concern us in the business of "working out our salvation," which St Paul exhorts us to do "in fear and trembling" (Phil. ii. 12), than to be sure (1.) that we have the clear warranty of the holy Apostles' words for what we do; and (2.) that we are not living in the habitual disregard of any of their great precepts, of which we cannot but very well know, from the great earnestness with which they are again and again repeated, that there can be no indifference to them on our part without the greatest detriment to our souls.

It should, then, by no means escape our vigilance, that St Peter most distinctly preaches the labour of acquiring the knowledge of God as a duty of religion incumbent upon all. St Peter's words are, "And do you, brethren, using all diligence, minister in your faith virtue, and in your virtue *knowledge*" (2 Peter i. 5). St Paul also says in substance exactly the same, "Let your charity abound more and more in all *knowledge* and in all understanding" (Phil. i. 9). Again, "See that you walk worthy of God, pleasing Him in all things, bearing fruit in every good work, and *increasing in the knowledge of God*" (Col. i. 10). Again, "Let us exhibit ourselves in all things as ministers of God, in chastity, in *knowledge*, and in long suffering" (2 Cor. vi. 6). No one will deny here that the knowledge which, according to the one Apostle, is to be the companion of charity, and, according to the other, the associate of virtue, is the "knowledge of God."

That the Apostles are not here insisting on anything that could have a new or strange sound to the people of God, but only on old and perfectly familar truth, is plain the moment we refer to the words of one of the prophets. Osee, the prophet of Israel, bitterly complains of the neglect and unworthy conduct of the degenerate priests of Israel, and says, "There is no knowledge of God in the land" (Osee iv. 1). And again, he complains, "My people are silent because they have no knowledge," and then, addressing himself to the priests through whose neglect it had come to pass that the people were without knowledge, he says to that priesthood, in the name of God, "Because thou hast rejected knowledge, I will reject thee, that thou mayest no longer perform the functions of the priesthood to me: thou hast forgotten the law of thy God, and I will forget thee and thy children" (Osee iv. 6).

To take pains, then, according to the means which it may please God to place within our reach to store the mind with the "knowledge of God," is thus, according to the doctrine of both St Peter and St Paul, a clear and plain duty of religion, and in enforcing this duty they are not enforcing any other except old and familiar truth.

But for every clear and plain duty of religion, it must be possible to bring forward good and intelligible reasons. For the Apostle never seeks for any servile compliance with his precepts, but is at all times careful to call only for our reasonable compliance, *rationabile obsequium vestrum* (Rom. xii. 1). And as nothing is better fitted to encourage and animate to the careful discharge of a duty than to see good and convincing reasons brought forward in its favour, we may properly pause here for a while to review some of the grounds on which the labour of acquiring a knowledge of God claims to be ranked as a plain duty of our religion.

It is St Paul, then, who assures us that to labour to acquire this knowledge is one of the ways by which God is to be pleased; and what can a Christian desire better than to please God?

Again, it may be easily perceived how very necessary for the encouragement and direction of Christian life is the knowledge of God, from the following consideration.

St Paul, at the end of his career, says, "I have fought the good fight, I have kept the faith." Can we understand how St Paul could have been able to do this without an adequate knowledge of the religion of which he was the preacher, and, apart from a corresponding clear perception of the motives which it placed before him, to induce him to continue faithful to his calling? Doubtless, it is perfectly true that there will be incomparably higher toils and dangers proper to the life and career of an Apostle of the Faith, than can, in the ordinary course of God's providence, be expected to become the lot of Christian life in general; but if there is one truth more clearly marked out for our guidance than another, it is, that a Christian way of life is in such permanent opposition to the ways of a fallen world, that every one who at the last may be able to say with St Paul, "I have kept the faith," will have also to say with the Apostle, "I have (in my degree also) fought my fight." The world at the present hour is well known to be full of those who make a mock of faith, and laugh at all the restraints of virtue; we are surrounded also by the world's literature, which in every page insinuates the folly of faith and the pleasures of a life free from restraints; and what sort of safety can there be for the keeping the faith in the case of those who, weak and feeble as they undoubtedly will be if they are mere children of nature, and unprotected by the knowledge proper to their calling, have still to take their chance all the same, such as it may be, in the arena of life?

The knowledge of God may be thus easily perceived to be not less than a real necessity of Christian life, and the homely poet who has said,

"They are most firmly good, who best know why,"

has expressed a very great and valuable truth.

Again, our Lord says to us, "Be ye perfect, as your Father in heaven is perfect" (Matt. v. 48). But it is part of the perfection of God that He knows His own work. "Known unto the Lord," says St James, in the council in Jerusalem, "from the beginning is His own work" (Acts xv. 18); and as God is an object of knowledge to Himself in His own works, it must plainly be, to say the very least, a great privilege to us to be admitted to share in the knowledge of God and of His works. And if the Scripture truly says that the fear of God is the beginning of wisdom, how shall this fear of God come into existence without a knowledge of the works of God, of which the Wise Man says, "I have learned that all the works of God shall last for ever, the works which He has done, that He may be feared" (Eccles. iii. 14).

Again, the Wise Man says, "It is not good where the soul is without knowledge" (Prov. xix. 2); and St Paul speaks of the condition of the nations, as having their understanding obscured by darkness, and as alienated from the life of God, by the ignorance that is in them (Eph. iv. 18). It is thus perfectly intelligible why the apostles should so earnestly insist on the truth, that a becoming measure of knowledge indispensably belongs to the dignity of the Christian calling, and that it is impossible for those who omit to improve the talent confided to their keeping, and to profit by the opportunities of acquiring a knowledge of God, which the providence of God puts in their way, to have the praise of "walking worthy of their calling." On the contrary, of such as these it must be said, that it is unhappily they who bring a very real scandal upon their calling, and who are in perpetual danger of losing their faith, and of falling back into a worse state than that of the heathen, "becoming alienated from the life of God, by the ignorance that is in them," and this frequently past the power of recovery.

Again, if omniscience is an attribute of the Godhead itself, it would be out of harmony with the order of the creation if the duty of acquiring knowledge, or, to use the language of the apostle, " of increasing in knowledge," had not been made an integral part of the Christian redemption, to those who, being created in the image of God, are consequently fitted by nature for the acquisition of knowledge. God is the Author of human society, which is ordered after His image and likeness, and in whatever degree the inroads made by human sin and perversity may have deformed its likeness to the divine original, this is never wholly effaced. Now, we invariably find that in civil life ignorance is branded with a note of disgrace. It not only justly passes, in the right-minded estimate of all sensible persons, for that which is culpable and hateful in itself, but also justly operates to the prejudice of the person guilty of the ignorance, by its being the bar to his admission to all the more honourable and eligible employments, whether of public or private life. The analogy, therefore, of the divine government undoubtedly requires that ignorance in religion should not only be held to be, in like manner, a thing hateful and culpable in itself, but also that serious positive forfeits and penalties should be incurred by it in the religious and spiritual life, corresponding to those which ignorance is well known to bring with it in the walks of civil life. That whole populations, as well as particular individuals, may most calamitously and largely forfeit the favour and blessing of God, through their culpable indifference to the duty of increasing in knowledge, is unhappily a sad truth of experience, showing how much of human sin and imperfection still remains in the world; but we must in justice entirely acquit the holy apostles St Peter and St Paul from all share in the responsibility of this. For what can be plainer than that no such culpable ignorance could exist anywhere, if we were all as solicitous as we ought to be to give due heed to the words of the one apostle, who says to us, "Brethren, I would not have you ignorant," and of the other, who says, "Using all diligence, minister in your virtue knowledge."

§ 2. *The benefit to be derived from acquiring a knowledge of God from the Sacred Scriptures.*

The Sacred Scriptures are the divine gift of a merciful God, desiring the welfare and the salvation of men, both in this present life and in the life to come; and they are given for the use of the Christian people. Who will deny this? The very nature of the gift will imply both the custody and the interpreting power of such a living body as the Church, to pledge its own authority for their authenticity, and to control and regulate their use, so as to secure them from the danger of misapplication to deception and other perverse ends. But subject to this necessary and indispensable control, the Sacred Scriptures are undeniably the good gift of God for the uses and needs of the Christian people; and that it has been the uniform tradition of the Catholic Church so to deal with them, none but a virulent fanatic can attempt to deny. There have been exceptional times and circumstances, such as the age of Luther's schism, when it was found necessary to impose for a time an unusual restraint upon their use and circulation. But allowing for such abnormal occurrences, the traditional mind of the Catholic Church with regard to the Scriptures is expressed in the example of St Jerome, a doctor of the Universal Church, recommending the mother of a young Roman lady to take care that her daughter was well read in the Scriptures, and advising her to begin with the Book of Ecclesiastes, and so to proceed to the Books of the Prophets.

In the letter written by command of the Macchabees and the Jewish people to the Senate of Sparta, the whole Hebrew nation make a noble confession of their attachment to their Sacred Scriptures. They desire, indeed, to renew their ancient friendship with the Spartan people; but this not from any sense of need, inasmuch, say they, "as we have our holy books for our consolation" (1 Macch. xii. 9). Again, when our Lord makes His reply to the Sadducees, who thought to propose an unanswerable difficulty to Him, and when He says, "You err, being ignorant of the Scriptures and the power of God" (Matt. xxii. 29), His words have this effect for all times, that wherever there is found ignorance of the Scriptures, there will be found ignorance of the power of God, and error. Again, nothing tends more, according to St Paul, to firmness of faith and perseverance than a knowledge of the Sacred Scriptures. "Do thou continue firm in those things which thou hast learned and which have been intrusted to thee, knowing from whom thou hast learned them, and *because from infancy* thou hast known the Sacred Scriptures, which are able to instruct thee unto salvation" (2 Tim. iii. 15). Nothing, also, is more confirmatory of faith in the apostolic preaching and doctrines of the Church than this knowledge. "The Jews of Berœa," says St Luke, "were more noble than those of Thessalonica, for they received the Word with great eagerness, searching the Scriptures daily for the confirmation of their faith" (Acts xvii. 11). And when our Lord replied to the reiterated cavillings of the Jews in the Temple, He said to them, "Search the Scriptures, for in them ye think ye have eternal life, and it is they that bear testimony of Me" (John v. 39).

It may be easily understood that the revelation which it has pleased God to make of Himself to the world, could not possibly have possessed the requisite permanent resting-place in the world without being embodied in a written record; and such a written record must, from the nature of human life, be vouched for by a living keeper and guardian, who is able to satisfy all reasonable inquiry. Here, however, we are dealing with the actual volume of these inspired writings as the "*fait accompli*" of the love and mercy of God, the good gift of God actually in our hands; and we justly conclude from the fact of the good gift, that there is a holy and good use to be made of it by all, that is, by each one in his own degree. This good gift of the holy and good God, who causes His sun to shine upon all alike, so far as it is used with thankfulness to the honour of the merciful Giver, can but bring a blessing with it. He who gave the gift will be sure to bless every humble and religious effort that is made to turn it to the good account for which He Himself intended it.

§ 3. *The testimony of the types and figures of the Old Testament to the mysteries of the New.*

With this conclusion, then, in the way of an encouragement to acquiring a knowledge of the Sacred Scriptures, we may proceed to a brief word or two touching the value of the confirmatory evidence which the Scriptures of the Old Testament bear in their numerous types and figures to the truth of the Christian mysteries of the New Covenant. "It is these," our Lord may still say to us, as formerly to the Jews, "that bear testimony of Me," therefore, "search the Scriptures."

"I would not have you ignorant," says

St Paul, "how our fathers passed through the cloud" (1 Cor. x. 1); and then enumerating many of the events recorded in the books of Moses, he says, "These things happened to them in a figure, and they are written for our instruction, on whom the ends of the world are come" (1 Cor. x. 11). Many other instances could be referred to in St Paul's writings, in which he himself gives the figurative interpretation of the facts recorded in the Old Testament; but for brevity's sake it will be sufficient to say here, that the study of the figurative sense of the Sacred Scriptures has always been held in the highest esteem in the Church, and its conditions are thus laid down by St Augustine. There are three things, according to this great doctor, to be observed in the Scriptures—First, the literal sense (*dictum proprium*); secondly, the figurative sense of its words (*dictum figuratum*); and lastly, the figurative or typical meaning of its facts (*factum figuratum*). It is the latter of these, the "figurative fact," which constitutes the type or figure of the Old Testament. And before we proceed to our task of the exposition of the mysteries of the Rosary, in which these types and figures, or "figurative facts," will be seen to play so very important a part, we may be reasonably permitted a brief remark, to point attention to their great value and importance as instructive and even entertaining witnesses on the Christian side.

In the first place, then, as so many figurative facts, they are precisely the very facts of the sacred narrative of which the apostle says, "Brethren, I would not have you ignorant of them." For before we can attempt to appreciate the figure, we must, of necessity, first be in possession of an accurate knowledge of the fact; lest, as St Augustine says, were we to withdraw the foundation of the fact, we should be found, as it were, to seek to construct our building in the air. In this respect, then, whatever may hereafter become of the figurative interpretation, the student of the types and figures of the Old Testament at least makes sure of a certain amount of solid valuable knowledge, gathered from the contents of the sacred volume, consisting of the simple narrative of the facts; and this, by itself alone, will always more than repay the labour of acquiring. But when, in addition to the mere knowledge of the fact, the Christian reader comes into possession of the figurative interpretation, he, as it were, lights upon the discovery of some new and unlooked for jewel or prize. The inspired proverb has said, "Diligently prepare thy field, and afterwards thou shalt build thy house." Where then can there be a more instructive study than the one in which we are perpetually finding new and unexpected proofs that God Himself, in the most wonderful way, has diligently beforehand prepared His own field in the shadows and figures of the ancient covenant, that He might afterwards build up with the better effect the new edifice of our own Christian redemption. The poor Hebrew student, for example, finds in them the simple matter of fact as this happens to be narrated, and alas! nothing whatever more than this. To him the wisdom of God, as it reveals itself to the inquiring Christian mind, in all the beauty and richness of figure, shadow, and parable, leading the understanding into the presence of truths, for which the way is seen to have been prepared, often in so surprising and even playful a manner, remains a simple profitless blank. Surely the Christian, then, is bound to bow his head in gratitude and admiration, in the presence of such winning and beautiful tokens of the wisdom which he thus perceives "to reach from end to end in its strength, and sweetly to dispose all things" (Wisd. viii. 1), that they may minister in their degree to the accomplishment of the Divine purpose of the redemption of man. Beware, then, good Christian, to whom God has so abundantly, and without reserve, made over all the riches of His household, as to a dear son, lest the poor forlorn Hebrew be found to show that he has a greater veneration, and a deeper love for the bare letter of the sacred text, than thou, in thy degenerate thoughtlessness and disdain, art found to have for all the treasures of its letter and its spirit combined.

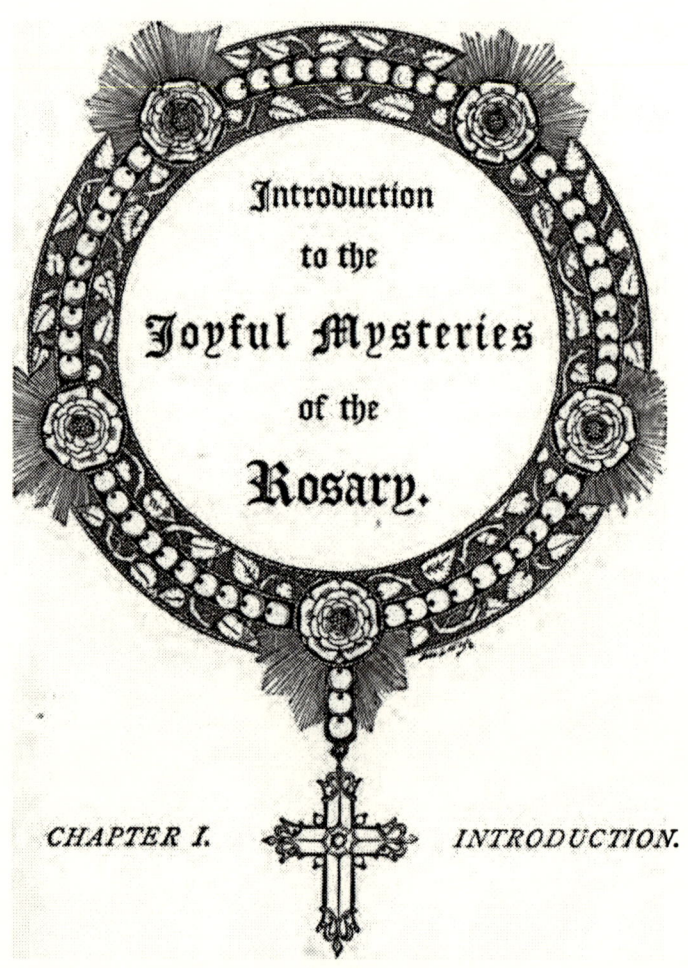

Introduction to the Joyful Mysteries of the Rosary.

CHAPTER I.   INTRODUCTION.

THE JOY THAT WAS BROUGHT TO ALL MANKIND THROUGH MARY, THE ARK OF THE NEW COVENANT, PREFIGURED BY THE JUBILEE OF THE WHOLE PEOPLE OF ISRAEL ON THE OCCASION OF THE ARK OF THE MOSAIC COVENANT BEING BROUGHT TO THE MOUNT SION, THE CITY OF DAVID.

"BEHOLD," says God, speaking by His prophet Isaias, "I create Jerusalem a rejoicing, and her people a joy." Although God had said to Adam, "In the sweat of thy brow thou shalt eat bread;" and to Eve, "In sorrow shalt thou bring forth children, for cursed is the earth for your sake;" still, notwithstanding, even on the earth, thus laid under a curse by reason of transgression, days of lightness of heart and rejoicing are to return; for "behold I create Jerusalem a rejoicing, and her people a joy" (Isaias lxv. 18).

In the royal David's life, we are permitted to see a figure of the manner in which it has pleased the wisdom of God

The Joys brought again to the Lost World by Mary the Ark of the New Covenant

are prefigured by

the joy of David and all the people bringing the Ark of the Covenant to the Mount Sion.

to work out His scheme for the restoration to the fallen world of its forfeited joy. David began his career in hardship and privation, as the youngest and least esteemed son of his father. Early in life he received the divinely-appointed anointing to his throne, of which he did not come into possession till he had reached an advanced time of life, matured in dangers and trials. He was pursued by his adversary Saul, as if he had been a wild beast, over the mountains of Israel, and was, as it were, hunted from one rocky fastness to another. He had thus to pass through a long term of watchings and labours, eating the bread of sorrow, while patiently waiting for God to bring about the accomplishment of His purpose. At length, however, his own inspired words were fulfilled—" Lamentation shall endure until the evening, but in the morning there cometh joy" (Ps. xxix. 6). In the end joy came to David, and it came to him through the Ark of the Covenant of the Lord his God. "Behold, I create Jerusalem a rejoicing, and her people a joy." From the day that David accomplished his purpose of bringing the Ark of the Lord God of Israel, in the midst of the universal jubilee and acclamations of the people of Israel, within the walls of his city on the Mount Sion, the Lord whom he served began to give him rest from his enemies, and to establish his throne. Then, in the inspired words of Sacred Writ, Mount Sion began to be founded in the exultation of the whole earth, and attained the honour of being the city of the great king (Ps. xlvii. 2).

But these things, as St Paul would say to us, happened to them in a figure, and are written for our instruction, on whom the ends of the world are come. The same came to pass in like manner, as we shall see, on a far larger scale with the whole of the vast world. In the entire world there had been heard nothing but the voice of its lamentation up to its eventide, up to the very dawn of the morning when Mary was chosen to be the Ark of the New Covenant, and when the Mount Sion became no more in figure but in truth, "founded in the exultation of the whole earth, the city of the great king."

All the polished literature of the world before the day of the glad tidings of great joy, which were accomplished in the Ark of the New Covenant, is one continued mirror that reflects the world's sorrow and uneasiness, and utters its voice of lamentation. The thought of the future, to the fallen world, is always one that is wrapped in gloom, and ever, as far as possible, one to be drowned in the sense of present enjoyment.

" Quid sit futurum cras, fuge quærere," says one of its poets, who perhaps best of all represents the pleasant, witty, and right-minded intelligence of a polished man of the world in its palmiest days— " Never trouble about the morrow, but enjoy the present hour."

Let not to-morrow's change or chance
Perplex thee, but as gain
Count each new day. Let beauty's glance
Engage thee, and the merry dance,
Nor deem such pleasures vain.
Gloom is for age.
—*Horace, Martin's Version.**

" The time of our life, says the heathen," in the Book of Wisdom, " is short and full of weariness. There is no comfort in the end of a man, nor has any one ever been known to return from the dead. For we are born out of nothing, and afterwards we shall be as if we had never been. Since the breath in our nostrils is as it were smoke, and our speech is as it were a spark wherewith our hearts have movement, the which when it is put out our body becomes dust, and our spirit is dissolved as though it were thin air, and our life vanishes as the vapour which is dispersed by the rays of the sun, being overpowered by its heat. Wherefore come, let us enjoy all the good things upon which we can lay our hands. Let us fill ourselves with costly wines and ointments, let not the flower of our time slip away from us. Let us crown ourselves with roses before they fade, for this is our lot and this is our portion." (Wisdom ii. 1, &c.)

There is no effectual balm in the fallen world for the knowledge of the dread

* Quem sors dierum cunque dabit, lucro
Appone, nec dulces amores
Sperne puer, neque tu choreas,
Donec virenti canities abest
Morosa.   —*Hor.*, Od. ix. Lib. i.

necessity of the death that is to come, and which is mercilessly to put an end to all its joy. The thought of it can never be excluded. There it stands, and say what you will, do what you will, it persists to utter its voice of lamentation.

For all must view Cocytus' pitchy tide
Meandering slow— . . . .
Land, home, and winsome wife must all be left,
And cypresses abhorred
Alone of all the trees
That now your fancy please
Shall shade his dust who was a little while their lord.   —*Horace, Martin's Version.**

Yet so natural to the whole being and constitution of the human soul is the thought of joy, and so inborn is the desire to live in a continual state of rejoicing, that this can but be one of the surviving lineaments of the original condition of the soul, as it came forth from the hands of its Divine Creator. "To crown the head with roses only before they fade" may doubtless be a poor, erring mortal's best actual attempt, in the absence of a better, to seize hold of the joy for which his nature tells him he has ample capacities; but who can fail to perceive that in thus acting he is but seizing upon the short-lived counterfeit, while true joy is eluding his grasp.

In the first book of the Sacred Writ we have the secret of the world's joyless existence fully revealed. The original joyous condition of the creation has been forfeited, and a life of penal labour has been substituted, to be terminated, beyond all doubt, at some unknown time by death; but which in the meantime, in particular cases, may also be vastly embittered by the injustice, cruelty, and unnatural conduct of others, as also by the personal visitations of many different mental and bodily ailments, the result of our own fault or misfortune. "Why hast thou eaten of the fruit of the tree of which I commanded thee that thou shouldest not eat?" said God to Adam. "Therefore, cursed is the earth in thy work; by labours shalt thou eat of it all the days of thy life, until thou return to the earth whence thou art taken; for dust thou art, and unto dust shalt thou return" (Gen. iii. 19). God might have dealt with the two first transgressors of His law as He dealt with the rebel angels, whom "He reserves in everlasting chains in darkness" (St Jude). He might have shut out from them even the hope of any amelioration of their condition. But God loves mercy as well as judgment (Ps. xxxv. 2); and while a certain measure of present consolation is not denied to them, they receive a distinct pledge which opens up a prospect of hope for the future. A promise is given to them of one to be born who shall crush the head of the serpent, their subtle adversary and betrayer. When this, therefore, shall be accomplished, then there will be a fountain of joy once more open for the whole earth.

In the meantime, the great secret of life, as taught and inculcated by the Divine Wisdom, is something totally distinct from the vain attempts at seizing the counterfeit joy "of crowning the head with roses before they fade." The people of God are made to understand that such happiness as is still to be found in this life is obtainable only in a life of honourable industry and labour, cheered and sustained by looking forward in faith to the accomplishment of the Divine promises, as it were, anticipating the joy which God had pledged Himself to give back to the earth. It was said to the people of God, "that it was better to go into the house of mourning than into the house of feasting, for in it might be found a useful warning as to the end of all men; for the heart of the wise is where there is sorrow, and the heart of fools where there is laughter" (Eccles. vii. 3.) "What is a man better," says the same inspired moralist, "for having spent his labour on the wind? This it is, therefore, that has appeared to me to be good: that a man should eat and drink, and that he should enjoy with gladness the fruit of his labour with which he has laboured under the sun all the days of his life which God has given to him, for this is his portion" (v. 17).

---

* Visendus ater flumine languido
   Cocytus errans, ...
   Linquenda tellus et domus et placens
   Uxor, neque harum quas colis arborum
   Te præter invisas cupressus
     Ulla brevem dominum sequetur.
         —*Hor.*, Lib. I. Ode xiv.

The son of Sirach inculcates the same lesson, that the proper life of man is one of labour. "Vast labour," he says, "has been created for all men, and a heavy yoke is laid on the sons of Adam, from the day of their birth to the day of their burial, in the common mother of all" (Ecclus. xl. 1). Speaking of the life of the industrious artizan, he says, "that he gives his heart to the completion of his work, and rises early to bring it to perfection. All these trust in their hands, and each one is wise in his own art. These are the men who shall strengthen the framework of the world, whose prayer is in the midst of the works of their art, and whose search is in the law of the Most High" (Ecclus. xxxviii.)

Everywhere, again, throughout the Sacred Writers, there is to be heard a voice of warning against trusting to the vain and short-lived joys of the heathen. "The eye," says Solomon, "is not satisfied with seeing, nor is the ear filled with hearing" (Eccles. i. 8). "Remember thy Creator," says the same moralist, "in the days of thy youth, before the time of affliction comes, and the years draw near of which thou shalt say, they please me not" (Eccles. xii. 1). The uniform lesson of the inspired writers is, that mere fleeting pleasures of life are not to be relied upon, and that the best that a man can do is to rejoice from the fruit of his labour; "for this," says Solomon, " is the gift of God" (Eccles. v. 18).

If then all the joys of the heathen are mere fleeting counterfeits of true joy; if it is perfectly sure that they will be followed by the years, of which men shall be forced to say, "they please me not;" nay, if even when they are at their very height, a poet (Lucretius) shall rise up to bear his testimony, and to betray the secret, that there is concealed bitterness in the cup,*—Where, we are entitled to ask, are the true and veritable joys to be found? The heart of man is plainly endowed by its Creator with the capacity for true and lasting joys, far higher and better than even those that God in His mercy has permitted to be found in the reaping in patience the modest fruits of prolonged and penitential toil. We ask our question, then, and what is the answer we receive. The voices of vast nations and peoples, the acclamation of many languages and tribes and kindreds of the earth, pour on their words from pole to pole, from shore to shore. They cry aloud with one accord, and say, It is none other than Mary the Virgin, blessed of all generations, who has brought true joy into the world. It is Mary, whom the Church salutes as the Ark of the New Covenant, who is the cause of the universal joy of the whole earth.

If the literature of the heathen world bears a certain testimony to the universal expectation of all nations as to a day of joy that was believed to be about to dawn, the inspired writers of the Holy Scripture abound in the most glowing anticipations of the joy which was, in the time and in the way predetermined in the counsels of God, to be restored to the fallen life of man. Our Lord tells us that Abraham, who, as St Paul says, was as it were a chief among the company of those who saw the Divine promises from afar, and who saluted them and confessed themselves to be but strangers and pilgrims upon earth (Heb. xi.), rejoiced to see His day; he saw it and was glad (John viii. 56). "How beautiful," says the soothsayer Balaam, "are thy tabernacles, O Israel, and thy tents, O Jacob, as the shady valleys, as the well-watered gardens, as the dwelling-places which the Lord hath planted, as the cedars near the waters" (Num. xxiv.) "Though the fig-tree blossom not," exclaims the prophet Habaccuc, "and the vine put not forth her shoots; though the sheep be cut off from the fold, and no herd be found in the stalls, yet I will rejoice in the Lord, and I will joy in God my Saviour" (Hab. iii.)

Again, the language of prophecy further determines the very spot of the earth which is to be the fountain, from whence this universal joy is to come. It is to be the city of Sion. "The Lord shall comfort Sion, and shall raise up all her ruins. He shall make the desert a delight, and the wilderness as the garden of the Lord.

* "Medio de fonte leporum,
Surgit amari aliquid, quod in ipsis floribus angit."

Joy and gladness shall be found in her, the giving of thanks and the voice of praise" (Isaias li.) And again, "Behold, I create Jerusalem a rejoicing, and her people a joy" (lxv.) And in the Psalms "Mount Sion is said to be founded in the exultation of the whole earth" (Ps. xlvii.) Nor is the favoured place only determined, but also the very person in whom the Divine promises are to be accomplished. He is to spring from the root of Jesse, and to be the Son of David, born in the royal house and family of David. His mother, also, a prodigy unknown over the whole earth, is to be a virgin. "Behold," says Isaias, "a virgin shall conceive, and shall bring forth a son, and His name shall be called Emmanuel" (Isaias vii. xiv.)

Thus the eyes of the whole world, both of Jew and Gentile, of all the tribes and kindreds of the earth, as well as of the chosen people, are concentrated on the expected coming of a Heavenly Visitor, who will bring back to the earth, and to the children of Adam, the joys that were lost in their fall and banishment from Paradise. This Heavenly Visitor is no other than the long-expected Son of the ever blessed Virgin Mother Mary, whom St John Damascene thus addresses:—

"Hail Mary, full of grace! O name and creature more gracious than every joy! O thou from whom Jesus, the Eternal Joy, the Medicine of all the sorrows inflicted on Adam, has deigned to come into the world, hail to thee, most beautiful Paradise! Hail to thee, thou Garden more choice than Eden, in which every plant of virtue has freely germinated, in the midst of whom the tree of life has sprung up! Hail to thee, by whose presence we gain our lost estate, through whom the flaming sword that barred our return is taken away! Hail to thee, thou City of the Great King, in whom the courts of heaven have again been opened to us mortals, enrolled in the ranks of whose heavenly citizenship we poor sojourners of the earth again clap our hands for joy! O thou whose memory and whose annals are glorious in the tongues and acclamations of the people of the entire earth, O Virgin Mother of Jesus, who in thee has looked down in mercy on me, notwithstanding that in my poverty and want of eloquence, words have failed me in which to celebrate thy countless praises!" (Sermon on the Nativity of Mary.)

Thus when full four thousand years of labour and sorrow and fruitless attempts at rejoicing had passed over the world; when one after another its great empires had failed, and were failing, and the shades of its evening were settling upon it, the morning of its joy begins to dawn. The heavenly messenger is sent to Nazareth to the pre-elect Virgin, espoused to Joseph, of the house and family of David. She hears the gracious words of the Holy and Ever-blessed Trinity to her, and she replies, "Behold the Handmaiden of the Lord. Be it unto me according to Thy Word." The Divine Word takes its effect, the expectation of the nations of the world is fulfilled, and henceforward its long-lost Joy is more than restored to a fallen world in Mary, who has become the "Ark of the New Covenant."

And now to return to our figure. The evening of David's troubled and agitated life is drawing towards its close. He has been a man of war from his youth up; and at length, after his long life of warfare and hair-breadth escapes, God appears to be about to give him rest. But in the midst of all his kingly glory David experiences a void in his heart that is not filled up. He says to the elders and princes of Israel, "Let us send to all our brethren who are dispersed, and let us bring back the Ark of the God of Israel, for we sought it not in the days of Saul" (1 Par. xiii.) And David swore to the Lord, and vowed a vow to the God of Jacob, saying, I will give no sleep to mine eyes, nor slumber to mine eyelids, nor rest to my temples, until I find a place for the Lord, and a tabernacle for the God of Jacob" (Ps. cxxxi.)

Therefore David and all Israel went out to bring the Ark of the Lord from Cariathiarim; and David and all the people rejoiced before the Lord with all their might in canticles, with stringed instruments, psalteries, dulcimers, cymbals, and trumpets. And David and all Israel sang this canticle to the Lord (Ps. civ.)

"Praise the Lord, and call upon His name; make His deeds known unto all people. Sing unto Him and give praise, and relate all His wonderful works."

Thus did the Mount Sion begin to be "founded in the exultation of the whole earth." And God created Jerusalem a rejoicing, and her people a joy, in the Ark of the Covenant of the God of Israel, a figure of the glad tidings of great joy which the angel announced to the shepherds of Bethlehem, "which shall be to you and all people;" and which came to the lost world through Mary, the Ark of the NEW COVENANT.

CHAPTER II.   THE ANNUNCIATION.

THE HOLY SCRIPTURE NARRATIVE.

"THE Angel Gabriel was sent from God, "into a city of Galilee, called Nazareth, "to a virgin espoused to a man whose "name was Joseph, of the house of David, "and the virgin's name was Mary.

"And the angel being come in said unto "her: Hail full of grace, the Lord is with "thee, blessed art thou among women. "Mary hearing these words was troubled "at his saying, and thought within herself "what manner of salutation this should "be. And the angel said to her: Fear not, "Mary, for thou hast found grace with "God. Behold thou shalt conceive in thy "womb, and shalt bring forth a son, and "thou shalt call His name Jesus. He shall "be great, and shall be called the Son of "the Most High; and the Lord God shall "give unto Him the throne of David His "father; and He shall reign in the house "of Jacob for ever, and of His kingdom "there shall be no end. And Mary said to "the angel: How shall this be done, be- "cause I know not man? And the angel "answering, said to her: The Holy Ghost "shall come upon thee, and the power of

THE FIRST JOYFUL MYSTERY.

Ave Maria Gratia Plena Dominus Tecum Benedicta Tu in mulieribus et Benedictus fructus ventris tui Jesus.

THE ANNUNCIATION.

Ecce Virgo concipiet et pariet filium; et vocabitur Nomen Ejus EMMANUEL. (*Isaias* vii. 14.)

Behold, a Virgin shall conceive, and shall bring forth a Son, and His name shall be called Emmanuel. (*Isaias* vii. 14.)

Revertere Virgo Israel. . . . Quia creavit Dominus novum super terras FEMINA CIRCUMDABIT VIRUM. (*Jer.* xxxi. 22.)

Return, O Virgin of Israel. For the Lord hath created a new thing on the earth, a Woman shall compass a Man. (*Jer. xxxi.* 22.)

"the Most High shall overshadow thee: and therefore also the Holy which shall be born of thee, shall be called the Son of God. And behold thy cousin Elizabeth, she also hath conceived a son in her old age; and this is the sixth month with her that is called barren: because no word shall be impossible with God. And Mary said: Behold the handmaid of the Lord; be it done to me according to thy word. And the angel departed from her" (St Luke i. 26).

On coming to consider the words spoken by the Archangel Gabriel, we cannot fail to perceive that he is in very truth made the messenger of wondrous tidings. Of such marvellous import indeed is the announcement of which he is the bearer, that, except the way for its being communicated had been, in methods too various to enumerate, diligently prepared beforehand by the wisdom of God, it would have been too stupendous for human belief. For what is it in sum that is announced? It is nothing less than that God Himself is about to come upon the earth, to make Himself visible, and to show Himself, that He may converse visibly face to face with His rational creatures. He is not about to come after the manner in which Enoch, the seventh from Adam, prophesied to the world before the Flood that He would come, saying: "Behold the Lord cometh with thousands of His saints to execute judgment upon all, and to reprove all the ungodly for all the works of their ungodliness" (Jude i. 14). He is to come to restore joy and gladness to the earth, and to show to His creatures, in His own Divine Person, the good way in which they may walk.

He sent, then, as we learn from this mystery, an archangel to announce His coming; for His coming is part of the divine plan that has been predetermined from all eternity. But all previous experience of such visitors from the unseen world has been that they have invariably inspired dread and terror to those to whom they have been sent. Of what kind, then, will the coming of the Lord of all be in His own person? For example, when the angel who came from heaven to announce to Manue and his wife the birth of their son Samson was seen by them to ascend towards heaven in the flame of the sacrifice from the altar, Manue and his wife fell flat on the ground in an extremity of terror (Judges xiii. 20). In the same manner, after the Archangel Raphael had made himself known to the family of Tobias, the whole family lay prostrate on their faces for the space of three hours (Tob. xii. 22). When Daniel saw the vision of the angel who appeared to him by the river Tigris, he says: "I fainted away, and I retained no strength, and when I heard the voice of his words I lay in a consternation on my face" (Dan. x. 8). If, then, those who were but messengers from the throne of God, and who came as fellow-servants to their other fellow-servants, could not help causing such consternation to those to whom they came that they fell on their faces to the ground, who will be able to survive the terror of the coming of the very King Himself who sitteth upon the throne? "Will not all flee from before His face, and hide themselves in the clefts of the rocks and in the holes of the mountains, from before the fear of the Lord and from the glory of His majesty" (Isa. ii. 21). How may it ever be made to come to pass that the Advent of the King who sitteth on the throne shall be a source of universal joy, and its record that of a joyful mystery of the faith of the Church?

The accomplishment of this wonder that the coming of the King of kings should be a cause of joy and gladness to the whole world, and not a cause of terror, we owe to the immaculate and blessed Virgin Mary. When she spoke the auspicious words to the holy archangel, "Behold the handmaiden of the Lord; be it unto me according to thy word," then the wonder was accomplished. It has been decreed, in the eternal counsels of God, that He who sitteth upon the throne between the cherubim should become the Son of Man and a child of Adam; and when He had condescended to make choice of the most blessed Virgin Mary for His mother, Mary set her seal to the joy of the world by accepting Him for her son.

St Peter Damian says, "That we owe in

this respect so great a debt of gratitude to Mary, that her very nativity is deservedly to be considered as an occasion of the most exalted joy; inasmuch as the whole of human redemption took its beginning from her. For as God Almighty foresaw, in His unspeakable providence, before He created man, that man would fall by the machinations of the devil, so in the bowels of His unfathomable mercy He predetermined His plan for the redemption of man before the world was made. For as it was impossible that the redemption of man could be accomplished unless God were to be born of a virgin, so it was necessary that a virgin should be born of whom the Eternal Word might take flesh. It was consequently requisite that the house should first be built in which the Heavenly King might condescend to take up His dwelling. Of this house it is that Solomon speaks when he says, 'Wisdom hath built herself a house, she hath hewn out for herself seven pillars' (Prov. ix.) Thus it was that the virginal house came into being, supported by its seven pillars; for the venerable Mother of God was endowed with the seven gifts of the Holy Ghost: wisdom, understanding, counsel, fortitude, knowledge, piety, and the fear of the Lord. She was the building which the Eternal Wisdom, that reacheth in its strength from end to end, and disposeth all things sweetly (Wisd. viii. 1), onstructed that it might be meet to receive Him, and clothe Him with flesh in her most pure womb" (St Peter Damian, Sermon on the Nativity of the Blessed Virgin).

"God dwells among men," exclaims St Andrew of Jerusalem. "God, to whom no space can set limits, is borne in the womb of a virgin. From hence human nature derives the prelude of its joy, and obtains the first beginnings of its union with the Godhead. From hence our first creation is renovated, and puts off its old apparel. 'Therefore let the heavens above rejoice, and the clouds rain down justice' (Isa. xlv. 8). 'Let the mountains distil sweetness, and the hills joy' (Joel iii. 18). For the Lord hath had mercy on His people. The 'mystery that was concealed for ages is now made manifest' (Eph. iii. 9), and all things are taken up again, and restored in Christ as the Head (Eph. i. 10). This is the counsel of God at which the angels rejoice, and men share their joy; the whole world is renewed, and is again restored to itself. What mind, what tongue can worthily conceive of these things? Words cannot utter them, and the ear cannot comprehend them. With reason, therefore, do we hold our joyous festive solemnity, and meet together to celebrate with rejoicing the wonderful mercy shown to the whole human race. But what, I shall be asked, is the joy that we celebrate? Plainly it is the rejoicing of the whole of creation at its renewal and restoration. We rejoice for the glad tidings of great joy in that the goodness of God has condescended to look in mercy upon His creation of men. This is our festive rejoicing for the salvation of the whole world. But from whence and from whom do these glad tidings come, and to whom are they sent? They come from heaven—from God; and they are sent to a virgin espoused to a man named Joseph, and the name of the virgin is MARY" (Sermon on the Annunciation).

"This day (the Annunciation)," says St John Damascene, "is the beginning of our salvation. On this day the Son of God, who was anterior to all time, becomes the Son of Man. This day is the beginning of the restoration of human nature, and of the blotting out of the sin of creation. On this day our nature has been sanctified by the indwelling in it of its Creator. On this day it has been raised to the dignity of holding dominion over archangels. On this day the time predicted by the prophets is fully come. This is the day which saints have desired to see. On this day Adam has built a temple for his Creator in one of his own daughters, in which He might deign to dwell concealed, and thus become our Redeemer. This temple is Mary, the virgin; precious, blessed, and holy, the pure and stainless offshoot of Adam's nature, the Queen of the whole family of men. So pure that none can be found purer in the whole human race; so holy that none among all intelligent creatures shall ever surpass her in holiness. She is the glory of the people of Israel, and the light of the house of David. This is she, the Beauty whose purity the Heavenly King desired, sending to her His ministering spirit Gabriel to salute her with a salutation of great joy, and to acquaint her that she has been chosen by her Creator, saying, 'Hail full of grace, the Lord is with thee; blessed art thou among women!'" (Sermon on the Annunciation.)

"Gabriel," says the Bishop of Ancyra, "marvels at her calmness of composure and self-possession; and on coming to lay at her feet a double crown of joy and benediction, he addresses her, 'Hail full of grace, the Lord is with thee! Blessed art thou, O most comely and most beautiful of women. The Lord is with thee, O thou who art all that is good, glorious, and venerable! The Lord is with thee, thou chosen and peerless one, surpassing all created brightness, in whom every beam of light finds its centre! Worthy art thou of God, that thou shouldest be blessed of Him! I greatly admire thy modesty, O thou elect one! Fear not, Mary, thou Bride of God, and pledge given to His saints! It is no conceiving in iniquity or birth in sin' (Ps. l.) that I am about to announce to thee, but tidings of great joy, that are to blot out and cancel the sorrow of Eve! It is no intelligence of a childbirth of pain and suffering that I communicate to thee, but of one that will cause joy and consolation! It is no sad and mournful maternity of which I bring to thee the tidings, but the rising of the Day Star of light for the whole world! Through thee the sorrows of Eve have passed away, calamities have ceased, error is put to flight, the malediction is blotted out, and Eve is redeemed!" (Theodotus, Sermon on the Glories of Mary.)

David, Mary's royal forefather, had said, "My brethren, hear me: the Lord God of Israel hath chosen His chief men from the house of Juda, and from the house of Juda He hath chosen the house of my father; but from the house of my father it hath pleased Him to choose me, that I should be king over all Israel" (1 Par. xxviii. 4). Mary, the daughter of the royal tribe of Juda, and of the house of David, says of her election in the same manner, " My soul doth magnify the Lord, for He hath had respect to the lowliness of His handmaiden." From among all the virgins of Juda, and all the daughters of the house of David, Mary may say, It hath pleased Him to choose me. "Hearken, ye isles, and give ear, ye people that are afar off, the Lord hath called me from the womb; from the womb of my mother hath He remembered my name. He hath set me as His chosen arrow, and hath hid me in His quiver" (Isa. xlix. 1, 2).

"God is not a man that He should lie, or the son of man that He should be changed" (Num. xxiii. 19); "and the gifts and calling of God," says St Paul, "are without repentance" (Rom. xi. 29). In making choice of Mary, therefore, God has challenged all generations of men to behold and contemplate on what sort of a daughter of man He Himself has fixed His choice. "What can be more noble," writes St Ambrose, "than the Mother of God? What can exceed in brightness her whom the Brightness itself has chosen? What can be more chaste than she who has been raised to the dignity of a virgin maternity? Of all her other excellences," he says, "how shall I dare to speak? She was a virgin, not in person only, but also in mind. One who never tainted the sincerity of her affection by any admixture of deceit. Humble of heart, grave of utterance, prudent in mind, reserved in speech, fond of reading, placing her trust not in uncertain riches, but rather in the prayers of the poor, intent on her work, modest in her words, wont to refer her thoughts to God as their judge rather than to man, careful to hurt no one, full of good-will to all, an enemy to all boasting, a listener to reason, and a lover of virtue" (Treatise on Virgins, book ii.)

Of a truth in Mary, the calling of God is without repentance. Let us hear St Peter Chrysologus: "It is Mary who has given glory to the heavens, to the earth a God, to vices an end, to life its good order, to morals their rule of discipline. The grace of which an angel was the messenger a virgin hath accepted to communicate it to all generations. O thou of a truth most blessed Virgin, to whom it has been given to unite the glory of virginity with the dignity of mother! O most blessed among women, who hast merited to obtain the privilege of a heaven-sent conception, and the crown of virginal integrity! Most truly blessed daughter, that has gained God for thine own Son, and yet remainest Queen of virgins!" (Sermon on the Prerogatives of Mary.)

"As the cool water," says the sacred proverb, "is to the thirsty soul, so is a messenger of good tidings from a far country" (Prov. xxv. 25). When, up to that time, had a messenger ever come to the earth the bearer of more joyful tidings than those which were entrusted to the holy Archangel Gabriel? "Forasmuch," says St Leo, "as the devil boasted that man, deceived by his machinations, now lay stripped of his divine gifts and denuded of the dowry of his immortality, being subjected to the hard penalty of death; and forasmuch as his seducer found a kind of consolation in the thought of having gained for himself a companion in his guilt, there was need of a secret dispensation in the counsels of God, in virtue of which, God, who is unchangeable, might fill up the measure of His mercy, and man, who was brought into transgression by the deceit of the devil, might not perish, contrary to the purpose of God. When the time, therefore, for the redemption of man, which had been predetermined, was come, Jesus Christ, lowering Himself down from His throne in heaven, yet not departing from the glory of the Father, entered our lower world in a new order, and by a miraculous birth" (Sermon on the Birth of Christ).

This new order, and this miraculous birth, was accomplished in Mary, to whom, first of all creatures, the glad tidings were brought by the heavenly messenger. "Hail Virgin, most blessed among women!" exclaims St Ephrem. "Hail most beautiful and precious vessel chosen of God! Hail Lady full of grace! Hail thou brightest star from whom Christ has come forth! Hail thou joy of the whole human race! Hail thou praise and glory of the patriarchs and prophets! Hail thou bright ornament of the martyrs and crown of the saints! Hail thou sweet flower of the religious, and joy of the solitaries! Hail thou most shining gem of the ecclesiastical hierarchy! Hail thou surpassing wonder of the whole world! Hail thou delight of the inhabitants of the earth! Hail thou paradise of pleasure, fountain of every sweetness and of immortality!" (St Ephrem, Sermon on the Praises of Mary.)

> Oh, how can we enough record
> Our grateful thanks to Israel's Lord,
> For sending us, in this the hour
> Of Juda's fast departing power,
> Of Juda's crime, and Juda's shame,
> This treasure of immortal fame,
> This earnest of the Father's love,
> This pure and spotless turtle-dove,
> This paradisal prodigy,
> This flower of immortality?"
>
> —*The Masque of Mary*, E.C.

THE OLD TESTAMENT TYPES OF THE I. JOYFUL MYSTERY.
Eve Banished from Paradise. Anna's Prayer in presence of the Tabernacle.

ROSA·MYSTICA·PASSIM·IN·LEGE·ET·IN·PROPHETIS
TENEBRAS·ORTA·SOLE·FUGANS·CUM·FILIUM

THE MOTHER WHO BROUGHT SIN INTO THE WORLD.
THE MOTHER WHO OBTAINED HER SON BY PRAYER.

CHAPTER III.

THE SCRIPTURE TYPES OF THE FIRST JOYFUL MYSTERY.

I. THE COMPARISON BETWEEN EVE, THE MOTHER OF ALL THE LIVING, AND MARY THE MOTHER OF THE LIFE OF OUR LIFE.
II. ANNA, THE MOTHER WHO OBTAINED HER SON BY EARNEST PRAYER.

1. *The comparison between Eve and Mary.*

THERE are two mothers to whom all of human kind are united by the most near, and, in a certain sense, even kindred ties—Eve and Mary. Eve, so-called by Adam, because she was the "mother of all the living" (Gen. iii. 20), and Mary, chosen and elect of God to be the Mother of Jesus, the "Life of our life."

From the first mother, Eve, are born all the living, for whom the Virgin Mother Mary has brought Jesus into the world. From the first we derive that birth of which the Sacred Writ thus speaks, "In the womb of my mother I was fashioned to be flesh; and being born, I drew in the common air, and fell upon the earth that is made alike to all; and the first voice I uttered was crying, as all others do. I was nursed in swaddling clothes with great care; for none other among kings has had any other beginning of birth, and all men have one entrance into life, and all the like going out" (Wisd. vii. 1–6). The second and the Virgin Mother, Mary, is she from whom "A Child is born to us, and a Son is given to us; and the government is upon His shoulder; and His name shall be called Wonderful, Counsellor, God the Mighty, the Father of the world to come, the Prince of Peace. He shall sit upon the throne of David in His kingdom, to establish it and to strengthen it with judgment and with justice from henceforth and for ever" (Isa. ix. 6). Or, to sum up all that has been said in the Sacred Scriptures and the Christian Theology of these two mothers, in the words of St Augustine, *Peccatrix Eva, Reparatrix Maria*—Eve who fell into transgression, Mary the repairer of her fall.

But to proceed without further preface to the particulars of our comparison. The history of the fall of Eve is thus related in the Book of Genesis :—" Now the serpent was more subtle than any of the beasts of the earth which the Lord God had made. And he said to the woman : Why hath God commanded you that you should not eat of every tree of paradise ? And the woman answered him, saying : Of the fruit of the trees that are in paradise we do eat; but of the fruit of the tree which is in the midst of paradise, God hath commanded us that we should not eat, and that we should not touch it, lest perhaps we die. And the serpent said to the woman : No, you shall not die the death. For God doth know that in what day soever you shall eat thereof, your eyes shall be opened : and you shall be as gods, knowing good and evil. And the woman saw that the tree was good to eat, and fair to the eyes, and delightful to behold; and she took of the fruit thereof, and did eat, and gave to her husband, who did eat. And the eyes of them both were opened; and when they perceived themselves to be naked, they sewed together fig-leaves, and made themselves aprons" (Gen. iii. 1–7).

It will not need more than a moderate attention to this narrative to be able to perceive in what way Eve's fall was brought about, in the form of a gradual progress from one misguided step to another, during each of which she was led onward with no ordinary daring and subtlety by her merciless deceiver, counting from her first formal act of indiscretion to the last final completion of her sin; it having been, as we must not fail to observe, notwithstanding always in her power, at each step of her gradual surrender, to have torn herself away from the fatal persuasion which effected her ruin. Indeed, what is Eve's history in this respect, but the history of almost all subsequent human transgression, which perhaps in no known example has ever reached its climax otherwise than in the way of a similar gradual surrender. No one ever became completely base all at once, is the Roman satirist's trustworthy testimony to this truth,* which the French nation, we may incidentally observe, also acknowledges in one of their remarkable proverbs, " *C'est le premier pas qui coute* " (it is the first step which works the mischief).

But to proceed. Eve's first formal act of indiscretion lay in consenting to any kind of interchange of words with a speaker whom the Scripture narrative shows to have been a perfect stranger to her. As the queen of paradise, and the royal consort of its king, Adam, it was clearly, on Eve's part, an indiscreet act of surrender of her dignity to permit any unknown speaker whatever to approach her person. For what form of presentation had the unknown visitor gone through, which was Eve's guarantee that he was a fitting person to whom the queen of paradise might grant the honour of an audience? Here, then, is her first false step. She admits a perfect stranger to the privilege of a colloquy, without taking the precaution to inquire if he is even known to Adam, or has Adam's warranty for seeking and holding any kind of interview with her.

The visitor appears to know that he has a very difficult point to gain, and that he must make the most of his chance. Extreme boldness is, therefore, his wisest course, so, omitting all ceremonious preliminaries, he goes straight to his purpose, and boldly puts the queen of paradise through an interrogatory, saying to her, " *Why hath God commanded you that you should not eat of every tree of Paradise?* " Here Eve makes a second false step, and falls into a second complete surrender of her dignity. If she had only asked in return, as her dignity required that she should have asked, " In whose name, pray,

* " Nemo repente venit turpissimus " (Juv. ii. Sat. 83).

do you come to put this question to me, and what reason have you for wanting to know?" the spell of the temptation would probably have been there and then broken; at least the speaker would then have been obliged to have given something like an account of himself; and it not being very easy to see how he could possibly have done this without raising some just alarm in Eve's mind, this would, in all probability, have brought their colloquy to an abrupt end.

It is worthy of note, then, that Eve tamely submits herself to the interrogatory of the stranger, and from the nature of her answer, we are led to infer the springing up of a certain fascination which the presence of her unknown visitor is already beginning to exercise. If we may guess from her answer what is passing in her mind, the queen of paradise does not appear to wish that the stranger should go away with the idea that their sovereignty in paradise had been subjected to any material limitation. " Of the fruit of the trees that are in the garden," she replies, " we do eat. It is only of the fruit of the tree in the middle of the garden that we do not eat ; " and the reason is, adds Eve, (disposed, under the influence of the fascination, to attenuate as far as possible both the urgency of the divine command, and the extent of the limitation of her own prerogatives,) " lest *perhaps* we die." Now, there was no "*perhaps*" at all in the case, as Eve must have very well known. The words of God had been clear and express, " In the day that you eat thereof you shall die the death" (Gen. ii. 17), and Eve must have known this. But it is one of the evils of a first false step that it draws on another; and under the influence of a fascination to which from the first she ought never to have trusted herself, the terrible express threat of God dwindles away to a comparatively unimportant "*perhaps.*"

The subtle deceiver is not slow in perceiving both how much he has gained, and in what way he will have the best chance to improve his advantage. Here, again, his policy is to put no limit to his daring. "No," he says to Eve, " you shall not die the death," but you shall gain by eating of the fruit. "Your eyes shall be opened, and you shall become as gods, knowing good and evil. And this your God knows."

Here, certainly, there is a new prospect opened for the first time before Eve's mind. And how does the case stand now? Who the Lord her God was who had given the command not to eat of the tree, she knew; and though in the presence of the serpent she affects to speak of His threat as only a *perhaps*, she also knew very well that it was much more than this. But who is the stranger who takes upon himself to insinuate in her presence that the threat of her God is an idle threat, to impute sinister motives as the reason of the command being given, and to assert that the path of progress to an increase of dignity and knowledge, lies in the transgression of the command? Eve does not know so much as who he is. Yet evidently here are extremely grave and serious questions at issue, and by her creation Eve is the associate of Adam. The very first condition of her being plainly requires that, as the associate of Adam, she should not even now, notwithstanding that she has gone so far, proceed to act in so grave a matter without first consulting him. But no; Eve has already entered the path of danger in her previous surrenders of her dignity in the presence of the stranger, and she now totally fails to recover herself. The fascination exercised by her visitor appears to have already obscured her conscience of the Lord her God, equally with the sense of her duty to Adam; and under the influence of this fascination she proceeds to fix her gaze on the fruit. This, as it was only natural to expect, appeared to be good to eat, fair to the eyes, and delightful to behold. All then that now remained was to put forth her hand and take possession of it, which she was not long in doing; and when she had brought Adam to join with her in eating of the fruit, then their joint sin was consummated.

Thus it was that, by one ill-advised step following close upon another, in the end Eve had completely surrendered herself into the power of the deceiver, and had suffered herself to be led by him, step by step, into her transgression. And thus, she who was created in dependence, and as the companion of another stronger than herself, through presuming to act by herself alone, ended in leading Adam himself into her sin, when even at the last, by having recourse to Adam's guidance, she ought to have been able to have rescued herself from committing it.

But the deceiver's triumph is not to be permanent. There was One to be born in due time who was to crush his head, whose very different example it is now time to compare with the conduct of Eve.

Mary is in her humble habitation in Nazareth, engaged in prayer, when the holy Archangel Gabriel, coming upon his mission from the throne of God, enters her chamber, and salutes her with the gracious salutation, "Hail, full of grace! The Lord is with thee. Blessed art thou among women!" Here are the very demonstrations of veneration and regard, spontaneously offered by a heavenly visitor, the hope of which Eve appeared to be so unwilling to imperil on the part of a very questionable stranger, that she is ashamed in his presence to own her subjection to her God. Mary, in place of being captivated or carried away with them, is rather troubled at his words, as expressive of far greater honour than any to which she has ever been wont to think herself entitled. And then, with admirable wariness and caution, she begins to consider within herself what such a salutation could mean. Hardly had the serpent spoken to Eve before she had begun to surrender her judgment to his; but Mary remains perfectly self-possessed in the presence of an archangel. Mary has been a pupil in the Temple, where she has been fed with wisdom from the Sacred Scriptures, and she has learned from thence that deceiving spirits are suffered to roam about the world equally with holy angels; and, besides, she would also be sure to know the inspired proverb, "Whoso believes quickly is light of heart, and shall come to grief" (Ecclus. xix. 4). She, therefore, observes a respectful silence, neither surrendering her judgment, for she is not secure against illusion, nor does she exhibit any disbelief, for she is a daughter of the house of David, and knows much too well the promises of God to her people and to her father's house. For the present, then, she wisely suspends her judgment, neither accepting nor rejecting the salutation, but taking, in the meanwhile, the necessary time to consider within herself "what manner of salutation this might be."

The holy archangel, perceiving Mary to be still revolving within herself what could be the meaning of his salutation, proceeds to unfold the further delivery of his message, "Fear not, Mary," he says, for thou hast found favour with God. "Behold, thou shalt conceive in thy womb, and bear a son, and thou shalt call His name Jesus; and God shall give unto Him the throne of His father David, and He shall reign in the house of Jacob for ever, and of His kingdom there shall be no end." The prospect of becoming as one of the gods, knowing good and evil, without its being possible for her to have had any very clear idea of what this could precisely be, still exercised such a power of fascination over Eve's mind, that neither the fear of offending God, nor the dread of incurring His threatened penalty of death, could stand in the way of her eagerness to obtain it. Let us, then, pause here for a moment, to contemplate some of the details of the unspeakably joyful prospect which Mary now perceived to be placed before her. There was not, as there must have been in Eve's case, merely the confused and dazzled sense of something that was attractive; the prospect here was just as precise as it was marvellous. Mary was to become nothing less than the Queen-Mother of the King of her people, who was to sit on the throne of His father David, to reign in the house of Jacob for ever, and to possess a kingdom without limit or end. Had a prospect such as this burst upon a mind in no way prepared for it, with the suddenness, as it were, of a celestial vision, beyond all possibility of expectation or knowledge, it may be reasonably supposed that no mere human power of self-possession could have borne up under it. But this could not apply to our present case. For, in the prospect placed before Mary, it was not anything unheard of, but the one known and darling hope of every maiden of the house of Israel that was proposed to her acceptance. Mary is able to perceive, assuming her visitor to be in truth an angel from heaven, that she herself is the maiden to whom it is offered to become the mother of the Child in whom all the hopes of her own nation, and the expectation of all the nations of the earth, are to be fulfilled.

Shall she then at once consent? Had Eve been in Mary's place, there could have been no room for any hesitation whatsoever; she, who made so little account of the divine command that stood in the way of her delusive prospect, may be easily supposed, more than likely, dismissing every other thought, to have at once embraced for herself the darling hope of all her people. But in Mary's mind there are thoughts that outweigh even such a prospect as the one that is placed before her. While she was a pupil in the Temple, she had bound herself by the vow of perpetual virginity. Similarly circumstanced, Eve might still have persuaded herself that the archangel's words bore with them the sufficient dispensation from her vow. Not so Mary. Her thoughts are, "I have bound myself by a vow to none other than the Lord Himself of the angels, and here is but the word of an angel." Let us study her reply to the archangel, in which, perfectly unconquered by the indescribable attraction of the prospect, the memory of her vow appears as the one reigning thought. "How shall these things be," says Mary, "seeing I know not man." Whatever may become of the marvellous prospect, Mary's one thought is "fidelity to her vow."

This answer of Mary draws from the archangel a further unfolding of the divine plan in her regard. He says to her, "The Holy Ghost shall come upon thee, and the power of the Most High shall overshadow thee; therefore the Holy One that shall be born of thee shall be called the Son of God." Mary, now satisfied as to her vow, to which she has given the signal proof of her inviolable fidelity, finds herself subjected to a new difficulty. The angel's words announce to her nothing less than a stupendous miracle, of which, since the world began, there has been no known example. Can she believe this to be possible? Here we may see how opportunely Mary's knowledge of the Holy Scripture comes to her aid. Her education in the Temple has happily prevented her being one of the class of persons to whom our Lord said, "Ye do err, not knowing the Scriptures or the power of God" (Matt. xxii. 29). She remembers then that Isaias had prophesied the birth of Messias from a virgin (Isa. vii. 14), and that God had pledged Himself by His prophet Jeremias to do a new thing on the earth, that a "woman should compass a man" (Jer. xxxi. 22). When, therefore, the archangel proceeds to inform her, "Behold thy kinswoman Elizabeth hath herself conceived a son in her old age, and this is the sixth month with her who is called barren; for there shall be no word impossible with God," Mary, as a daughter of faithful Abraham, is quite prepared to believe. Yet to one so cautious and self-possessed, and at the same time so humble and retiring as Mary, there might still have been valid grounds on which rather to wish to decline the proffered honour of the public life of the Queen-Mother of the King of Israel; but so eminently pious and prudent a virgin as Mary would also not fail to say to herself, "If God, who is Almighty, has sent a holy archangel from His throne to be the bearer of such a message as this to one who is so lowly and humble as I am, this can only be because He has purposes of His own to accomplish through me, for which He has condescended to make choice of my humble person; who am I, therefore, that I can resist the choice and election of God?" So Mary answers the heavenly messenger, "Behold the handmaiden of the Lord; be it unto me according to thy word."

How wonderful, then, is the difference between the two mothers, Eve and Mary! Eve, ashamed to make an open confession in the presence of a visitor of her subjection to the law of her God, yields an ear to the voice of a seducing spirit, and is led by him, step by step, into the breach of the divine law. Mary, glorying in her subjection to her vow of virginity, and not willing to accept even the words of an archangel sent from heaven as containing a release from it, obtains from God not only the full measure of the glorious prospect that has been proposed to her, but over and above, the singular and unexampled prerogative of uniting with the joys of her maternity the glory and grace of remaining a virgin. Eve, who for the sake of a delusive prospect of advancement tramples under foot the law of her God, not only discovers the particular prospect proposed to her to have been a cheat, but is compelled to forfeit the dignity she already had, and to become subject to death with all her children. Mary, esteeming her duty to God sovereign over every other thought, obtains God Himself for her son, and to be called "Blessed" by all generations.

"Peccatrix Eva sed Reparatrix Maria."

2. *Anna, the mother who obtained her son by prayer on the condition of giving him up to the service of God.*

As Mary's special prerogative of virgin maternity is without a parallel upon earth, we are not to expect to find in the Old Covenant one who can be more than, in a remote and collateral degree, a figure of the glorious Virgin Mother of the New Covenant. In Anna, however, the mother who by earnest supplication obtained her son Samuel from God, and afterwards gave him up without reserve to the service of God, we have a beautiful figure of this remote and collateral kind.

The mother of the sons of Zebedee came to Christ with the prayer, "Lord, grant that my two sons may sit, the one at Thy right hand and the other at Thy left in Thy kingdom." But the Son of Mary came into the world pledged to suffer humiliation and death for the benefit of others, and as He was also to be a perfect model of the deference and subjection which a son owes to his mother, it was necessary, in the counsels of God, that His mother should be one who would not in any way interpose her maternal authority to withdraw Him from the accomplishment of His death and passion, but one who should, on the contrary, conform her mind in all respects, as His mother, to the will of God, in obedience to which her Son became, as St Paul says, "obedient to death, even the death of the Cross;" and this, however much it might cost her affection as mother thus freely to surrender Him up to become the victim who was to take away the sins of the world. A mother who had the spirit of the mother of the sons of Zebedee was, therefore, most plainly in no way fitted to occupy Mary's place; and thus incidentally a beautiful light is thrown by the figure of Anna on the character of Mary, which justifies the wisdom of the Holy Trinity in their choice of her. For when the time came for the sacrifice of her Son to be offered, Mary was found not only willing to surrender her only Son up to die for the sins of the world, but was not afraid even to stand by His Cross, and so to share in His passion, as He was dying upon it. Anna's history occurs in the Holy Scripture as follows:—The divine promise of a Redeemer to be born of the seed of the woman, had caused all Hebrew women to be extremely desirous to be blessed with children; and as Anna was childless, in her affliction "she betook herself to prayer before the tabernacle in Silo." And with her heart full of grief, and shedding many tears, she made a vow saying: "O Lord of Hosts, if Thou wilt look down on the affliction of Thy servant, and wilt be mindful of me, and not forget Thy handmaid, and wilt give to Thy servant a man child, I will give him to the Lord all his days, and no razor shall come upon his head. And it came to pass as she multiplied her prayers before the Lord, that Heli observed her mouth. Now, Anna spoke in her heart, and only her lips moved, but her voice was not heard at all; Heli therefore thought her to be drunk, and said: How long wilt thou be drunk? Digest a little the wine of which thou hast taken too much. Anna, answering, said: Not so, my lord; for I am an exceedingly unhappy woman, and have drunk neither wine nor any strong drink; but I have poured out my soul before the Lord. Count not thy handmaid for one of the daughters of Belial, for out of the abundance of my sorrow and grief have I spoken till now. And Heli said: Go in peace, and the God of Israel grant thee thy petition, which thou hast asked of Him" (1 Kings i. 10, &c.)

Anna is thus the mother in the Mosaic Covenant who so pleased God by her piety and persevering trust in the efficacy of prayer addressed to Him, that she obtained from Him the gift of her son Samuel. And the Church sings of Mary, "Thou Sanctuary of the Holy Ghost, alone without an equal, thou hast pleased the Lord Jesus Christ." And again, "Rejoice with me, all ye who love God; for even when but a little one I pleased the Most High, and gave forth from my womb the God-Man" (Office of the Circumcision). The Bull of Pope Pius IX. proclaiming the dogma of the Immaculate Conception of Mary also says, "That the incarnation of the Eternal Word being decreed from all eternity, God, from the beginning and before the creation of the world, chose and appointed a mother for His only-begotten Son, from whom, BEING MADE FLESH, He might be born in the blessed fulness of time; and on this mother He has vouchsafed to bestow so surpassing a love above all other creatures, as to be in the highest degree well pleased in her."

How Anna fulfilled her vow of giving up her son to the service of God, we shall learn when we come to the type of the fourth joyful mystery, the Presentation of Jesus in the Temple.

THE ✠ SECOND JOY- ✠ -FUL MYS- ✠ -TERY.

Ave ✠ Maria ✠ Gratia ✠ Plena ✠ Dominus ✠ Tecum ✠

Tempus
putationis
advenit vox
turturis
audita est
in terrâ
nostra.
(*Cant.* ii. 12.)

Ecce tu
pulchra es
amica mea,
ecce tu
pulchra es.
Oculi tui
columbarum.
(*Cant.* i. 14.)

Benedicta ✠ Tu in mulieribus et Benedictus fructus ventris ✠ tui Jesus ✠

THE VISITATION OF ST ELIZABETH.

Behold, thou art beautiful, my beloved one; behold thou art beautiful. Thine eyes are as the eyes of doves. (*Canticles* i. 14.)

The time of pruning is come, the voice of the turtle dove has been heard in our land. (*Canticles* ii. 12.)

The Second Joyful Mystery of the Rosary.

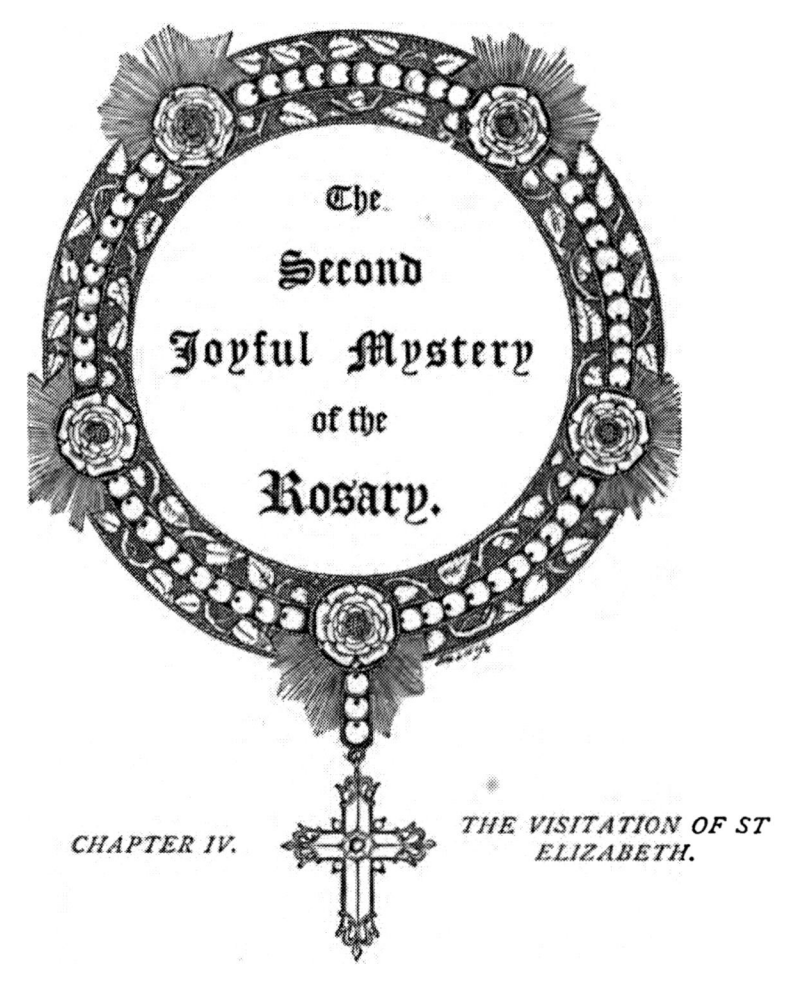

CHAPTER IV.   THE VISITATION OF ST ELIZABETH.

THE HOLY SCRIPTURE NARRATIVE.

"And Mary rising up in those days, went into the hill country with haste, into a city of Juda. And she entered into the house of Zachary, and saluted Elizabeth. And it came to pass, that when Elizabeth heard the salutation of Mary, the infant leaped in her womb. And Elizabeth was filled with the Holy Ghost: and she cried out with a loud voice, and said: Blessed art thou among women, and blessed is the fruit of thy womb. And whence is this to me, that the mother of my Lord should come to me? For behold, as soon as the voice of thy salutation sounded in my ears, the infant in my womb leaped for joy. And blessed art thou that hast believed, because those things shall be accomplished that were spoken to thee by the Lord" (Luke i. 39–45).

"The highest in rank," writes Origen, "come to those lower than themselves, that by their coming they may impart some blessing to them. Thus Jesus came to John that He might sanctify John's baptism. And no sooner had Mary heard the words of the angel announcing to her that she had been chosen to be the mother of the long-expected Messias, and that her kinswoman Elizabeth also was with child, than she rose up and went with haste into the hill country, and entering into the house of Zacharias, saluted Elizabeth. Jesus, who was in her womb, hastens to sanctify John, who was in like manner in his mother's womb. Before Mary came and saluted Elizabeth the babe had shown no signs of joy, but no sooner had Mary spoken than the babe leaped for joy, and then for the first time, Jesus made John His forerunner" (Origen, Homily on St Luke i.).

Thus it was the tie of family affection, and the charity of Mary, which prompted this speedy visit to her kinswoman. But God in it had His own designs also which were to be duly accomplished. "No man lighteth a candle," says our Lord, "and hideth it, or putteth it under a bushel, but upon a candlestick, that all who enter may see the light" (Luke xi. 33); and as it had now pleased the Eternal Wisdom to make Mary the vessel of election bearing the Light of the whole world, it became an appropriate part of the divine counsels both that fitting witnesses should be found to bear their testimony to the marvellous wonder that was accomplished in Mary, and that an occasion should be placed in Mary's way to utter her own solemn testimony and acknowledgment of the great things which God had done for her, for the comfort and confirmation of the faith of the countless generations yet unborn, who were to participate in the salvation of which she was the bearer.

The witnesses, it must be observed, have here no ordinary event to attest. "God would not," writes the Patriarch of Nicomedia, "confide to His angels the business of human salvation, but He condescended in His mercy to lower Himself to our degraded condition. He was not satisfied with merely repairing, but He would Himself assume our nature, and place it on the throne given to Him by the Father. How shall I worthily reflect on this unspeakable goodness of the Godhead—this intensity of the divine love for the race of man? With what kind of praises shall I endeavour to celebrate His abasement of Himself to our infirmities? How shall I find words wherewith to extol the Holy Virgin, through whom these things have come to pass—the Virgin, I say, by whom our ruin has been repaired? Where can brightness be found equal to the purity of her in whom, captivated by her love, her own Creator built for Himself a tabernacle in which He abhorred not to dwell, in which the counsels of the Eternal Father have been accomplished, and in which the Holy Ghost hath found a resting-place? What glory is there that may compare with the excellence of her whom her Creator hath exalted high above all other beings, Himself alone excepted? O priceless gift! O treasure of inestimable value! O thou among countless beautiful things the most surpassingly beautiful! O Mother of God! Oh! of all lovely things the loveliest! Through thee the banished race of man returns to its lost post of honour. Through thee we have regained the undying pleasures of Paradise. Through thee the flaming sword that turned on all sides is withdrawn, and the barred doors that stopped our way to true joys have been thrown open. Through thee the longings of the prophets have been satisfied, and their testimony hath in thee received its fulfilment. Through thee we have gained the tokens of our future resurrection, and through thee we have received our hope of one day obtaining the kingdom of heaven. In thee we have the patroness of our salvation, and the advocate of our cause; and in thee we make a boast of our boldness and confidence" (Sermon on the Presentation in the Temple).

Such was Mary now become, in virtue of her words, "Behold the handmaiden of the Lord; be it unto me according to thy word;" but the mystery as yet is known to no one beside herself on the entire earth, although the whole world has in due time to be brought to the knowledge of it, and to glorify God for the salvation which He has sent. Though, therefore, nothing can stay the completion of the counsels of the Almighty, all events must, notwithstanding, move towards their accomplishment in the order that He has prescribed. In the same manner, then, as it has been the divine will, that the whole world should know the resurrection of Jesus from the dead in no other way than from the testimony of His apostles and other witnesses chosen for this end, so it is likewise here from the witnesses whom God has chosen that we first learn to know what great things are accomplished in Mary, and to read a just lesson to human pride; these first witnesses are an elderly female and an unborn babe.

"Mary, then," to cite the words of St Bernard, "enters the house of Zacharias and salutes Elizabeth, and immediately the singular glory of the Blessed Virgin is revealed to Elizabeth by the Holy Ghost. Elizabeth cries out with a loud voice— "BLESSED ART THOU AMONG WOMEN, AND BLESSED IS THE FRUIT OF THY WOMB!" She is lost in wonder at the person of her visitor, and says: "WHENCE IS IT THAT THE MOTHER OF MY LORD SHOULD COME TO ME?" Then she praises the voice of her visitor, and declares the wonder that has been effected by its very sound. "IT CAME TO PASS THAT AS THE VOICE OF THY SALUTATION SOUNDED IN MINE EARS, THE INFANT IN MY WOMB LEAPED FOR JOY." Then she congratulates with her on her promptitude in believing, saying— "BLESSED ART THOU THAT HAST BELIEVED, BECAUSE THOSE THINGS SHALL BE ACCOMPLISHED WHICH WERE SPOKEN TO THEE BY THE LORD" (Sermon on the Twelve Prerogatives of Mary).

St Elizabeth's testimony has by no means been given in vain, for it is now re-echoed over the world by the millions of every clime and language who ceaselessly repeat the words—"Blessed art thou among women, and blessed is the fruit of thy womb!" But the first to bear testimony to the mystery accomplished in Mary was the unborn babe—the future prophet, whom Jesus, at Mary's approach, now sanctifies in his mother's womb.

"Tell us, O John," writes St Chrysostom, "when thou wast hidden in the womb, how camest thou to see and hear? How couldest thou contemplate the things divine? How couldest thou exult? That which is come to pass is a great mystery, and far exceeds human comprehension. It is fitting that I should outstep the power of nature on account of Him who, Himself above nature, is about to renovate all things. True though it be that I am enclosed in the womb, I can still see the Sun of Justice borne in the womb. I hear, for I am about to be born as the Voice proclaiming the presence of the Eternal Word. I cry out, for I behold the Only-begotten of the Father clothed in flesh. I rejoice in spirit, for I see the Maker of the universe assume the form of man. I leap for joy, for I have present to my mind the Redeemer of the world in a body of flesh and blood. I, as it were, run before you to greet His coming, and am the first to give Him glory."

And next, Mary herself completes the chain of testimony by her own solemn thanksgiving. "My soul doth magnify the Lord, and my spirit hath rejoiced in God my Saviour. Because He hath regarded the humility of His handmaid; for behold from henceforth all generations shall call me blessed. Because He that is mighty hath done great things to me; and holy is His name. And His mercy is from generation unto generations, to them that fear Him. He hath showed might in His arm; He hath scattered the proud in the conceit of their heart. He hath put down the mighty from their seat, and hath exalted the humble. He hath filled the hungry with good things; and the rich He hath sent empty away. He hath received Israel His servant, being mindful of His mercy. As He spoke to our fathers, to Abraham, and to his seed for ever" (Luke i. 46-55).

Thus all is accomplished according to the inspired rule of the law of Moses: "In the mouth of two or three witnesses every word shall be established" (Deut. xix. 15). The unborn prophet, the venerable and aged Elizabeth, and Mary herself, bear their testimony. And Zacharias the priest, where is he? He is not admitted to give testimony. He had shown a disposition to doubt the announcement made by the holy Archangel Gabriel to himself, and he is in consequence become speechless, and can give no testimony until the words of the angel which he hesitated to believe, shall have received their full accomplishment. Then indeed his lips will be loosed, and he will join in the testimony in words which all generations to the end of the world will ceaselessly repeat, but at present his lips are sealed. Oh! blessed prerogative of faith, which endows men with the "wisdom that hath opened the mouth of the dumb, and given eloquence of the tongues of babes" (Wisd. x. 21).

CHAPTER V.

THE SCRIPTURE TYPES OF THE SECOND JOYFUL MYSTERY.

I. THE ARK OF THE COVENANT IN THE HOUSE OF OBEDEDOM.
II. THE BUSH THAT BURNED WITH FIRE AND WAS NOT CONSUMED.

1. *The Ark of the Covenant a visitor in the house of Obededom in the reign of King David.*

"HAIL, thou *Ark of the Covenant*," says the Patriarch of Constantinople, Germanus, addressing himself to Mary, "of whom David prophesied, saying, Arise, O Lord, to Thy rest, Thou, and the Ark of Thy Sanctification" (Ps. cxxxi. 8). *Ark of the Covenant*, pray for us, is a petition of the popular litany of Loretto; and, perhaps, there is no one of the Old Testament types of Mary on which the Fathers of the Church are so fond of dwelling as this.

"Of a truth, the Ark of Israel," writes Leo, an Emperor of Constantinople, "was an image of thy glory, O Mary, as having been a refuge and a protection for the conquered. Yet the things which were brought about through it were but a shadow of the things that have come to pass through thee; and far inferior to them. The Ark to the Israel of old was a source of help, only when they walked in the path of God's commandments; and so far from proving a help to the guilty, and to those who deserted the ways of God, the very Ark itself was brought into peril through their sin. Nothing of the kind can be said of thee. It is no mere defence of the kind that thou bringest to the Christian people, for not only at the time when all were lost didst thou make haste to come to their aid, but even now thou offerest thyself as a guide, not only to those who keep the straight path of the Divine commandments, but also to those who turn aside, and render themselves liable to most just punishments. For God, in thee, has respect to His own most sacred Ark, and reverences the stretched-out hands that were once His own support" (Leo, Emperor, on the death of the Blessed Virgin).

So dear to the Christian people, indeed, has this particular image of Mary always appeared to be, that we shall find our account, in taking a brief preliminary glance at some of the striking points of the resemblance, on which the Church writers delight to expatiate; which, taken together, certainly present a beautiful proof of the Divine forethought in preparing the way for the Christian mysteries.

(1.) The form and design of the Ark of the Mosaic Covenant, had been preconceived in the Divine mind, for God said to Moses, "See that thou make all things according to the pattern showed thee in the Mount" (Exod. xxv. 40); and the Church delights to understand of the Ark of the New Covenant the inspired words, "I was preordained from all eternity; of old, and before the earth was made, and while the depths were not, was I conceived" (Prov. viii. 23).

The Old Testament Types of the II. Joyful Mystery.

The Ark in the House of Obededom. · The Burning Bush in the Wilderness.

ROSA·MYSTICA·PASSIM·IN·ADUMBRA☩TA·ORA·PRO·NOBIS · LEGE·☩·IN·PROPHETIS·☩·EUM·☩·FILIUM·TUUM

A FAMILY BLESSED THROUGH THE ARK OF GOD. · THE MISSION OF MOSES TO DELIVER ISRAEL.

(2.) The Ark of Israel was to be constructed entirely from materials which were freely offered—"From every man that shall offer of his own free will, thou shalt receive them" (Exod. xxv. 2); and Mary, in the same manner, was not asked to offer herself otherwise than entirely of her own free will to become the Ark of the New Covenant, her consent being given in the words—"Behold the Handmaiden of the Lord; be it unto me according to Thy word."

(3.) "Thou shalt make it of setim wood." The setim-tree furnished an imperishable material, the shadow of the inviolable purity and virginity of the Ark of the New Covenant.

(4.) "Thou shalt line it with the purest gold within and without, and thou shalt make a golden crown round about it"—a figure of the care bestowed on the formation of the Ark of the New Covenant. "Almighty and everlasting God," says the Church in her prayer, "who by the power of the Holy Ghost didst prepare the body and soul of the glorious Virgin Mother Mary, to be a fit dwelling-place for Thy Son."

(5.) "Thou shalt place in the Ark the testimony which I will give thee." He who came to dwell in the Ark of the New Covenant, says of Himself, "I am the Way, the Truth, and the Life" (John xiv. 6).

(6.) "Thou shalt make a mercy seat of the purest gold with which the Ark is to be covered." The Church loves to call Mary the "Mother of Mercy," of whom St Bernard says, "Why should frail humanity fear to approach Mary. In her there is nothing that is austere, nothing that is terrible. She is all sweetness, offering milk and wool to all who are of her household. Turn over all that is written in the entire of the Gospel history of Mary, and if but the very smallest symptom of anything harsh and censorious, or so much as the least sign of any disposition to be stern and severe is found in her, then you may suspect and hesitate to approach her" (Twelve Prerogatives of Mary).

(7.) "From thence I will give laws, says God, and I will speak to thee from above the mercy seat, all the things which I will command to the children of Israel" (Exod. xxv. 1–25). "Behold, a Virgin shall conceive," says the prophet, "and shall bear a Son, and His name shall be called Emmanuel, or God with us" (Isa. vii. 14). It is the Emmanuel who is Mary's Son, who has sent His apostles into the whole world, to teach all its nations and people to observe all that He has commanded them.

"And Mary," says St Luke—to resume the subject of the particular parallel to the visit Mary paid to Elizabeth—"abode with Elizabeth about three months, and she returned to her own house" (Luke i. 56). It happened to the Ark of the Covenant of Israel to be, in like manner, also a visitor in the house of a sojourner in Israel, for the exactly similar space of time of three months, and this came to pass in the ensuing remarkable way. When all the people of Israel had received, with acclamations, David's proposal to bring the Ark of the Covenant to Mount Sion, and had answered "that so it should be, for the word pleased all the people" (1 Par. xiii. 4), David's pious design suffered a temporary interruption from the following cause:—"David and all Israel played before God with all their might with hymns, and with harps, and with psalteries, and timbrels, and cymbals, and trumpets. And when they came to the floor of Chidon, Oza put forth his hand, to hold up the Ark; for the ox being wanton had made it lean a little on one side. And the Lord was angry with Oza, and struck him, because he had touched the Ark; and he died there before the Lord. And David was troubled because the Lord had struck Oza; and he called that place the Breach of Oza to this day. And he feared God at that time, saying, How can I bring in the Ark of God to me? And, therefore, he brought it not home to himself, that is, into the city of David, but carried it aside into the house of Obed Edom the Gethite. And the Ark of God remained in the house of Obededom three months; and the Lord blessed his house, and all that he had" (1 Par. xiii. 7–14).

Thus, by the design of God, it was brought to pass, that both the Ark of the

Old and the Ark of the New Covenant, were each respectively visitors for the space of three months; each bringing moreover the blessing of God to the houses where they respectively sojourned. But the beauty of the parallel by no means terminates here. When the marvel that had been accomplished in Mary began to be apparent, "Joseph, her husband," as St Matthew relates, "being a just man, and not willing to expose her publicly, was minded to put her away privately; but while he thought on these things, behold, the Angel of the Lord appeared to him in his sleep, saying, 'Joseph, son of David, fear not to take unto thee Mary, thy wife, for that which is conceived in her is of the Holy Ghost ; and she shall bring forth a Son, and thou shalt call His Name Jesus, for He shall save His people from their sins.' And Joseph, arising from his sleep, did as the angel had commanded him, and took his wife" (Matt. i. 19, &c.)

And it was told to King David that the Lord had blessed Obededom, and all that he had, because of the Ark of God ; so David went and brought away the Ark of God into the city of David with great joy. Such is the remarkable parallel which the wisdom of God has preordained should be found between the Ark of the Old and the Ark of the New Covenant.

2. *The Bush which burned with fire and was not consumed.*

In the Vespers for the feast of the Circumcision the Church sings : "In the bush which Moses saw burning with fire, which yet was not consumed, we confess the preservation of thine admirable Virginity. Mother of God, intercede for us." The particular event to which these words refer is thus related in the Book of Exodus :—

"Moses fed the flocks of his father-in-law, Jethro, the priest of Madian, and when he had led his flock into the further part of the desert, he came to Horeb, the mount of God. And the Lord appeared to him in the flame of fire from the midst of the bush, and he saw that the bush was on fire and yet was not consumed. Moses therefore said : I will go and see this great vision why the bush is not burned. But the Lord seeing that he approached to behold, called him from the midst of the bush, and said, Moses, Moses. But he answered, Here I am. And the Lord said, Draw not nigh hither ; loose thy shoes from off thy feet : for the place whereon thou standest is holy ground. I am the God of thy fathers, the God of Abraham, the God of Isaac, and the God of Jacob. And Moses hid his face, for he was not able to look upon God" (Exodus iii. 1-6).

Some few of the particular details of this striking parallel will well repay the labour of a little careful study. Moses, for example, full of wonder and amazement, says : "I will go and see this great vision why the bush is not burned ;" and Elizabeth, full of awe and wonder at the mystery, the accomplishment of which in Mary has been revealed to her, goes forth to behold and greet her with the words— " Whence is this that the Mother of my Lord should come to me ?"

Moses, approaching the Burning Bush of the Old Law, receives the favour of being permitted to hear the Voice of God speaking from the midst of the bush, revealing to him circumstantially the nature of the salvation He is about to accomplish in behalf of the oppressed people of Israel ; and Elizabeth, in a transport of joy, hears the sweet voice proceeding from the Burning Bush of the New Law, in which the Holy Ghost, by the lips of Mary, reveals the nature of the salvation which is about to be accomplished in behalf of all the lost and oppressed tribes and kindreds of the whole earth.

Since St James, then, assures us that with God there is neither change nor shadow of turning (James i. 17), if it be granted that we have the remarkable parallel of the Divine Voice uttering its revelations respectively from the Burning Bush both of the Old and the New Covenants, we shall naturally expect, that whatever truly proceeds from the mouth of God will possess such traces of harmony and consonance that will bear ample internal testimony to the identity of the one Divine source from which they come. It is of course true that the circumstances in the two cases will very greatly differ. Mary as the mouthpiece of the Holy Ghost, uttering her inspired testimony in the hearing of the aged Elizabeth, speaks under quite other circumstances than the Divine Voice which condescends to engage in a colloquy with Moses on the subject of his mission to the people of Israel; and the salvation God promises to Israel by the hand of Moses is but a remote figure and shadow of the Divine salvation intended for all the tribes and nations of the earth to the end of time, to which Mary is bearing her testimony. Yet, taking all this into consideration, we may still look for traces of the identity of the one Divine source manifesting themselves in the words that proceed from both respectively; and thus we proceed to seek our edification in discovering some of the leading features of the parallel.

"I have seen," says the Divine Voice which speaks to Moses, "the affliction of My people in Egypt, and, knowing their misery, I am *come down* to relieve them." And the Church says, in the Nicene Creed, Who for us men, and for our salvation, *came down* from heaven, and was incarnate by the Holy Ghost, of the Virgin Mary, the Burning Bush of the New Law.

For *He that is mighty* hath done great things to me, and holy is His name, says the Voice that spoke to Elizabeth; and the Voice that spoke to Moses says: Thus shalt thou say to the children of Israel, *He who is* hath sent me to you. This is My name and My memorial to all generations.

"He hath put down the mighty from their seat, and hath exalted the humble," says the Divine Voice that spoke through Mary; and the Voice on Mount Sinai endowed the rod of Moses with the power to put down the mighty from their seat; for it was with the same rod that Moses called forth the waters of the Red Sea upon the hosts of Pharaoh, drowning him and his army in its waves.

"He hath filled the hungry with good things, and the rich He hath sent empty away," says the Voice from the Burning Bush of the Christian Covenant. There is nothing which the hungry soul so eagerly desires as to be cleansed from its sin. "Wash me," says the holy psalmist, "from mine iniquity, and cleanse me from my sin; restore to me the joy of Thy salvation, and strengthen me with Thy princely spirit" (Ps. l.) And the Voice which spoke to Moses gave him for a sign the sudden restoration of his hand, which had been smitten with leprosy, a figure of the cleansing from the leprosy of sin; and also the power of turning the water of the river into blood, at one and the same time a token of their redemption to the faithful Israelites, and of death to the proud Egyptians.

The Divine Voice which spoke in the Burning Bush of the New Law, concludes with the words—" He hath taken up the cause of Israel His servant, as He promised to our fathers, Abraham and his seed for ever." And the same Divine Voice which spoke to Moses, said—" Go, therefore, and I will be in thy mouth, and I will teach thee what thou mayest speak." And again, " I will be in thy mouth and in his mouth (Aaron's), and I will show you what you ought to do." "He that keepeth watch over Israel," says holy David, "neither slumbereth nor sleepeth." And He of whom Mary bears witness that He hath taken up the cause of Israel His servant, afterwards pledged His word to His apostles: "Behold I am with you all days, even to the end of the world." The Voice from the Burning Bush of both the Old and the New Law perfectly agree with each other in promising that God will for ever continue to be with His people, defending, protecting, and watching over them.

The Third Joyful Mystery of the Rosary.

CHAPTER VI.   THE NATIVITY.

THE HOLY SCRIPTURE NARRATIVE.

"And it came to pass, that in those days there went out a decree from Cæsar Augustus, that the whole world should be enrolled. This enrolling was first made by Cyrinus, the governor of Syria. And all went to be enrolled, every one into his own city.

"And Joseph went up also from Galilee, out of the city of Nazareth into Judea, to the city of David which is called Bethlehem, because he was of the house and family of David, to be enrolled, with Mary, his espoused wife, who was with child. And it came to pass, that when they were there, her days were accomplished that she should be delivered; and she brought forth her first-born Son, and wrapped Him in swaddling clothes, and laid Him in a manger, because there was no room for Him in the inn.

"And there were in the same country shepherds watching, and keeping the night watches over their flock. And

THE THIRD JOYFUL MYSTERY.

THE NATIVITY.

Ave ~ Maria ~ Gratia ~ Plena ~ Dominus ~ Tecum ~
Benedicta ~ Tu in mulieribus et Benedictus fructus ventris, tui Jesus.

Parvulus enim natus est nobis et filius datus est nobis, et vocabitur Nomen Ejus Deus Fortis. (*Isaias* ix. 6.)

Unto us a Child is born; and unto us a Son is given, and His Name shall be called the Mighty God. (*Isaias* ix. 6.)

In diebus illis germinare faciam David germen justitiæ et faciat judicium in terra. (*Jer.* xxxiii. 15.)

In those days the Lord shall cause a bud of justice to bud forth unto David, and he shall execute judgement in the earth. (*Jer.* xxxiii. 15.)

"behold an angel of the Lord stood by them, and the brightness of God shone round about them; and they feared with a great fear. And the angel said to them: Fear not; for, behold, I bring you good tidings of great joy, that shall be to all the people: for this day is born to you a Saviour, who is Christ the Lord, in the city of David. And this shall be a sign unto you. You shall find the Infant wrapped in swaddling clothes, and laid in a manger. And suddenly there was with the angel a multitude of the heavenly army, praising God, and saying: Glory to God in the highest; and on earth peace to men of good-will. And it came to pass, after the angels departed from them into heaven, the shepherds said one to another: Let us go over to Bethlehem, and let us see this word that is come to pass, which the Lord hath showed to us. And they came with haste; and they found Mary and Joseph, and the Infant lying in the manger. And seeing, they understood of the word that had been spoken to them concerning this Child. And all that heard wondered at those things that were told them by the shepherds. But Mary kept all these words, pondering them in her heart. And the shepherds returned, glorifying and praising God, for all the things they had heard and seen, as it was told unto them" (St Luke ii. 1–20).

"While all things were moving silently on their way, and the night was in the midst of her course, Thine almighty word came down from heaven from Thy royal throne" (Wisd. xviii. 14). Such were the words of inspired prophecy in which the accomplishment of this holy mystery of the nativity was foretold to the faithful under the old covenant. Isaias, who is often called the evangelical prophet, had spoken of it in the following glowing language:—

"For a Child is born to us, and a Son is given to us, and the government is upon His shoulder: and His name shall be called Wonderful, Counsellor, God the Mighty, the Father of the world to come, the Prince of Peace. His empire shall be multiplied, and there shall be no end of His peace: He shall sit upon the throne of David, and upon his kingdom, to establish it and strengthen it with judgment and with justice, from henceforth and for ever: the zeal of the Lord of hosts will perform this" (Isaias ix. 6, 7).

Jeremias had in the same manner foretold of the stupendous wonder which God was going to accomplish, and of the mercies which would follow in its train, thus:—

"The Lord hath created a new thing upon the earth; A WOMAN SHALL COMPASS A MAN. Behold the days shall come, saith the Lord, and I will make a new covenant with the house of Israel, and with the house of Juda. Not according to the covenant which I made with their fathers, in the day I took them by the hand to bring them out of the land of Egypt: the covenant which they made void, and I had dominion over them, saith the Lord. But this shall be the covenant that I will make the house of Israel, after those days, saith the Lord: I will give my law in their bowels, and I will write it in their hearts, saith the Lord: and I will be their God, and they shall be my people" (Jer. xxxi. 22, &c.)

"Mary," writes the Cistercian Abbot Amedeus, "filled with the knowledge of God as the waters cover the sea, and rapt in the deepest contemplation, wonders to behold herself a virgin chosen to become a mother, and rejoices to know that she is the Mother of God. She understands that the promises given to the patriarchs are fulfilled in her. She knows that the longing desires of the old fathers and the oracles of the prophets who foretold that Christ should be born of a Virgin, and who, with the utmost powers of their soul, desired to see His coming, are now accomplished. She sees the Son of God entrusted to her, and she rejoices that the salvation of the world is committed to her keeping. She hears the voice of the Lord Himself speaking in her, and saying —'Behold, I have chosen thee out of all flesh (Ecclus. xlv. 4), and I have blessed thee among all women.' See, I have committed My Son, My only Son, to thee. Fear not to nurse thy child at the breast;

nor to bring Him up to whom thou hast given birth. Behold in Him not God alone, but thine own Son. My Son is thy Son. My Son as regards the Godhead; thy Son as regards the humanity He has assumed" (Amedeus' Sermon on the Praises of Mary).

"We must remember," writes St Augustine, "that there are two nativities of Jesus Christ taught by the Catholic faith—the one Divine, the other human; the one from all eternity, the other in time. Both marvellous—the one without a Mother, the other without a Father. If we are not able to comprehend the latter, how shall we be able to declare the former? And who is there who can comprehend a marvel so entirely beyond all human experience; so completely a thing alone and by itself in the world; so incredible, and yet, in fact, actually received, and even universally believed, in spite of its incredibility—to wit, that a virgin should conceive, give birth, and yet remain a virgin? What human reason cannot grasp, faith holds fast; where reason fails, faith advances. Who is there who would say that the Eternal Word, by whom all things were made, could not have taken flesh without a mother, as He made the first man without either father or mother? But, inasmuch as beyond all doubt He was the Creator of both sexes, the male and the female, so in His birth He wished to pay honour to them both, seeing that He came to redeem both. In neither sex, therefore, ought we to do any injury to our Creator, for our Lord, in His holy nativity, has opened the way for both sexes to hold fast to the hope of their salvation. The honour of the male sex is in the Humanity of Christ; the honour of the female sex is in the Mother of Christ. The grace of Jesus Christ has overcome the craftiness of the serpent" (St Augustine, Seventh Sermon on the Nativity of Christ).

"Eve's maternity," writes the same Abbot Amedeus, "was in the way of nature; Mary's was that of mother and virgin. Eve's maternity was in pain and sorrow; Mary's in joy. Eve's maternity belonged to the old world; Mary's to the new. Eve became the mother of a servant; and Mary of the Lord of all. Eve gave birth to a transgressor; and Mary to the Just One. Eve brought into the world a sinner; Mary Him who justifies from sin. Eve's parturition multiplies deaths; Mary's delivers from death. The serpent stands by at the side of Eve's childbirth to watch for his occasion; Mary is ministered to by angels. Eve is seized with trembling of heart; Mary is filled with heavenly joy. Eve exposes those to whom she gives birth to many dangers; Mary preserves her children from every evil. Wickedness follows close upon Eve's childbirth; grace on that of the Virgin Mary. In the maternity of Mary the heavens rejoiced and the earth was glad, hell also was moved to its depths. The clouds above displayed the brightness of their star, and sent forth a glorious company of the angels praising God, and saying, Glory to God in the highest, and on earth peace to men of good-will" (Sermon on the Virgin Childbirth of Mary).

"Think not, O man," writes St Proclus, the Archbishop of Constantinople, "that this birth is a thing to be ashamed of; for it is become the cause of our salvation. For if God had not been born of a woman, He would not have subjected Himself to death; nor would He "by His death have overcome him who hath the dominion of death, that is, the devil" (Heb. ii. 14). It is no disparagement to the honour of the architect to dwell in the house which he has himself made; nor does the clay reproach the potter when he remoulds the vessel which he had formed; and in the like manner God, who is all pure, contracts no stain by His being born from the womb of a Virgin. O most blessed womb! in which the writing of discharge from their prison was accomplished for the whole race of man, and a spiritual armoury forged against the deceits of the devil. O blessed field! in which the Husbandman has reaped the ears of corn that sprung up without being sown. O temple! in which God was made Priest, not changing His own nature, but in His mercy clothing Himself with that which is according to the order of Melchisedec" (St Proclus of Constantinople, Sermon on the Praises of Mary).

Let us hear the words of St Leo, Pope and Doctor of the Universal Church, on the subject of this great mystery:—

"Our Saviour, dearly beloved, is born on this day. Let us rejoice! For it would not be right that any place should be given to sorrow on the birthday of Life; that Life, I say, which, swallowing up the terror of death, introduces to us the joys of the eternity of which we have received the promise. No one can be put aside from his share in this rejoicing. The cause of our joy is one that is common for all; for as our Lord, the destroyer of death and sin, finds no one free from guilt, so He came for the common delivery of all alike. Let the saint rejoice, for he draws near to his reward; let the sinner rejoice, for he is invited to pardon; let the heathen take courage, for he is called to life. For the Son of God, according to the fulness of time which the unsearchable depth of the Divine counsel had brought about, assumed to Himself the nature of the human race, that it might be reconciled to its Maker, and that the devil, the instigator of death, might be overcome by that which he himself had conquered.

"In this conflict, entered into on our behalf, the battle was fought on a great and marvellous footing of equal justice. For the Almighty Lord joins issue with His most ferocious adversary, not in His own majesty, but in our humility, opposing to him the same form and the same nature with ours, being a sharer to the full in our mortality, though entirely exempt from our sin. For His nativity has no part whatsoever in that which is said of all others: 'No one is free from stain, not even the babe whose life has been but of one day on the earth.' Nothing, therefore, of the concupiscence of the flesh passed into this birth, and nothing flowed into it from the law of sin. A royal Virgin of the family of David is chosen, who, when about to become the bearer of the sacred burden, first conceived in her mind the Divine and human offspring prior to His conception in the womb. And lest, for want of a right understanding of the Divine counsel, she might take alarm at the unwonted nature of that which was proposed to her, she learns from a colloquy with an Angel what it was that was to be wrought in her by the Holy Ghost, and she fully believes that she may become the mother of God, without detriment to her virginity.

"Let us then, dearly beloved, give thanks to God the Father by His Son, in the Holy Ghost, who, through the abundance of the love with which He hath loved us, hath had pity upon us; and when we were dead in sin, hath raised us again to life with Christ, that we might be in Him new creatures and a new creation. Let us lay aside, then, the old man with his works, and as we have been admitted to a share in the generation of Christ, let us renounce the works of the flesh. Acknowledge, O Christian, thy dignity; and now that thou art become a partaker of the Divine nature, refuse to turn back to thy former degradation, by a degenerate life. Bear in mind of whose head and of whose body thou hast been made a member. Recollect that having been delivered from the power of darkness, thou hast been translated into the light and kingdom of God" (St Leo, Sermon on the Nativity).

St Augustine writes: "He is born in a stable; He is wrapped in poor swaddling clothes by His mother, Mary, and laid in a manger. For her there was no house of cedar nor throne of ivory, on which she might give birth to her Creator, and lay to rest the Redeemer of all. As an exile and as a wanderer, in the house of another, she brought forth the Lord of the world; and as a poor woman, she wrapped Him up in poor, and not in silken clothing. When her child was born, she adored Him as God. O favoured stable! O blessed manger in which Christ is born, and the God of all is laid to rest! There stood by at His birth the heavenly powers, and angels ministered comfort. There were present the thousands of thousands singing for joy. There was heard the cry of the infant Christ in the stable, and great joy in the heavens. Christ weeping in the manger, and the multitude of the heavenly host exulting around Him, and sounding forth, Glory to God in the highest, and announcing 'peace on earth to men of good-will,' for heavenly goodness was born upon earth. True peace had come down from heaven, and the rejoicing angels sang, Glory to God in the highest. The angels exult for joy. Mary trembles at having become the mother of God. The angels crowd together joyfully, without fear, in the presence of the Christ, before whom His mother stands, before whom she exults with great fear and trembling, and timidly perseveres in her joy" (Sermon on the Nativity).

"Rejoice, ye just men," says St Augustine; "it is the birthday of Him who justifieth. Rejoice, ye that are sick and infirm, it is the birthday of your Saviour. Rejoice, ye captives, it is the birthday of your Redeemer. Rejoice, ye servants, it is the birthday of the Master over all. Rejoice, ye freemen, it is the birthday of Him who maketh all free. All Christians rejoice, it is the birthday of Christ" (St Augustine, Third Sermon on the Nativity).

"But if all things on earth rejoice at the birth of Christ," writes the Cistercian Abbot above quoted, "what must have been the joy of Mary. The lips stammer, the heart shrinks, and the mind trembles at the thought of such joy. Whence came it that a vessel, still frail and mortal, was able to endure under the burden of such joy? It was because He still overshadowed her in the birth of Christ, who had previously overshadowed her in His conception. He gave her power to bear the joy, who had given to her its abundance; and the same marvellous power of the Godhead sustained her, which had already filled her with the wonderful overflowing of His glory and majesty."

CHORUS OF PRIESTS.

Who can count the starry jewels
   Set in Mary's crown of light?
    Who can estimate her greatness?
      Who can guess her glory's height?
What can measure its extent,
Save the depth of God's descent?

CHORUS OF VIRGINS.

Hail! O Queen of nature's kingdoms,
   Queen of Angels, hail to thee!
Greater none have been before thee,
   Greater none shall ever be:
Hail, divine Receptacle
Of th' Incomprehensible!

—From "The Masque of Mary."

But we must by no means here fail to take note in what way the Third Mystery of the Rosary shows the Divine plan of the Incarnation, making good one further and very signal step in unfolding itself to human belief. The time is now come for an entirely fresh order of witnesses to appear on the scene, to bear their testimony to the wonder which has been brought to pass. The infirmity of human faith, we may observe, will assuredly fail, except there comes to its aid a testimony consonant with the magnitude of that which has been accomplished. St Paul writes: "When He brings the First-born into the world, He says, Let all the angels of God worship Him" (Heb. i. 6). And to provide for the difficulty of human belief in the truth of so surpassingly great a mystery, an Angel is sent to shepherds watching their flocks by night, to bring to them the glad tidings. The brightness of God shone around them as they heard the Angel's words telling them what had come to pass in Bethlehem, and giving them a sign, "You shall find the infant wrapped in swaddling clothes, and laid in a manger." Then suddenly there was with the Angel a multitude of the heavenly host, praising God, and saying, "Glory to God in the Highest, and on earth peace to men of good-will." Here, then, we have given to aid our infirmity in believing, the testimony of the multitude of the Host of heaven, corroborating the words of the Angel; and there are theologians who say, that the sin on Satan's part which caused his fall, was the pride which revolted from joining the other angels in their adoration of an Incarnate King of the angels, when this mystery was made known to them as hereafter to be accomplished.

Yet, however fitting it was that the multitude of the heavenly host should bear its unanimous testimony, still, as the inspired proverb says, "As in water face answereth to face, so the heart of man to man." The heart of man surrenders better to the testimony that comes from its own world which it can see, than even to that of the angels, and hence we shall be more effectually drawn by the testimony of the shepherds than even by theirs. The shep-

The Old Testament Types of the III. Joyful Mystery.

The Fleece of Gideon. — The manna which came from Heaven.

ROSA MYSTICA PASSIM IN LEGE ET IN PROPHETIS

ADUMBRATA ORA PRO NOBIS CUM ET FILIUM

THE SIGN GIVEN TO THE SOLDIER OF GOD. — THE HEAVENLY FOOD GIVEN TO THE PEOPLE OF GOD.

herds then said to one another, Let us go to Bethlehem "to see." And they went with haste, and found all things according to the sign that had been given them. "And they understood," says the evangelist, "of the word that had been spoken to them of this Child." They tell the wondrous story to others, "And all that heard wondered at those things which were told them by the shepherds." Thus we reach, in the third mystery of the Rosary, a fresh stage in the unfolding of the Divine plan. The great mystery of the Incarnation begins to be known and talked of in Bethlehem, and there begin to be those who fall down and adore the first fruits of the great company of the faithful upon earth, which is to see the end of the world.

CHAPTER VII.

THE SCRIPTURE TYPES OF THE THIRD JOYFUL MYSTERY.

I. THE FLEECE OF GIDEON.
II. THE MANNA THAT CAME DOWN FROM HEAVEN, AND WHICH WAS LAID UP IN THE GOLDEN URN.

1. *Type—The fleece of Gideon.*

AROUND the subject of the third joyful mystery, the birth into our lost world of the "long-waited-for Messias, the Prince," and the "Desired of all Nations," the types and figures of the old law congregate together with a richness and profusion, in which, however, we can see no possible cause for surprise, when we reflect that the Almighty has designed, in His wisdom and mercy, that the Mosaic Covenant should be, as St Augustine says, "*Gravida Christo*"—pregnant with Christ. God, as we may rejoice to repeat again and again, has intended that the old law should be the schoolmaster of the nations of the world to bring them to Christ; and as it is by its types and figures that it performs a very important portion of its duty in this respect, nothing can be judged more agreeable to the designs of God, than that the crowning event of the long-matured plan, the advent of the Eternal Son of God into our world as the Son of Mary, should be foreshadowed in almost innumerable types and figures; "for where the body is," says our Lord, "thither will the eagles be gathered together" (Luke xvii. 37). The same truth, as we shall see in its proper place, applies equally to His sacrifice of Himself on the Cross; the types and figures of which will be found to be equally numerous and various. But to proceed with our proper subject, the particular manner in which the Mosaic Covenant has prefigured the Nativity of Jesus Christ from a Virgin Mother.

As the Christian people spread over the earth in their various nations and languages, with one unanimous voice proclaim and testify to the truth of Mary's peerless prerogative, her inviolable virginity, inseparably associated with the birth of her Divine Infant, our object must be to show in what way the Mosaic Law has been made to reveal in its figurative method to future ages the special and peculiar glory of the New Covenant.

The Church sings in the vespers for the feast of the circumcision, "When Thou wast born after an unspeakable manner from a Virgin, then the Scriptures were fulfilled. Thou didst descend like the rain unto the fleece. We praise Thee, O our God." The narrative here referred to occurs in the Book of Judges, and runs as follows:—"In the days of the Judges of Israel, Gideon, the son of Joas, was thrashing and winnowing the wheat by the wine-press, in the territory of the tribe of Manasses, to prepare to fly from before the face of the Madianites, when an Angel of the Lord appeared to him, and said, 'The Lord is with thee, O most valiant of men.'" Gideon was directed by the Angel to destroy the altar of Baal, which stood on his father's land, and to cut down his grove.

Gideon, fearing his father's house, and the men of the city, went by night with ten men of his father's house, and destroyed the altar, and cut down the grove.

The men of the city, in the morning, saw the grove cut down, and Baal's altar overthrown, and it was told to them that Gideon had done this. Soon after this all Madian and Amalec assembled their people, and came and pitched their tents in the valley of Jezrahel. But the Spirit of the Lord came upon Gideon, and he called together the house of Abiezer to follow him, and he sent messengers to all Manasses, and to the tribes of Aser, Zabulon, and Nepthali. And Gideon said to God, "If Thou wilt save Israel by my hand, as Thou hast said, I will put this fleece of wool on the floor ; if there be dew on the fleece only, and it be dry on all the ground beside, I shall know that, by my hand, as Thou hast said, Thou wilt deliver Israel. And it was so. And rising before day, wringing the fleece, he filled a vessel with the dew. And he said again to God, Let not Thy wrath be kindled against me if I try once more, seeking a sign in the fleece. I pray that the fleece only may be dry, and all the ground wet with dew. And God did that night as he had requested ; and it was dry on the fleece only, and there was dew on all the ground" (Judges vi. 36).

The Book of Psalms foretells the manner of the miraculous birth of Jesus, by a reference to this very sign that was given to Gideon. "He shall come down as the dew unto the fleece, and as the drops of rain that distil upon the earth" (Ps. lxxi. 6). But the Cistercian Abbot, Amedeus, shall give us in his own words the explanation of the type. "The fleece," he says, "is a figure of Mary ; and the falling of dew first upon the fleece, signifies the conception and birth of Jesus, without detriment to the virginity of His Mother; while the subsequent falling of the dew on all the earth around, and not upon the fleece, signifies the Divine grace which Jesus afterwards communicated in the heavenly dew of His holy baptism to all the world ; while Mary, by the privilege of her immaculate conception, in no way stood in any need of this grace,—the fleece alone remaining unmoistened, when all the earth besides was covered with the dew."

"Hail, fleece of Gideon," say also both St Ephrem and St Germanus, addressing themselves to Mary, "into which the dew from heaven fell noiselessly." As Moses says in his canticle, "My speech shall distil as the dew, as a shower upon the herbs, and as drops upon the grass" (Deut. xxxii. 2).

2. *The Type of the Manna which fell from Heaven, and which was laid up and preserved in the Golden Urn.*

"I am the bread of life," said Christ to the Jews ; "your fathers did eat manna in the wilderness, and are dead. I am the living bread which came down from heaven ; if any man eat of this bread he shall live for ever; and the bread which I will give is my flesh for the life of the world" (John vi.)

And St Paul writes referring to the passage in Exod. xvi. 33, and speaking generally of the Mosaic tabernacle, "After the second veil was the tabernacle called the holy of holies, containing the golden thurible, and the Ark of the Covenant, covered round about with gold on every side, in which were laid up the GOLDEN URN CONTAINING THE MANNA, the rod of Aaron which had blossomed, and the tables of the covenant" (Heb. ix. 3).

"Hail, Thou vessel made of purest gold !" exclaims St Germanus; "preserving Christ, the heavenly manna, the bread of life for all." "Hail, full of grace," writes St Ephrem, "Thou that art the golden urn, which preservest the manna from heaven."

"Hail, O urn, beaten out of purest gold!" writes St John Damascene "apart from every other vessel, in which the whole world receives the manna that has been given for it, the bread of life prepared in the fire of the Godhead itself."

"Urn of sinless mortal clay,
In which the manna immortal lay;
Destined in God's prophetic page
To be the life of a future age.
  Glory, glory, glory to Thee,
  Mother of Immortality!"
—*The Masque of Mary* (*Caswall*).

The Fourth Joyful Mystery of the Rosary.

CHAPTER VIII.

THE PRESENTATION OF THE INFANT JESUS IN THE TEMPLE.

THE HOLY SCRIPTURE NARRATIVE.

"And after the days of her purification, according to the law of Moses, were accomplished, they carried Him to Jerusalem, to present Him to the Lord, as it is written in the law of the Lord, '*Every male opening the womb shall be called holy to the Lord*,' and to offer a sacrifice, according as it is written in the law of the Lord, a pair of turtle doves, and two young pigeons. 'And behold there was a man in Jerusalem named Simeon, and this man was just and devout, waiting for the consolation of Israel; and the Holy Ghost was in him. And he had received an answer from the Holy Ghost, that he should not see death, before he had seen the CHRIST of the Lord. And he came by the Spirit into the Temple. And when his parents brought in the child Jesus, to do for Him according to the custom of the law, he also took

The Fourth Joyful Mystery.

Ave Maria Gratia Plena Dominus Tecum

Dicite filiæ Sion, Ecce Salvator tuus venit, ecce merces ejus cum eo et opus ejus coram eo. (*Isaias* lxii. 11.)

Tu in mulieribus et Benedictus fructus ventris tui Jesus.

Tell it forth to the daughter of Sion, Behold, thy Saviour cometh. Behold, His reward is with Him, and His work is before Him. (*Isaias* lxii. 11.)

Pro puero isto oravi, et dedit mihi Dominus petitionem meam pro quâ postulavi eum. (1 *Reg.* i. 27.)

Benedicta

For this child I prayed, and the Lord hath granted my petition for which I asked Him. (1 *Kings* i. 27.)

THE PRESENTATION OF THE INFANT JESUS IN THE TEMPLE.

"Him in his arms, and blessed God, and said:—

THE CANTICLE "NUNC DIMITTIS."

"Now, Thou dost dismiss Thy ser-
"vant, O Lord, according to Thy word,
"in peace, because my eyes have seen
"Thy salvation, which Thou hast pre-
"pared before the face of all peoples; a
"light to the revelation of the Gentiles,
"and the glory of Thy people Israel.
"And His father and mother were
"wondering at those things which were
"spoken concerning Him. And Simeon
"blessed them, and said to Mary, His
"mother, Behold, this Child is set for
"the fall and for the resurrection of many
"in Israel, and for a sign which shall be
"contradicted; and thy own soul a sword
"shall pierce, that, out of many hearts,
"thoughts may be revealed. And there
"was one Anna, a prophetess, the daugh-
"ter of Phanuel, of the tribe of Aser.
"She was far advanced in years, and had
"lived with her husband seven years from
"her virginity. And she was a widow
"until four score and four years, who
"departed not from the Temple by fast-
"ings and prayers, serving night and day.
"Now she at the same hour coming in,
"confessed to the Lord, and spoke of
"Him to all that looked for the redemp-
"tion of Israel. And after they had
"performed all things according to the
"law of the Lord, they returned into
"Galilee to their city Nazareth" (Luke
ii. 22–39).

The prophets of Israel had promised that the glory of the Second Temple should be greater than that of the first. "Who is left among you," says the prophet Aggeus, addressing himself to the people, "that saw this house in its first glory, and how do you see it now? Is it not in comparison to that as nothing in your eyes? For thus saith the Lord of Hosts, Yet a little while and the 'Desired of all Nations' shall come, and I will fill this house with glory, saith the Lord of Hosts" (Aggeus ii. 4). Malachy, the last of the prophets, had foretold, "And immediately the Ruler whom you seek, and the Angel of the Covenant whom you desire, shall come to His Temple."

The fourth mystery of the Rosary bears witness to the merciful fulfilment of these predictions; and in all that is recorded of the holy Simeon, and the aged widow Anna, it expresses the exceeding and heartfelt joy of those who, having received tidings of the great mystery of the Nativity being accomplished, now go forth to meet the Divine Visitor, who has come down from heaven, and to behold with their eyes the salvation which God has wrought. The cry has been heard, "Behold, the Bridegroom cometh, go ye forth to meet Him" (Matt. xxv. 6); and the wise virgins rise, trim their lamps, and set out on their way to meet Him.

The occasion of this going forth to meet the Holy Infant, was furnished by the act of compliance on the part of Mary and St Joseph, with the enactment of the law of Moses, which prescribed a legal term of purification to the mother, and the offering of a sacrifice for the infant that had been born (Lev. xii. 6); which, in the case of the male first born, was to be a sacrifice of redemption, as the law claimed every male first born as holy to the Lord (Exod. xiii. 2), except it were redeemed in the manner commanded by the law.

"And after the days of her purification were accomplished," writes St Luke, "they carried Him to Jerusalem." "But hold!" writes Bishop Leontius, "what is that thou sayest, most venerable evangelist? What means this word of thine, O Luke? Have a care, lest you may have forgotten what you have written above, for this which you have now said seems to be at variance with it. Do you not bring in the blessed archangel Gabriel addressing these words to the most holy Virgin, the Mother of God, 'The Holy Ghost shall come upon thee, and the power of the Most High shall overshadow thee?' How then comes it to pass that she who conceived through the Holy Ghost, and not according to the laws of humanity, should stand in need of purification? How is it that she whom the power of the Most High overshadowed, should not be full of all holiness and purity?" What will the evangelist reply to this? "I have by no means forgotten," he will say, "what I have previously written, nor is what I have just written at all at variance with what I have said before. If, indeed, the Divine Word had chosen to remain in the heights of heaven, and had never condescended to lower Himself to our weakness, then what you urge would indeed sorely perplex me. But when He who sits above the cherubim suffers Himself to be carried in the arms of His Virgin Mother, and He who gives life to all created things endures to be fed with milk from her breasts, where is the wonder that He who is all pure and undefiled, together with His Virgin Mother, who is alike pure and undefiled, should submit to undergo the purification prescribed by the law, inasmuch as the apostle says of Him, that He was, 'made under the law, that He might redeem those who were in bondage to the law?' (Gal. iv. 5)" (Leontius' Sermon on Holy Simeon).

"And, behold, there was a man in Jerusalem." "Listen," writes Timothy, the presbyter of Jerusalem, "and prudently consider these things. What the evangelist here says is, as if to the following effect:—"As Simeon was sitting at home meditating, and was in his inmost heart earnestly praying for this one thing, that the revelation which had been made to him might be speedily brought to pass, and as Joseph and Mary were in the act of setting out to bring the child Jesus to the Temple, that according to the custom prescribed by the law they might offer the legal sacrifice for Him, the Holy Ghost became present to him, and awakened his attention by such words as the following:—'Arise, old man, wherefore dost thou slumber? The time for the oracle to be accomplished is now come. Be quick, therefore, and make haste, for He that will set thee free is close at hand. Unroll thy funeral garments and thy winding-sheet, and make ready thy tomb. Set thine house in order, for He is at hand who shall send thee to thy home. The Emmanuel is come. Run across quickly to the Temple, and when thou art in the Temple, prophesy that which shall be foretold to thee concerning this Holy Child.'

"Simeon, therefore, as if suddenly filled with the vigour of youth, and carried forward with the vehemence of his desire as it were with wings, led, at the same time, by the Holy Ghost, ran with his utmost speed, and overtook Joseph and Mary as they were pursuing their way to the Temple. The Holy Child, indeed, who was being carried by them, he did not overtake; for how could he be said to overtake Him, who hath nowhere where He is not present. He overtook, then, none but Joseph and Mary, and entering the court of the Temple before them, he came and stood close by the sanctuary, there to wait for the inspiration which the Holy Ghost might send to him. Here he saw many mothers coming to present their sons, but alone amongst them he observed the Holy Virgin, with a Divine, and as it were indescribable, light shed around her. Running, therefore, he pushed the other matrons aside, crying out and saying before all, 'Make way for me that I may embrace Him whom I have so long desired. Behold, I now see Him who long ago hath seen me. I see Him, and my spirit revives. Why do you who are but servants press forward and contend with the free woman and the mistress? Why take your children to the altar? Hitherward turn yourselves, and offer your gifts to this Child who is older than Abraham'" (Timothy, presbyter of Jerusalem. Sermon on the "Nunc Dimittis.")

"Mary, His mother," writes St Augustine, "was carrying her infant in her arms when Simeon saw Him and recognised Him. Whence and how did he come to know and recognise Him? Was He who was outwardly born inwardly revealed? He saw Him, and he recognised Him. Simeon knew who the babe was that was speechless, and yet the Jews could put the grown-up Man who worked miracles to death. When, therefore, he had recognised Him, he took Him, that is, he embraced Him, in his arms. He upheld Him by whom he was himself upholden. For He was no other than the Christ, the wisdom of God, which reaches in its strength from end to end, and disposes all things sweetly. What greatness, what immensity was there! and yet how little He had become. Having become little, He sought those who were little. How is

The Old Testament Types of the IV. Joyful Mystery.

Moses sees the Promised Land.
LEGE · ES · IN · PROPHETIS · SEUM · FILIUM · TUUM

THE PROPHET WHOSE DEATH ENABLES HIS PEOPLE TO ENTER THE PROMISED LAND.

Anna presents Samuel in the Temple.
ROSA · MYSTICA · PASSIM · IN · UMBRA · ORA · PRO · NOBIS

THE MOTHER WHO GAVE HER SON FOR THE WORK OF GOD.

this? He gathered about Him not the proud but the humble. Simeon took Him into his arms, and said, 'Now, dost Thou, O Lord, dismiss Thy servant in peace?' Dismiss him in peace? Yes, for I have seen Thy peace. Why dost Thou dismiss him in peace? 'For mine eyes have seen Thy salvation.' The salvation of God is the Lord Jesus Christ. 'Tell of His salvation from day to day' (Ps. xcv. 2)." (St Augustine's Sermon on the Purification).

"But," writes the Bishop of Ancyra, "what has the holy and never sufficiently to be praised Virgin Mother to say to these things?" She, indeed, wondered, and with reason, at the things which were uttered, and she treasured them together with all that had previously happened in her heart. To her, then, Simeon now purposely addresses his discourse. "O most pure and innocent dove! O holy tabernacle of our hope, in whom all sanctity and pre-eminence resides. This Child to whom thou hast given birth" (and thou knowest it not) "is set for the ruin and the rising again of many in Israel, and for a sign that shall be contradicted; and a sword shall pierce through thine own soul, that the thoughts may be revealed out of many hearts" (Luke ii. 34). What is this, O aged man, that makes thee thus mix up sadness with thy words of joy?

Hitherto thou hast spoken of "light" and "glory," but now thou announcest "ruin," and to the Mother of the Child thou depictest a sword? "Of a perfect certainty," he says, "all these things shall come to pass in their time." "Ruin" shall come on them that refuse to believe, and "rising again" to those that believe. And "for a sign that shall be contradicted" throughout the entire world, inasmuch as it is to be received in no light and easy spirit of credulity on the part of men, but through open trials and acts of heroism. And, moreover, there will be much suffering to thy virgin mind, through many thoughts coming in and going away. For the question will not be concerning small things, but concerning God, the abolishing of customs and laws, the changing of men, the union of people, the concord of nations, the fusion of languages, the undivided unity of worship; and how can such things as these be brought about without great agitation and disturbance of minds? Some, therefore, will fall; others will rise again. Some will be raised to life; others will be blotted out. Some will contradict the sign, as a thing novel and extraneous; others will surrender themselves to its life-giving and wonder-working power (Theodotus' Sermon on Holy Simeon).

CHAPTER IX.

SCRIPTURE TYPES OF THE FOURTH JOYFUL MYSTERY.

I. THE PRESENTATION OF SAMUEL TO THE HIGH PRIEST HELI.
II. MOSES ALLOWED TO SEE THE PROMISED LAND PREVIOUS TO HIS DEATH.

1. *Anna presents her son Samuel to the High Priest Heli for the service of the tabernacle for the whole of his life.*

WE have already become familiar, in the First Joyful Mystery, with the peculiar circumstances attending the birth of Samuel, and with the beautiful character of his mother Anna, as prefiguring the Mother of Jesus, in respect of her spirit of piety and earnest supplication, through which she obtained the precious gift of her son Samuel. We have now to make the further acquaintance of Anna, in the new and still more affecting character of the mother who presented her son, in the presence of the altar of God, to be henceforward entirely devoted to the service of God and of His people: she, as his mother, formally renouncing all her maternal right in her son, and giving him up entirely to the work to which it might please God to call him.

The Scripture relates the history as follows:—" And after she had weaned him, she carried him with her, with three calves, and three bushels of flour, and a bottle of wine, and she brought him to the house of the Lord in Silo. Now the child was yet very young, and they immolated a calf, and offered the child to Heli. And Anna said, 'I beseech thee, my lord, as my soul liveth, I am that woman who stood before thee praying to the Lord. For this child did I pray, and the Lord hath granted me my petition which I asked of Him. Therefore, I also have lent him to the Lord; all the days of his life he shall be lent to the Lord.' And they adored the Lord there. And Anna prayed and said—

"CANTICLE OF ANNA.

"My heart hath exulted in the Lord, and my horn is exalted in my God. My mouth is enlarged above my enemies, for I have rejoiced in Thy salvation. There is none holy like unto the Lord, for there is none other beside Thee, and there is none mighty like unto our God. Forbear to speak high things and multiply boastings. Let the old things depart from thy mouth; for the Lord He is the God of knowledge, to Him shall all thoughts be turned. The bow of the strong is broken, and the feeble are clothed with strength. For they that were full before have hired themselves out for bread, and the hungry are filled. Until she that was barren hath brought forth many children, and she that had many sons hath become weak. The Lord killeth and maketh alive; He bringeth down to the grave and bringeth back again. The Lord maketh poor and maketh rich. He bringeth down and raiseth up. He lifted up the needy from the dust, and raiseth the poor man from the dunghill, that he may sit with the princes, and hold the throne of glory. For in the hands of the Lord are the hinges of the earth, and He hath set the world upon them. He shall preserve the feet of His saints, and the ungodly shall be silenced in the darkness, for no man shall prevail by his own strength. All His enemies shall fear the Lord. He shall cast down lightning upon them from heaven. The Lord shall judge the ends of the earth, and He shall give dominion unto His King, and shall exalt the horn of His Christ" (1 Kings ii. 1–10).

Anna presents Samuel, the son whom she had obtained from God by her earnest prayer, to be made over for the whole of his life to the service of the tabernacle, in fulfilment of her vow. And Mary presents her Son Jesus in the temple, to do honour to the law of Moses, notwithstanding that she did not come under its obligation, and to signify that, as His Mother, she gave Him up to God to the work of saving His people from their sins. "When," writes St Athanasius, "was the Lord hid from the eye of His Father, or what place is exempted from His dominion, that by remaining in it, He should be separate from the Father, except He were brought to Jerusalem and presented in the temple? for, as He was made man and circumcised, not to obtain grace for Himself, but that we might obtain grace and be circumcised in spirit, so it is entirely for our sakes that Mary presents Him in the temple to the Father, that we may learn from thence to give ourselves to God."

Again, Anna having presented her son for the service of God to be henceforward a servant of the tabernacle, rejoices in spirit, and says, "For I have rejoiced in Thy salvation;" and Mary rejoices to hear the words of holy Simeon: "Mine eyes have seen Thy salvation."

Again, Anna's son, even before his conception and birth, is irrevocably pledged by his mother to the service of God in His sanctuary, and Mary is the Mother of a Son who also previous to His birth was irrevocably pledged to save His people from their sins, which involved His becoming obedient to death, even the death of the cross.

Anna, again, was blessed of God in an especial manner for thus surrendering up her son to the service of the sanctuary, and she was afterwards rewarded with numerous children, so that her name has even become celebrated in prophecy: "Rejoice, thou barren that bearest not; sing praise, and cry out for joy, thou that didst not bring forth, for more are the children of the forsaken than of her that hath a husband" (Isa. liv. 1). Mary also freely surrendered up her Son Jesus to save His people from their sins, and now all generations make it their glory to vie with each other for the right to call themselves her children, and to place themselves under her maternal love and protection. Of a truth He that is mighty hath done great things for Mary.

2. *Moses is allowed to see the promised land before his death.*

Simeon was a just and devout man waiting for the consolation of Israel, to whom it had been revealed by the Holy Ghost that he should not taste death before He had seen the "Christ of the Lord."

He was not to live to hear the words spoken on the cross, "It is finished;" he was not to benefit by the cleansing bath or to hear the words of regeneration, "I baptize thee in the name of the Father, and of the Son, and of the Holy Ghost;" it was only reserved to him to see with his bodily eyes the Christ of the Lord, and after he had seen Him to die in peace: "Lord, now dost Thou let Thy servant depart in peace, for mine eyes have seen Thy salvation."

So it was with Moses, of whom St Paul says, that he was faithful as a servant in all his house; he waited patiently for the consolation of Israel. He bore with the iniquities and transgressions of his people, and the last act of his long life was to assemble the whole people of Israel together, and to recapitulate to them all that the Lord their God had done for them.

For this faithful service, like holy Simeon, Moses receives the reward of being permitted to see with his bodily eyes the salvation which he is not personally to enjoy, and to behold the promised land which he is not himself to enter.

"The Lord," says the sacred Scripture, "spoke to Moses the same day, saying, Go up to this mountain, Abarim, to Mount Nebo, which is in the land of Moab, over against Jericho, and see the land of Canaan which I will give to the children of Israel to possess, and die thou in the mountain" (Deut. xxxii. 48).

"Then Moses went up from the plains of Moab, upon Mount Nebo, to the top of Phasga, over against Jericho, and the Lord showed him the land of Galaad as far as Dan, and all Nephthali, and the land of Ephraim and Manasses, and the land of Juda to the furthermost sea, and the south part, and the breadth of the plain of Jericho, the city of palm-trees, as far as Segor.

"And the Lord said to him, This is the land which I sware to Abraham, Isaac, and Jacob, saying, I will give it to thy seed: thou hast seen it with thy eyes, and shalt not pass over to it.

"And Moses, the servant of the Lord, died there in the land of Moab, by the commandment of the Lord.

"And He buried him in the valley of the land of Moab over against Phogor, and no man hath known of his sepulchre until this present day" (Deut. xxxiv. 1-6).

Abraham saw the day of Jesus Christ afar off; he saw it and was glad. Moses saw with his eyes the land which God had promised to give to the seed of Abraham, Isaac, and Jacob; he saw it and died in peace. Simeon saw with his eyes the Christ of the Lord, and he blessed God that he was thus enabled to depart in peace. And yet, dear fellow-Christians, is not our Christian blessedness far greater than this. Let us hear St John telling us what it is that we possess: "That which our ears have heard, our eyes have seen, and our hands have handled of the Word of life" (1 John i. 1). Of a truth, "Many prophets and kings have desired to see *the things which we see*, and have not seen them; and to hear the things that we hear, and have not heard them" (Luke x. 24). Where then, dear Christians, is our gratitude?

The Fifth Joyful Mystery of the Rosary.

CHAPTER X.   THE FINDING OF JESUS IN THE TEMPLE.

THE HOLY SCRIPTURE NARRATIVE.

"And His parents went every year to "Jerusalem, at the solemn day of the "Pasch. And when he was twelve years "old, they going up into Jerusalem, ac-"cording to the custom of the feast, and "having fulfilled the days, when they "returned the Child Jesus remained in "Jerusalem, and His parents knew it not. "And thinking that He was in the com-"pany, they came a day's journey, and "*sought* Him among their kinsfolks and "acquaintance, and not finding Him, they "returned into Jerusalem, seeking Him. "And it came to pass, that, after three "days, they found Him in the temple "sitting in the midst of the doctors, "hearing them, and asking them ques-"tions. And all that heard Him were "astonished at His wisdom and His "answers. And seeing Him, they won-"dered. And His mother said to Him: "Son, why hast Thou done so to us?

The Fifth Joyful Mystery.

Ave — Maria — Gratia — Plena — Dominus — Tecum

Benedicta — tu in mulieribus et Benedictus fructus ventris — tui Jesus

Solatium vitæ nostræ. Omnia simul in te uno habentes, te non debuimus dimittere a nobis. (Tob. x. 5.)

The comfort of our life. Having all things in Thee, we ought not to have suffered Thee to go away from us. (Tob. x. 5.)

Benedico te Domine Deus Israel: tu salvasti me; et ecce ego video Tobiam filium meum. (Tob. xi. 17.)

I bless Thee, O Lord God of Israel: Thou hast saved me. And, behold, I see Tobias my son. (Tob. xi. 17.)

THE FINDING OF JESUS IN THE TEMPLE.

"Behold, Thy father and I have sought "Thee sorrowing. And He said unto them: "How is it that you sought Me? did you "not know that I must be about My "Father's business? And they under-"stood not the words that He spoke unto "them. And He went down with them "and came into Nazareth, and was sub-"ject to them. And His mother kept all "these words in her heart. And Jesus "advanced in wisdom and age, and in "grace with God and men" (St Luke ii. 41, 52).

Before entering upon any consideration of the Fifth and last Joyful Mystery, we shall do well to pause for a moment to take a brief retrospect of the steady progressive unfolding of the Divine plan which we have hitherto witnessed.

The one great mystery which is the groundwork of the entire fifteen mysteries of the Rosary is the *Incarnation of God*, namely, *God manifest in the flesh*. And the fifteen mysteries are but so many steps or stages in the unfolding of the one supreme Divine Mystery, the "Incarnation of God."

The progress of the Divine plan then has been as follows, as we have witnessed it:—

The first of all human creatures who is conscious of this supreme mystery is the Blessed Mary herself. As she alone of all the daughters of Eve is chosen for the dignity of being both Virgin and Mother, so there is a time when she alone of the whole race of Adam is chosen as witness of the accomplishment of the Divine counsel that was pre-ordained from all eternity to be accomplished in her. God has in the world one solitary human voice to bear testimony to the truth of His promises, and this one chosen and elect witness is the Blessed Virgin and Mother Mary. This is the First Mystery of the Holy Rosary, and the first stage of the Divine plan.

But the designs of God do not stand still, for who can say to Him, "What doest Thou?" Others beside Mary must be brought to bear their testimony. Mary, therefore, by a Divine inspiration, goes in haste to the house of her cousin Elizabeth, who, on seeing her, is filled with the Holy Ghost, and together with the infant Baptist in her womb, becomes a new witness to the work of God. This is the Second Joyful Mystery, and the second stage of the accomplishment of the plan of God.

God, then, is now incarnate in the womb of one who is both Virgin and Mother, and the days will be accomplished when He must be born. He is born, and His Mother still retains the honour and privilege of her virginity. There must now be new voices to bear fresh witness to the work of God, and to proclaim who it is that is born. God, therefore, sends His own angels to bear witness to His work, and the angels pass on their testimony to shepherds, who kept their flocks by night, who come and present themselves and bear their witness that God has fulfilled His word. This is the Third Joyful Mystery, and the third stage of the Divine plan.

But there must be other witnesses besides the heavenly angels and the unlearned shepherds. The temple of Jerusalem must bear its testimony, and therefore Mary again, by a Divine inspiration, and not because she is obliged by the Law, which does not apply to her case, goes to Jerusalem, to the house of the Lord, to present her Divine Son in the temple, and to offer for Him the sacrifices prescribed by the Law. Here the aged prophet Simeon, and Anna, the widowed prophetess, neither of whom departed from the temple, serving God night and day, come forward and bear their testimony. This is the Fourth Joyful Mystery, and the fourth stage of the accomplishment of the Divine plan.

Then follow, in order, as we may learn from the evangelist, the testimony borne by the adoration of the wise men of the East; next, the testimony of Herod's bloodthirsty jealousy and malice, which plunged the mothers of Bethlehem in mourning; next, the testimony of the idols of the land of Egypt, which like Dagon heretofore in the presence of the Ark of the Covenant, fell prostrate before the Christ of the Lord, as His Mother, accompanied by St Joseph, carried Him into the land of Egypt. Something, however, is yet wanting to follow on in the natural order of the Divine plan which is by its sovereign wisdom to challenge the captious understandings of men, and to impress the conviction of its simple reality and truth upon the mind of the observer. This is some irresistible public testimony that God has really become the Son of Mary, in which Mary gives proof of her being His Mother by being publicly seen to assume and to exercise over Him the rightful jurisdiction and authority of the mother over the son. God may possibly have not gone beyond merely making use of Mary as no more than a simple instrument from whom to assume His sacred Humanity, and may never have intended to place one of His own creatures in a position to exercise authority and control over Himself. If, however, He really has done this, and if He has truly placed Himself under subjection to the control of His mother, nothing seems more conformable to the Divine plan than that there should be some public manifestation before a competent assembly of witnesses, that the Divine Person of the ever blessed Trinity, who has assumed our humanity, owns the control of His Mother Mary as being her Son. And if there is in the gospel history any such public manifestation of the subjection of the Divine Son to the authority of the human Mother, this will be at once the most joyful of all possible testimony to the marvellous truth of the Divine maternity of Mary, and it will form the Fifth most Joyful Mystery or stage in the fulfilment of the Divine plan of the manifestation of God in the flesh, the true and veritable Son, of the Holy Virgin who was promised to crush the serpent's head. This is precisely what does form the subject of the Fifth Joyful Mystery of the Rosary, viz., the finding of Jesus in the temple in the midst of the doctors of the law, when this very public manifestation was made before them all, and when they all became witnesses of the authority which Mary exercised over her Son. Here there is no ambiguity or faltering, but the plain and simple assertion of the authority of the Mother over the Son. Mary, in nothing like the mothers who spoil their children by over-indulgence, falls into no lavish display of her tenderness before the doctors of the law. She allows no immediate signs to appear of her being overjoyed at finding Him again after her sorrowing search of three days. There is nothing in what takes place in the temple that in the remotest manner gives rise to any other thought than that of the authority of the mother. With the calm and conscious dignity of one who is fully aware of her rights, she says in their presence to the Divine Youth of twelve years of age, whose wisdom and answers had filled the minds of the doctors of the law with amazement, "Son! why hast Thou done so to us? behold, I and Thy father have sought Thee sorrowing."

Let St Bernard be heard on the subject of this mystery. "But there is something greater still, at which you may be filled with wonder in Mary—Maternity united to Virginity. For, since the beginning of the world, it has never been heard of that one should be both mother and virgin. And oh, if you will but attend, whither will not your wonder at her exalted dignity lead you? Will it not bring you to the conviction that you cannot wonder enough? Is not she, who has God for her Son, to be deemed in your judgment—yea, rather in the judgment of truth itself—exalted above all the choirs of the angels? Does not Mary boldly call God and the Lord of the angels, Son? saying to Him, '*Son, why hast Thou done so to us?*' Which of the angels would have dared to do this? It is enough for them, and they esteem it a great thing, that being spirits by creation, they have been called and made angels by grace, as holy David bears witness: 'He maketh His spirits angels' (Ps. ciii. 4). But Mary, conscious that she is Mother, with the greatest confidence calls the very Majesty whom they serve Son. Nor does God object to be called what He has not abhorred to become. For a little afterwards the Evangelist adds, '*And He was subject to them.*' Who subject? and to whom? God to man! God, I say, to whom the angels are subject, and whom the powers and principalities obey, was subject to Mary, and not only to Mary, but also to Joseph, for the sake of Mary. Wonder therefore at either, and choose at which of the two you will wonder most,

The Old Testament Types of the V. Joyful Mystery.

The joyful meeting with the son who returns.

ROSA · MYSTICA · PASSIM · IN

The mother of Tobias watches for her son's return.

LEGE · ET · IN · PROPHETIS

THE HOUSEHOLD MADE JOYFUL BY THE SON'S RETURN.

EUM · FILIUM · ES

AGNUM · BRA · ORA · PRO · NOBIS

THE MOTHER WHO GRIEVED FOR HER ABSENT SON.

whether at the most gentle condescension of the Son, or at the most excellent dignity of the Mother. On either side there is wonder and marvel; humility without a parallel in that God should be obedient to a woman; and sublimity without a rival in that a woman should impose her will upon God. In the praises of virgins it is sung as a mark of their especial honour that they follow the Lamb whithersoever He goeth. But of what praise, I pray you, is she to be held worthy who goes before Him?" (St Bernard, Fourth Homily on the Praises of the Blessed Virgin.)

What communicates additional force still to this public manifestation of the authority of Mary as Mother over her Son, and therefore the more joyfully confirms the truth of God being in very deed incarnate as the Son of Mary, is the answer of the Son to His Mother, and what followed thereupon. The Son asks "How is it that you sought Me? Did you not know that I must be about My Father's business?" Here the same St Bernard observes: "Have ye not read in the Gospels what kind of an example Jesus gives to holy children? For, when He had remained behind in Jerusalem, and had pleaded that He was in duty bound to be occupied with the business of His Eternal Father, finding that His earthly parents would not consent, He did not despise to follow them to Nazareth. The Master was subject to the disciples! God to man! the Eternal Word and the uncreated Wisdom to an artisan and to a woman! For what does the sacred history go on to say? 'And He was subject to them.' How long then will you be thus wise in your own eyes? God intrusts and subjects Himself to mortal creatures, and will you continue to walk in ways of your own?" (Nineteenth Sermon on the Canticles.)

The very business of the Eternal Father Himself is postponed to the voice of the mortal Mother, recalling her Son to the domestic home of Nazareth. "O humility indeed, without a parallel! O exaltation, without equal! Mary is Mother of very truth, and the Eternal Son of God is become of a truth Mary's Son."

"Thee, the God of worlds foreseeing,
   In thy dignity supreme,
Loved thee, chose thee, gave thee being,
   Set thee in salvation's scheme;
Then with all perfections decked
   As His Mother pre-elect.

"Thine shall be a lot surpassing
   All that is of glory known,
In the earth, or in the heavens,
   Thine, but not for thee alone.
God, in whom thy life began
Made thee for Himself and man."
—*Masque of Mary, Caswall.*

CHAPTER XI.

THE TYPES OF THE FIFTH JOYFUL MYSTERY.

I. THE SORROW OF ANNA FOR THE ABSENCE OF TOBIAS.
II. THE JOY OF ANNA AND TOBIAS ON HIS RETURN.

The history of the departure and return of Tobias to his parents.

TOBIAS was one of the captive Jews whom Salman el Assur removed into his kingdom from the conquered land of Israel. He had married a wife from his own tribe, Anna by name, and they had one son, called by his own name Tobias. In his captivity he gained the goodwill of the Assyrian monarch, and was allowed freely to travel about from town to town, during which journeys, by his industry and sagacity in trade, he amassed a moderate fortune.

When Sennacherib succeeded his father Salman, and was defeated before Jerusalem by the visitation of God, the soldiery, on their return, were in the habit of wreaking their vengeance on the captive Jews, and often murdered them in the streets. Tobias, on these occasions, would go out and bring the dead bodies to his own house, to give them burial during the night.

In one of these works of mercy he lost his eyesight by an accident, and soon after fell into the greatest poverty, so that his kinsfolks and friends, and even his wife Anna, began to mock at him, saying, "Where is thy hope now, for which thou gavest alms, and buriedst the dead?"

In this state of poverty and distress he remembered the sum of ten talents in silver which he had deposited with his countryman Gabelus, in Media, and resolved to send his son Tobias to reclaim the money. And when all things were made ready, Tobias, the son, took his leave, with the guide whom they had carefully selected to be his companion, and they both set out on their way.

And when they were departed, his mother began to weep, and to say, "Thou hast taken the staff of our old age, and sent him away from us. I wish the money for which thou hast sent him had never been. For our poverty was sufficient for us, that we might account it as riches, that we saw our son." And Tobias said to her, "Weep not, our son will arrive thither safe, and will return safe to us, and thy eyes shall see him. For I believe that the good Angel of God doth accompany him, and doth order all things well that are done about him, so that he shall return to us with joy." At these words his mother ceased weeping, and held her peace.

In the meantime God had sent the holy Archangel Raphael, under the form of the young man chosen to be his guide. His heavenly companion delivered him from the jaws of the fish in the river, prospered his journey, and brought him in safety to the house of his kinsman Raguel, who gave him his daughter Sara in marriage. During the rejoicings of the marriage the angel went and recovered the sum of money from Gabelus.

But as Tobias made longer stay upon occasion of the marriage, Tobias his father was solicitous, saying, "Why thinkest thou doth my son tarry, or why is he detained there? Is Gabelus dead thinkest thou, and no man will pay him the money." And he began to be exceeding sad, both he and Anna his wife with him; and they began both to weep together, because their son did not return to them on the day appointed.

But his mother wept, and was quite disconsolate, and said, "Wo, wo, is me, my son, why did we send thee to go to a strange country, the light of our eyes, the staff of our old age, the comfort of our life, the hope of our family. We having all things together in thee, ought not to have let thee go from us. And Tobias said to her, "Hold thy peace, and be not troubled, our son is safe; the man with whom we sent him is very trusty." But she could by no means be comforted, but daily running out, looked round about, and went into all the ways by which there seemed any hope that he might return, that if possible she might see him coming afar off.

In the meantime, Anna sat by the way daily on the top of the hill, from whence she might see afar off. And while she watched his coming from that place, she saw him afar off, and presently she perceived it was her son coming, and returning she told her husband, saying, "Behold, thy son cometh." Then the dog which had been with them on the way ran before, and coming as if he had brought the news, showed his joy by his fawning and wagging his tail. And his father, who was blind, rising up, began to run, stumbling with his feet, and giving a servant his hand went to meet his son.

And receiving him, they kissed him, as did also his wife, and they began to weep for joy. And when they had adored God, and given Him thanks, they sat down together. Then, by the application of the gall of the fish, Tobias restored sight to his aged father, and they glorified God, both he and his wife, and all that knew him. And for seven days they feasted, and rejoiced all with great joy.

Mary, in like manner, sorrowed for the absence of her Son, and rejoiced to see Him again, the Light of her eyes, and of all the nations of the earth, the Staff of her age, the Comfort of her life, the Hope of her house, of all His people Israel, and of all the nations of the whole earth.

The Sufferings and Sacrifice of Jesus Christ in rebuilding the City of God

ARE PREFIGURED BY

THE MALICE AND DERISION WITH WHICH THE ENEMIES OF GOD MOCKED AND OPPOSED THE REBUILDING OF THE WALLS OF THE HOLY CITY JERUSALEM.

Introduction to the Sorrowful Mysteries of the Rosary.

CHAPTER I. *INTRODUCTION.*

THE REBUILDING THE CITY OF GOD IN DISTRESS OF TIMES.
(Dan. ix. 25.)

Sorrow and suffering cannot be supposed to have been the work of an Almighty and merciful Creator, or to have any place whatever of its own right in His creation. God is the Author and the Giver of life, while sorrow and suffering are at once the evidence that the precious gift of life lies under a forfeit, and the prelude to the approach of death. God, as the Book of Genesis relates, " created man in His own image, male and female created He them, and He blessed them, and said, Increase, and multiply, and fill the earth. Subdue it, and rule over the fishes of the sea, the fowls of the air, and all living creatures that move upon the earth. And God saw all things that He had made, and behold they were very good " (Gen. i. 28).

Into a world thus formally blessed and pronounced to be good by the voice of its own supreme Lord, if sorrow and suffering have found an entrance, it has certainly been owing to some cause or other foreign to the original plan of the All-wise and All-merciful Creator. "The gifts of God," says St Paul, "are without repentance;" and God having once freely given the good and precious gift of a life, not merely devoid of suffering, but abounding in joys, could never simply of His own act and deed have revoked His own gift, and with His own hand, as it were, have maimed and deformed His own work. If misery and suffering, therefore, have entered into the world which God has made, has pronounced to be good, and to which He has solemnly given His blessing, the hand of some one else, and not the hand of God, has been concerned in bringing them in. We have already seen in the explanation of the type of "Eve's colloquy with the serpent," how it was the transgression into which she was seduced which became the cause of God revoking His gifts, and pronouncing a curse where He had at first given a blessing.

Through the act of transgression of the law of Paradise, the whole condition of the world of man, which its Creator had blessed, undergoes a signal change. In the place of the unlimited gift of life, which accompanied the breathing into man a living soul, the gift of life has become a forfeit, which will in due time be claimed. The condition under which life is allowed its temporary respite is also changed. Paradise is gone. The banished pair no longer find, as before, the choice fruits of the earth grow spontaneously to their hands. It is no longer with them, as the poet describes—

"Nullo munuscula cultu
Errantes hederas passim cum baccare tellus
Mixtaque ridenti colocasia fundit acantho."
—Virgil, Ecl. iv. 18.

The word of God has gone forth, which He alone can revoke: "Maledicta terra in opere tuo"—"Cursed is the earth in thy labour, in the sweat of thy brow thou shalt eat of it all the days of thy life" (Gen. iii. 17). Life has become forfeit, and its Divine Giver not only announces that He will reclaim His forfeit whenever He shall think fit, but He says, "Though I may suffer you to retain for a certain time, to depend on My good pleasure, the possession of that which you have forfeited, you will retain possession of it no longer as before in a paradise, where everything will grow ready to your wants, but upon the earth, which is cursed for your sake, and where you must toil and labour in order to subdue it to the purposes of your life, until I reclaim my forfeit gift, for 'dust ye are, and unto dust ye shall return.'"

But if a mere limitation by itself of the gift of life, and an exchange of daily labour for the ease and abundance of Paradise be the whole of what has ensued from the transgression of Eve, this, it may be argued, does not at all account for the Christian doctrine of the necessity of God Himself coming into the world to offer a sacrifice and an atonement for it. The life of Paradise, with its ease and abundance, its peace and security, may have the palm easily conceded to it over the life of the world as it is, with its labour and short duration. A Divine gift of life not revoked, and in the full enjoyment of everything good for life, is no doubt much superior to the same gift, when it is only allowed to remain on the terms of a forfeit, to be reclaimed without any covenanted notice, and is deprived of every good which has not been won by hard labour. Still, it may be argued that life is quite enough worth having even on the inferior tenure, and that all mankind think so with the most perfect unanimity. Even Satan himself bears witness, where he says, "Skin for skin, everything that a man hath will he give for his life" (Job ii. 4). The mere exchange, therefore, of the thorns and the thistles of the earth for the flowers and fruit-trees of Paradise, cannot be any sufficient or satisfactory explanation of the Christian doctrine, that God took our human nature upon Himself, and died upon the Cross for the life of the world. The objector may also push his reasoning still further, and say, that even upon the Christian showing itself, the death upon the Cross of the God-

Man has not made matters, in the world of man, at least, perceptibly better: the gift of life continuing, under Christianity, subject to precisely the same forfeit as before, no single instance being on record in which it has not been rigorously exacted, while there remains exactly the same necessity as there ever was for toil and labour. For any visible proof, then, that we have to the contrary, the objector on the infidel side will say, Christianity had made no difference to the world, which is as far as we can see neither more nor less what it would have been, whether the Christian doctrine had ever been heard of in it or not.

To this it is to be replied, that such language expresses the mind of the person whom St Augustine would call a citizen of the "earthly city," of which he writes thus: "The earthly city will not last for ever (for when it shall have been condemned to eternal punishment, it will be no longer a city at all); and it has all its good things here, in the enjoyments of which it finds its delight, in the sort of way in which delight can be found in such kind of things" (City of God, Book xv., chap. 4). And secondly, that the Christian doctrine nowhere alleges that God became incarnate, and died upon the Cross, merely to effect an amelioration in the condition of this present mortal life. God came down, according to the Christian doctrine, for us men and our salvation, to rebuild in the midst of the earthly city—that is, in the present world—the city of God, or the heavenly city. And compared with each other, these are, as St Augustine says, two societies or companies of men, one of whom lives according to human ways, and is destined to undergo eternal punishment with the devil, and the other lives according to God, and is destined to reign for ever with God.

It is, of course, to be asserted that even the condition of the earthly city has derived incalculable benefits from the presence and the ministry of God, who became Incarnate, and who has rebuilt His own city in it, but this is by reason of the overflowing of His mercy, and the good measure with which the gifts of God are given, and not because Jesus Christ had received any direct mission to benefit the condition of the earthly city. "Let the dead bury their dead," said Jesus, "but go thou and preach the kingdom of God" (Luke ix. 60). The mission of God Incarnate into the world is to rebuild the city of God, in the midst of the earthly city; and for this purpose to take the very citizens of the earthly city, and convert them into the citizens of the heavenly city. He rebuilds, in short, His own city out of the fallen ruins themselves of the earthly city.

This rebuilding of the city of God by the Just One, who leaves the bosom of the Father, and comes among the unjust into their fallen world; who takes upon Himself their nature, being like unto them in all things, sin only except; who begins to teach them the doctrines and precepts of a world different to their own, and builds up His own heavenly city, which He binds, attaches to Himself, and to which He gives the obligation to practise all that He has taught;—this, we say, is a work which necessarily brings upon Him suffering and contradiction while He is engaged upon it, and which can only be accomplished by His perfect sacrifice of Himself.

"O fools, and slow of heart," says Christ Himself to His disciples on the way to Emmaus, "to believe in all things which the prophets have spoken. Ought not Christ to have suffered these things, and so to enter into His glory?" (Luke xxiv. 25.) "The wall and the streets of the city of God shall be rebuilt," says the prophet Daniel, "in straitness of times" (Dan. ix. 25).

Sorrowful mysteries are thus a necessary part of our salvation; for *Christ*, according to His own words, *must suffer;* and the wall and the street, according to His own prophet, can only be rebuilt in straitness of times.

God, who continues the same yesterday, to-day, and for ever, could not consistently with His eternity come into the world, whose life is already forfeit, merely to effect in it some temporary purpose, however merciful such purpose might be, during the time which the forfeit world has to run before the forfeiture is claimed. But He comes into the world as Man, to effect an eternal purpose, to collect about Himself the citizens of an eternal kingdom, the life of which is not to be subject to any forfeit.

The first point that He has to secure in the accomplishment of His eternal purpose, is to redeem the forfeit which stands *in limine* as the bar to every citizen of the world which is subject to death by reason of its birth-sin, gaining the rights of citizenship in His eternal kingdom. This, St Anselm teaches,* He alone could do, who could redeem His fellow-citizens by the voluntary laying down of a life which had incurred no forfeit. No ordinary man could redeem his fellow-men by a voluntary death, because, in the case of any ordinary man, even a voluntary death could never be anything more than the surrendering, possibly a little earlier in point of time, that which was already a forfeit. Death, in the case of every one born of Adam, is nothing more than the payment of the debt due by the person himself, a thing which can never, in the nature of things, become the ransom of the debt of another. When, therefore, God Himself lowered Himself to take our nature, He took a life which, not being forfeit like that of the rest of men, its voluntary laying down could be an all-sufficient ransom for the debt of those whom He came to redeem. Thus the plan of human redemption was, that God should become Man, and should lay down His life, as His apostle says, a "ransom for many." And it is by His death that God the Son made Man redeems the forfeit life of all the children of Adam, and purchases from the Eternal Father the right to make all whom He may choose and elect citizens in His eternal kingdom. The death of God made Man is thus the necessary condition of the fulfilment of His eternal purpose. God takes our nature to come into our world; and in consequence of our fall He comes into our world to die; and by His death He redeems the citizens of the earthly city, which is destined to eternal punishment with the devil, and purchases for them rights of citizenship in His own eternal kingdom, where there is to be no death.

* Cur deus homo.—Lib. ii. ch. xviii.

But God does not only come into the world to die. He also lives and dwells in the world to suffer. For He is Just, and those to whom He is sent are unjust. He is therefore contrary to their ways, and they are contrary to His ways. His brethren, says St John, did not believe in Him; and Jesus said to them, "Your time is always ready. The world cannot hate you, but Me it hateth, because I give testimony of it that the works thereof are evil" (St John vii. 7). "God had spoken in times past," says St Paul, "by the prophets to the fathers;" and Jesus Himself says, "Which of the prophets have not your fathers stoned." The hatred of the fallen world against the voice of the Just One preaching in it the words and the doctrines of His eternal kingdom, is so clearly foretold, and so circumstantially described beforehand in the language of prophecy, that there can be no further wonder when we read them, how Christ comes to say to His disciples, "O fools and slow of heart to believe all that is written in the prophets. Ought not Christ to suffer?"

The citizens of the earthly city are thus represented in the Book of Wisdom as clubbing together to maltreat the Just One, and they say one to another, "Let us therefore lie in wait for the Just, because He is not for our turn, and He is contrary to our doings, and upbraideth us with transgressions of the law, and divulgeth against us the sins of our way of life. He boasteth that He hath the knowledge of God, and calleth Himself the Son of God. He is become a censurer of our thoughts. He is grievous unto us, even to behold: for His life is not like other men's, and His ways are very different. We are esteemed by Him as triflers, and He abstaineth from our ways as from filthiness, and He preferreth the latter end of the just, and glorieth that He hath God for His Father. Let us see, then, if His words be true, and let us prove what shall happen to Him, and we shall know what His end shall be. For if He be the true Son of God, He will defend Him, and will deliver Him from the hands of His enemies. Let us examine Him by outrages and tortures,

Introduction to the Sorrowful Mysteries.

that we may know His meekness and try His patience. Let us condemn Him to a most shameful death: for there shall be respect had unto Him by His words. These things they thought, and were deceived: for their own malice blinded them" (Wisdom ii. 12–21).

The prophet of God is never acceptable to the citizens of the earthly city: "Take, my brethren," says St James, "for an example of suffering evil, of labour and patience, the prophets who have spoken in the name of the Lord" (James v. 10). "There is one more prophet, Micheas, the son of Jemla," says Achab, the King of Israel, to Josaphat, " but I hate him; for he doth not prophesy of me good, but evil." And when Micheas had prophesied at the special request of Josaphat, the King of Israel said, " Put this man in prison, and feed him with the bread of affliction and the water of distress till I come again in peace" (3 Kings xxii. 27). The book of Ecclesiasticus bears witness to what befell the prophet Jeremias, in the execution of his ministry, " They maltreated him that was consecrated a prophet from his mother's womb, to overthrow, to pluck up, and to destroy, and to build again, and to renew" (Ecclus. xlix. 9). How still less acceptable to the world, then, could that Prophet be, who, in His denunciations, spake as never man spake. How could such a Prophet upbraid men with His Divine voice for their transgressions of the law, and they not turn against Him? How could He say to the Scribes and Pharisees, "Wo to you, Scribes and Pharisees, hypocrites, for you make clean the outside of the cup and platter, but within you are full of all rapine and uncleanness" (Matt. xxiii. 25); and they, who had no mind to change, not fiercely and malignantly hate Him? How could He say to them, "Ye serpents, ye generation of vipers, how will ye flee from the judgment of hell?" and they not conspire together to put Him to death? Thus Christ *must* suffer. The Just One who rebuilds the City of God in the fallen world must encounter contradiction in His own person, and must leave suffering as a heritage to all who succeed Him in the carrying on His work, for "if they have called the Master of the house Beelzebub, how much more those of His household " (Matt. x. 25).

If all mankind could be brought to be unanimous in preferring the City of God to the earthly city, or the Babel of the world, in which they hold the insecure tenure of their already forfeit life, the rebuilding of the city of God might still be a work of peace, as the angels announced on making known the birth of the great Prophet, when they sang, " Peace on earth to men of good will," but notwithstanding "all the glorious things that are said of the City of God," the citizens of the earthly city, says St Augustine, " each notwithstanding prefer their own idols to the Founder and Builder of the city which is eternal " (City of God, book xi. c. 1). Hence there can never be any lasting peace between its citizens and those of the City of God; precisely as St Paul says, "As then he that was born according to the flesh persecuted him that was born according to the Spirit, so also it is now " (Gal. iv. 29). St Augustine further on explains this at some length when he says, " But because the citizens of the earthly city are each running after their own ends, one his vineyard, one his merchandise, one his wars and victory, another his match-making,— one after one thing and another after another,—while the citizens of the City of God look up to God alone as the sole object of the worship which is called *latria*, it comes to pass that the City of God cannot have its laws in common with the earthly city, and therefore it is obliged to be at variance with it; and as those who think differently are necessarily disagreeable to each other, the City of God has to sustain the anger and hatred, the attacks and persecution of the earthly city, except where it terrifies its adversary by its numbers, and repels their assault by the help of God " (Book xix. c. 17).

The City of God, whilst it is in its pilgrimage in this world, St Augustine continues, nevertheless seeks its citizens from the midst of the earthly city that is thus opposed to it out of every nation and people, and it gathers together its own pilgrims from every language. Jesus

Christ is its rebuilder, and He reconstructs it out of stones that have fallen down to the ground, and to which He alone can restore life. And, as we have seen, this rebuilding of the City of God brings suffering and sacrifice upon Jesus Christ.

Of this rebuilding the streets and walls of the heavenly Jerusalem, in straitness of times, in sorrow and suffering, the old law affords us a striking figure. After Solomon had built the house of the Lord, and had firmly established the holy city, with its walls and towers for the first time, the Queen of Saba came bringing rich presents to hear his wisdom, and all the kings of the earth desired to see the face of Solomon, that they might hear the wisdom that God had given him in his heart, and every year they brought him presents (2 Par. ix. 24). So it was also when God first established His City when the foundations of the world were laid. Then, "the morning stars praised Him together, and all the sons of God made a joyful melody" (Job xxxviii. 7). But after "the holy house of sanctification that Solomon had built in Jerusalem, where their fathers had praised him, had been burned by the Chaldeans with fire;" and after Jerusalem, "the city that was full of people, had sat solitary as a widow among nations for the sins of her people," during the appointed time; when it pleased God to show His mercy, and to cause the walls to be rebuilt, then the kings of all countries no longer brought presents as they did to Solomon; but, on the contrary, they hired counsellors in the court of the King of Persia, to speak against the rebuilding, so that the Scripture describing the rebuilding says, "Of them that built the wall, and that carried burdens, and that laded, with one of his hands he did the work, and with the other he held a sword" (2 Esdras iv. 17).

"And it came to pass," as Nehemias, who was charged with the rebuilding of the wall, relates, "that when Sanaballat heard that we were building the wall, he was angry: and being moved exceedingly he scoffed at the Jews. And said before his brethren, and the multitude of the Samaritans, What are the silly Jews doing? Will the Gentiles let them alone? will they sacrifice and make an end in a day? are they able to raise stones out of the heaps of the rubbish, which are burnt? Tobias also the Ammonite who was by him said, Let them build; if a fox go up, he will leap over their stone wall. Hear Thou our God, for we are despised; turn their reproach upon their own head, and give them to be despised in a land of captivity. Cover not their iniquity, and let not their sin be blotted out from before Thy face, because they have mocked Thy builders" (2 Esdras iv. 1-5).

How truly, as St Paul writes, did these things happen to them in a figure, and how strikingly is the rebuilding of the city of Jerusalem amid dangers and insults the figure of the sufferings, mockery, and derision that Jesus Christ endured in rebuilding, by His passion and death, out of the fallen children of Adam, His eternal kingdom, the City of God, "the Jerusalem that is above, the mother of us all" (Gal. iv.)

THE FIRST SORROWFUL MYSTERY.

Ave — Maria — Gratia — Plena — Dominus — Tecum

Pro eo quod laboravit anima Ejus videbit et saturabitur; ideo dispertiam Ei plurimos. (Isaias liii. 11.)

For that His soul suffered anguish, He shall behold and shall have His fill; therefore will I set apart tui Jesus.

Si posuerit pro peccato animam suam, videbit semen longaevum; et voluntas Dei in manu Ejus dirigetur. (Isaias liii. 10.)

If He shall lay down His life for sin, He shall see a long-lived seed, and the Will of God shall be Benedicta

Tu in mulieribus et Benedictus fructus ventris.

THE PRAYER AND THE AGONY OF JESUS IN THE GARDEN OF GETHSEMANI.

The First Sorrowful Mystery of the Rosary.

CHAPTER II.

THE PRAYER AND THE AGONY OF JESUS IN THE GARDEN OF GETHSEMANE.

THE HOLY SCRIPTURE NARRATIVE.

"And going out, He went, according to "His custom, to the Mount of Olives. "And His disciples also followed Him. "And when He was come to the place, He "said to them: Pray, lest ye enter into "temptation. And He was withdrawn "away from them a stone's cast; and "kneeling down, He prayed, saying: "Father, if Thou wilt, remove this chalice "from me: but yet not My will, but "Thine be done. And there appeared to "Him an angel from heaven, strengthen-"ing Him. And being in an agony, He "prayed the longer. And His sweat be-"came as drops of blood, trickling down "upon the ground. And when He arose "up from prayer, and was come to "His disciples, He found them sleeping "for sorrow. And He said to them: "Why sleep you? arise, pray, lest you "enter into temptation. As He was yet "speaking, behold a multitude; and he "that was called Judas, one of the twelve, went before them, and drew near to Jesus, for to kiss Him. And Jesus said to him, Judas, dost thou betray the Son of Man with a kiss?" (St Luke xxii.)

We have seen in the preceding introduction how our Divine Saviour Jesus Christ, in undertaking to rebuild the city of God in our fallen world, had taken upon Himself a work of suffering which *must* terminate in death. We now prepare to follow Him through the five stages of His suffering which form the Five Sorrowful Mysteries of the Holy Rosary.

Jesus, then, we must call to mind, lest we should be tempted with the temptation to suffer a feeling of shame for what we are about to see Him suffer, is, as St Proclus writes, "In His Divine nature impassible,—that is, incapable of suffering; and it was only in obedience to the Eternal Father, and moved by mercy for us, that He took to Himself our nature, in which He has made Himself liable to sufferings. Christ did not advance in perfection till at length He became God. God forbid! But being God, as the faith teaches, moved by mercy He became man. We do not preach a man who was raised to be God, but we confess God who has taken our flesh." "He took not on Him the nature of angels," writes St Paul, "but of the seed of Abraham, that He might be made in all things like unto His brethren, to become a merciful and faithful High Priest before God, and a propitiation for the sins of the people" (Heb. ii. 16).

Jesus, therefore, in all the humiliations and indignities through which we are now about to follow Him, stands before us as a voluntary sufferer. "He was offered," says Isaias, "because He willed it." He came to suffer, not because fallen men had a claim to His coming, for they had no claim, but because He loved them, though they were lost, and desired to redeem them, and make them members of His eternal kingdom. "In this He commendeth His love," writes St Paul, "because when as yet we were sinners, according to the time, Christ died for us" (Rom. v. 8). Who could have brought Him down from heaven into the hands of those from whom He suffered insults and death, except, out of love to us, He had been pleased to place Himself in their power, and to subject Himself to their will? In return, then, for this so great love, "Let us," says St Paul, "go forth to Him without the camp bearing His reproach" (Heb. xiii. 13). Let us do this in faith, and we shall find for our reward that these Sorrowful Mysteries of the Rosary are full, as the Patriarch of Nicomedia writes, of a dread and a most august majesty: "To us they are titles of nobility; to the Jews who perpetrated them, they are horrible and terrific;—to them, they are despair; to us, they are radiant with hope;—to them, they are the punishment of their Deicide; to us, they are the gift of the knowledge of God;—to them, they are mourning; to us, joy and gladness. Theirs is the act of butchery; ours is the benefit. Far other is our part in them than theirs. They have rejected Him, we have received Him. They have cast the Heir out of the vineyard; we, by receiving Him, have been restored to life. They have the cross, we the salvation gained by the cross; they have the spear and the nails, we the immortality that has flowed forth from them" (Sermon on the words "Stabant juxta Crucem").

In the outset of these Mysteries which record the humiliations and death of our Captain and Deliverer, we thus do well to fortify ourselves against any inroad of the temptation to a feeling of shame for the spectacle of apparent powerlessness and inability to help Himself which Jesus is about to exhibit. This is the mystery of the cross, as St Paul says, "to the Jews a scandal, to the Greeks foolishness, but to him that believeth the power of God." We would not that our Divine Saviour should say to us, as He said to the disciples going to Emmaus, "O fools and slow of heart to believe all that is written in the prophets! *Ought not Christ to suffer these things?* Therefore we will study to have the spirit of the Holy Apostle, who says, "God forbid that I should glory save in the cross of our Lord Jesus Christ, by whom the world is crucified to me, and I to the world" (Gal. vi. 14).

The drama, so to speak, using the word

The First Sorrowful Mystery.

in a pious and religious sense, of the sufferings and humiliations which Jesus voluntarily undertook for our salvation, as set forth in the Mysteries of the Rosary, opens and exhibits our Divine Saviour falling to the ground in the garden of Gethsemane in a mental agony. His three chosen disciples, whom He had taken with Him that they might be witnesses of His humiliation, as they had been witnesses a few months before of His being transfigured in glory, are fallen fast asleep.

Jesus had withdrawn Himself from them about a stone's-throw to pray; and in the midst of His prayer He falls into an agony of mind, and His agony of mind becomes so terrible that His sweat falls from Him in large drops of blood rolling to the ground. Wherefore this prayer? and wherefore this terrible agony?

St Paul, writing to the Hebrews, after applying to Jesus the verse of the 109th Psalm, "Thou art a priest for ever after the order of Melchisedec," says, "Who in the days of His flesh, with strong cries and tears, offering up prayers and supplications to Him that was able to save Him from death, was heard for His reverence" (Heb. v. 7).

"Jesus," writes St Anselm, commenting on the preceding words of St Paul, "as a true High Priest, offered up prayers. For we often read in the Gospels, particularly in St Luke, who describes Him in His character of Priest, that He went to pray. Now all that He did in the days of His flesh, all His prayers and supplications, were for men. All His life long He prayed His Father to grant Him the resurrection of His flesh, and our salvation; and at the approach of His Passion, He offered supplications—that is, the most humble and urgent entreaties—with the utmost devotion and affection of heart; when, falling into an agony, He prayed the longer, and His sweat became great drops of blood trickling down to the ground. And these prayers and supplications He offered, or rather He laid them before His Father, who came out as it were to meet Him and to hear Him. He offered them to Him who was able to save Him from death—that is, to raise Him from the dead,—to Him whom He knew to have power to save Him—that is, to make Him immortal and impassible, by delivering Him from death, so that neither His soul should remain in hell nor His flesh see corruption in the tomb. And these prayers He offered with strong cries and supplications—that is, with the most vehement and efficacious intention of a pious devotion; so that when He prayed more intently, shedding tears—for He is to be believed to have shed tears during that most earnest prayer when His sweat fell from Him as great drops of blood—then He was heard; for that which He asked He obtained in His resurrection. He was heard above all others who have prayed, since after the warfare of His Passion was finished, He was raised by the Father above every creature" (St Anselm, Commentary on Epistle to the Hebrews).

Jesus having terminated His personal ministry of going about from city to city and from village to village preaching the kingdom of God, by the act of instituting the adorable sacrifice of the New Law, and the perpetual priesthood of the Church, into whose hands He committed it, now enters upon the work of His Passion and death. And how does Jesus commence this great work of His Passion, which He undertakes of His own will for our sakes? As an example to thee, O Christian! which Thou shouldst be careful to follow in every work which Thou undertakest, Jesus begins the work of His Passion by prayer, "Sit down here," He says, "while I go and pray yonder." Canst thou then hope, O Christian! to spend any day to the honour and glory of God, in which thou hast not followed this example, by first praying for the blessing of God on all the works thou purposest to do. See here is Jesus, moved solely by love, about to undertake sufferings for thy sake, which are to end in His ignominious death! Is it not enough for Him that He is about to suffer, the Just One for the unjust? Consider well! No; it is not enough! He will first throw Himself before His Eternal Father. He will first assure Himself through prayer that He is about to suffer by the will of His Heavenly Father, and after this He will pray that His work may be blessed and prospered, to thy salvation. In this, O Christian! behold thy pattern, and never put thy hand to any work respecting which thou hast not first consulted God in prayer, and never proceed in any work except thou knowest that in proceeding with it thou art doing not thine own will but the will of God. Neither canst thou stop here; if thou followest the pattern of Jesus, thou must also earnestly pray that thy work may be blessed in the event. All these things Jesus did at the beginning of His most blessed Passion. Blessed is he that followeth in all his own works this most holy example!

Wherefore, then, this prayer of Jesus? For an example for all faithful people, and especially for thee, O Christian reader! saying to thee, "Watch and pray lest ye enter into temptation."

But wherefore this great and terrible agony of Jesus? To prove to thee, O Christian! that Jesus had a true human soul, and was like unto thee in all things, sin only except. Jesus knows that His Gospel will cause thee to suffer in this present life, "for *all* that will live godly in Christ Jesus shall suffer persecution" (2 Tim. iii. 12), says the apostle of Christ; and, therefore, He is mercifully pleased to show Himself unto thee in His agony, that thou mayest see thy Master and Teacher under the influence of all the terror and affliction that the soul of man can suffer. He even bears to be blasphemed, as showing faintness where other martyrs have shown unquailing courage, that He might give thee this proof of His having compassion for all thy infirmities.

Jesus has come into a garden of olives, the symbol of peace and joy, to commence in it His expiation of the sin which Adam perpetrated in the garden of Eden. It is in a garden that Adam eats of the forbidden fruit with a perverse delight, and it is also in a garden that Jesus in agony and sore affliction receives the chalice of His Passion.

Jesus is very and true man; and while many martyrs by supernatural grace have been delivered from the fear of death, and have been able to mock and deride their tormentors in the midst of their sufferings, Jesus refuses to be delivered from any suffering to which human nature is subject, and therefore submits Himself to become subject to the fear of death, despising the shame. His soul foresees all and each of the torments,—the scourging, the buffetings, the insults, the mockeries, the blasphemies, and the death of the Cross, which He is about to suffer; and the fear and agony of death falls upon him. "Cœpit pavere," says St Mark,—"He began to be afraid."

Jesus foresees the cowardice of His chosen Disciples, how on the first sight of danger they would all forsake Him and flee. He sees the obstinate and impenetrable malice of the Jews; the cowardly and miserable friendship of Pilate, that, after exposing Him to needless suffering and insult, will sacrifice Him in the end; the fickle ingratitude of the multitude, who, notwithstanding that they were so lately all on His side with their loud Hosannas to the Son of David, will soon cry with one voice, "Crucify Him!" and He is overwhelmed with weariness and disgust. "Cœpit tædere," says St Mark,—"He began to be weary."

Jesus sees all the countless sins of the children of Adam, their sacrileges, murders, adulteries, calumnies, blasphemies, and all the horrible crimes that have been perpetrated, and will continue to be perpetrated in spite of His sufferings; and He elicits acts of contrition for them.

Jesus foresees all the countless torments of the martyrs and of the prelates and pastors of His Church, and all the sufferings that the rage of the devil and of impious men will soon inflict upon His faithful people; and His compassionate soul is overcome with grief. "Cœpit mœstus esse," says St Matthew,—"He began to be sorrowful."

Jesus foresees the obduracy and ingratitude of so many of His own people, to whom His bitter Passion and death will not bring salvation by reason of their own impenitence, and upon whom He will hereafter have to pass the sentence, "Go ye into the eternal fires prepared for the devil and his angels;" and His infinite love grieves over their impenitence. "My soul is sorrowful even unto death,"

The Old Testament Types of The I. Sorrowful Mystery.

Elias prays for the dead son of the Widow.
Elias in his affliction is comforted by an Angel.

ROSA ☩ MYSTICA ☩ PASSIM ☩ IN ☩ LEGE ☩ ☩ IN PROPHETIS

SUMBRÆ ☩ ORA ☩ PRO ☩ NOBIS ☩ ☩ CUM ☩ MUTIH ☩ MUM

THE PRAYER WHICH RESTORES LIFE TO THE DEAD.
THE PROPHET WEARIED OF HIS LIFE FOR THE SINS OF HIS PEOPLE.

says the merciful Jesus. So the zealous Apostle, who thought he had the mind of Christ, cries out "that he would fain be anathema for his brethren."

Wherefore, then, did Jesus submit Himself to this mortal agony? That He might give thee an example, O Christian! by which thou mightest learn not to be terrified through the weakness of the flesh from encountering the trials which God may be pleased to send to thee, but rather be emboldened to follow the example of thy Lord, who, notwithstanding the terrible agony to which He submitted for thy sake, still endured the Cross, despising the shame; and now, as the Apostle says, "sitteth at the right hand of God."

CHAPTER III.

SCRIPTURE TYPES OF THE FIRST SORROWFUL MYSTERY.

I. THE PRAYER OF ELIAS FOR THE DEAD CHILD.
II. THE WEARINESS OF ELIAS FOR THE SINS OF HIS PEOPLE.

1. *The prayer of Elias for the restoration to life of the dead child of the widowed mother.*

JESUS retired from His disciples to pray, and St Anselm, as we have seen, teaches us that He went to pray for His own resurrection from the dead. He was about to commit Himself to death, and He prayed to Him who was able to save Him from death, that He would not leave "His soul in hell, neither suffer His flesh to see corruption." What was there that depended upon His resurrection from the dead? Let St Paul answer us: "He was delivered up for our sins, and He rose again for our justification" (Rom. iv. 25). In His resurrection from the dead, the rising again of the lost world, dead in trespasses and sin, to the life of grace was bound up. In praying, therefore, for His resurrection from the dead, He was praying for the restoration of the life of faith to the world, which had lost its life; for this restoration of the world to life was most intimately bound up in His resurrection.

These reflections conduct us to the circumstance in the life of the prophet Elias, which St Augustine, as we shall see, treats as the figure of the prayer of Jesus in the Garden of Olives.

"And it came to pass," the Scripture relates, "after this that the son of the woman, the mistress of the house, fell sick, and the sickness was very grievous, so that there was no breath left in him. And she said to Elias, 'What have I to do with thee, thou man of God? art thou come to me that my iniquities should be remembered, and that thou shouldst kill my son?' And Elias said to her, 'Give me thy son.' And he took him out of her bosom, and carried him into the upper chamber where he abode, and laid him upon his own bed. And he cried to the Lord, and said, 'O Lord my God, hast Thou afflicted also the widow, with whom I am after a sort maintained, so as to kill her son?' And he stretched and measured himself upon the child three times, and cried to the Lord and said, 'O Lord my God, let the soul of this child, I beseech Thee, return into his body.' And the Lord heard the voice of Elias, and the soul of the child returned to him, and he revived. And Elias took the child, and brought him down from the upper chamber to the house below, and delivered him to his mother, and said to her, 'Behold, thy son liveth.' And the woman said to Elias, 'Now by this I know that thou art a man of God, and that the word of the Lord in thy mouth is true'" (3 Kings xvii. 17–24).

"The son of the widow," says St

Augustine, commenting on this Scripture, "lay dead; for the son of the Church, the people of the Gentiles, lay dead in innumerable trespasses and sins. At the prayer of Elias the son of the widow is raised up; at the coming of Christ, the son of the Church, that is, the Christian people, is brought back from the prison-house of death. Elias bows himself down in his prayer, and the son of the widow is brought to life again. Christ falls to the earth in His Passion, and the Christian people is raised up to life. For in that Christ fell to the ground three times, the mystery of the Holy Trinity is shown; for the widow's son, that is, the people of the Gentiles, was not raised to life by the Father without the Son, nor by the Father and Son without the Holy Ghost, but by the joint act of the whole undivided Trinity. The same mystery is still further shown in the Sacrament of Baptism, in which, by a threefold immersion, the old Adam is washed away in order that the new man may be raised up." (St Augustine, Serm. 201).

2. *The weariness and agony of Elias for the sins of his people a figure of the weariness and agony of Jesus in the Garden of Gethsemane.*

Jesus, as we have seen, would not put away from Himself any of the sufferings which He foresaw that His Gospel might hereafter bring upon His faithful disciples, and therefore He was graciously pleased to endure the agony and dread to which His soul was subject in the Garden of Gethsemane. He willed to be like unto us in all things, sin only except; and He has most graciously despised the shame of being seen struggling with the fear of death, that He might thereby strengthen all His faithful people in their last agony and struggle with death, in whatever form it might come upon them. Jesus saw Himself about to die as a Victim, sacrificed by the wickedness of the world. Hence His soul struggled with the sacrifice required from Him: "If it be possible, let this chalice pass from me." "Perchance," says St Paul, "for a good man one would dare to die." But Jesus was required to submit to death at the hands of a wicked world for its life. A figure or similitude of this gracious agony befell the prophet Elias.

The Scripture relates, "And Achab told Jezabel all that Elias had done, how he had slain all the prophets of Baal with the sword. And Jezabel sent a messenger to Elias, saying, 'Such and such things may the gods do to me, and add still more, if by this hour to-morrow I make not thy life as the life of one of them.' Then Elias was afraid, and rising up he went whithersoever he had a mind: and he came to Bersabee of Juda, and left his servant there. And he went forward one day's journey into the wilderness, and sat down under a juniper-tree, and requested for his soul that he might die, and said, 'It is enough for me, Lord; take away my soul: for I am no better than my fathers.' And he cast himself down, and slept in the shadow of the juniper-tree: and behold, an angel of the Lord touched him, and said to him, 'Arise and eat.' He looked, and behold there was at his head a hearth-cake, and a vessel of water: and he ate and drank, and he fell asleep again. And the angel of the Lord came again the second time, and touched him, and said to him, 'Arise, eat; for thou hast yet a great way to go.' And he arose, and ate and drank, and walked in the strength of that food forty days and forty nights, unto the Mount of God, Horeb" (3 Kings xix.)

Achab, the apostate Jewish King, tells his idolatrous Gentile wife Jezabel of the zeal of Elias against her prophets, and Jezabel sends Elias a message to prepare for death. The apostate Synagogue pours its tales of the zeal of Jesus against the crimes of the fallen world into the ears of the idolatrous civil power, and Jesus knows that His hour is come to be delivered into the hands of the Gentiles.

Elias falls into an agony of fear, and dreading to be given up into the hands of a wicked woman, escapes for his life into the wilderness. Here he is ready to give

The Second Sorrowful Mystery.

Ave ~ Maria ~ Gratia ~ Plena ~ Dominus ~ Tecum

Benedicta ~ Tu in mulieribus et Benedictus fructus ventris ~ tui Jesus

JESUS IS SCOURGED AT THE PILLAR.

Sæpe expugnaverunt me a juventute mea. Supra dorsum meum fabricaverunt peccatores: prolongaverunt iniquitatem suam.
(*Psalm* cxxviii. 2.)

They have often fought against me from my youth up. The sinners have ploughed furrows on my back; they have prolonged their evil doings.
(*Psalm* cxxviii. 2.)

Attritus est propter scelera nostra; disciplina pacis nostræ super Eum, et livore Ejus sanati sumus.
(*Isaias* liii. 5.)

He was bruised for our transgressions; the chastisement of our peace was upon Him, and by His stripes we are healed. (*Isaias* liii. 5.)

up his soul into the hands of God, but not into the hands of a woman. For, as the Scripture says, "there is no head worse than the head of a serpent, and there is no anger above the anger of a woman" (Ecclus. xxv. 23). It is better "to dwell with a lion and a dragon than to be in the power of a wicked woman." He therefore prays that this chalice might pass from him: "Lord, do Thou take away my soul." Jesus was about to be given up into the hands of the fallen world, of which the wicked woman Jezabel is the figure; and He prays that, if it be possible, the chalice may pass from Him.

Hereupon an angel appears to Elias, and says to him, "Arise and eat." Elias obeys, and falls asleep. And the angel touched him again, and says, "Arise and eat; for thou hast yet a great way to go. And he arose and went forty days and forty nights, unto Horeb, the Mount of God." So in like manner an angel appears to Jesus, strengthening Him to drink of the chalice His Heavenly Father had given to Him. Jesus obeys, and drinks of it. He falls asleep on the Cross; and behold, again an angel comes down from Heaven and rolls away the stone from the mouth of the sepulchre; and Jesus rises from the dead, and continues forty days and forty nights walking and conversing with His disciples, till He ascends up from them to His throne on high, to sit in the Heavens at the right hand of the Eternal Father, upon the true Horeb, the Mount of God.

The Second Sorrowful Mystery of the Rosary.

CHAPTER IV. JESUS IS SCOURGED AT THE PILLAR.

THE HOLY SCRIPTURE NARRATIVE.

"And Pilate, calling together the chief priests, and the magistrates, and the people, said to them, 'You have presented unto me this Man, as one that perverteth the people; and behold, I having examined Him before you, find no cause in this man, in those things wherein you accuse Him: no, nor Herod neither. For I sent you to him, and behold, nothing worthy of death is done to Him. I will chastise Him, therefore, and release Him.' Now, of necessity, he was to release unto them one upon the feast-day. But the whole multitude together cried out, saying, ' Away with this Man, and release unto us Barabbas;' who, for a certain sedition made in the city, and for murder, was cast into prison. And Pilate again spoke to them, desiring to release Jesus. But they cried again, saying, 'Crucify Him, crucify Him.' And he said to

The Second Sorrowful Mystery.

" them the third time, 'Why, what evil hath this Man done? I find no cause of death in Him. I will chastise Him, therefore, and let Him go'" (St Luke xxiii.)

The better to contemplate, in the Second Sorrowful Mystery, our Divine Redeemer submitting Himself to bear for our sakes the "*multa flagella peccatoris*" (Ps. xxxi. 10)—"the many stripes of the sinner,"—piety seems to require that we should attempt to follow Him briefly through the chief intervening circumstances of His Passion, in the well-founded hope also of deriving thereby an additional insight into the reasons which He had for undergoing in our behalf this particular humiliation and suffering of a public scourging, which forms the subject of the " Second Sorrowful Mystery."

After the angel who was sent to strengthen Him had departed, and after He had risen the third time from His prayer, the traitor Apostle Judas comes into the garden, with a band of soldiers and servants of the high priest, and straightway going up to Him, says, "Hail, Rabbi," and kisses Him. Jesus answers, "Judas, betrayest thou the Son of Man with a kiss?" His disciples, seeing their Master overpowered by numbers, profit by His words to the multitude, " If therefore you seek Me, let these go their way," and all forsake Him, and seek for their own safety in flight.

Jesus is hereupon bound by the servants of the high priest; and, if we may accept a venerated tradition, He was taken down the valley of the Brook Cedron, and brought by a circuitous route through the Dung Gate to the house of Annas, the father-in-law of Caiphas, the high priest of that year, situated on the Mount Sion, there to be in safe keeping till the Sanhedrim or high court of the Jews could assemble for judgment on the morrow.

In the house of Annas He passes the night, exposed to indescribable insults and buffeting from the various servants of the high priest, all of which are to be repeated on the next day by the Roman soldiery and the mixed multitude; and it is during the course of these indignities that He is three times denied by His chosen disciple Peter.

At the early dawn of the morning, like the lamb that has been chosen for the morning sacrifice, Jesus is hurried off from the house of Annas to that of Caiphas, where the Sanhedrim assembles to sit in judgment upon Him. Various witnesses are brought forward, and the result is that He is judged by them to be worthy of death; upon which they adjourn, to have their Prisoner brought before the court of Pontius Pilate, the Roman Governor, as the sovereign jurisdiction over life and death has been taken away from them by the Romans, and reserved to the Roman court.

In the meantime, Judas appears before the Sanhedrim, filled with remorse on hearing of His Master having been condemned to death; and casting down the thirty pieces of silver in their presence, saying, "I have sinned in that I have betrayed the innocent blood," he goes and hangs himself in fruitless despair, a terrible warning to all future traitors.

Jesus is now brought before Pilate by the judges of the Sanhedrim, who at first merely inform Pilate that they have judged His case, and have passed sentence of death upon Him. But when Pilate answers by telling them to proceed in their own manner, they reply that they have no longer the power by law of putting any one to death; therein bearing witness out of their own mouths that the term fixed in Jacob's prophecy, " The sceptre shall not depart from Juda, nor a lawgiver from his thigh, until He that is to be sent shall come" (Gen. xlix. 10), was past and gone. The sceptre had now departed from Juda; and Jesus, after having been condemned as having forfeited His life under the law of Moses, must now be accused as one who has also forfeited it to the laws of the Roman empire. They consequently now proceed to lay to His charge state crimes against the Roman power, in order to force Pilate to give them a hearing, and to extort the Roman sentence of death from him. Their charges are three in number—

1. Of perverting their nation, and making them disaffected to the Roman power.
2. Of forbidding to give tribute to Cæsar.
3. Of making Himself a king, saying He is Christ the King.

Pilate, quite aware that their motive is nothing else than envy, is still unable to appear to make light of such charges as these, and therefore returns to his court to examine his prisoner; the doctors of the Sanhedrim refusing to enter with him on account of its being the eve of the great day of the Pasch. In due time Pilate returns to them, saying, "I find no cause of death in Him;" upon which the doctors insist, saying, "He disturbeth the people, teaching throughout all Judea, beginning from Galilee."

Pilate hearing Galilee named, forthwith seizes on it as a pretext for saying that the cause must in this case belong to Herod's jurisdiction, to whom, as Herod happened to be in Jerusalem, he sends Him and His accusers with Him. Herod, however, only mocks Him, and sends Him back.

Pilate finding His prisoner returned to his hands, and perceiving that it looks likely to end by his being forced to give some kind of satisfaction to the malice and hatred with which the principal men of the city are so deeply animated, thinks it will be best for all parties to propose a compromise; as if he had said, "I find no cause in Him, but to satisfy you I will scourge Him, and then set Him at liberty." This proposal does not appear to find acceptance, and Pilate tries one more way of escape for himself. The populace have the privilege at this season of the year of asking for the release of some one public prisoner, and he gives them the choice between Jesus and Barabbas: Barabbas being a well-known robber and murderer. To Pilate's great surprise and embarrassment, the populace cry out, "Not this Man, but Barabbas."

"What shall I do then," asks Pilate, "with Jesus who is called Christ?" They all answer, "Let Him be crucified! let Him be crucified!"

Pilate is now in this difficulty: the populace have manifestly taken sides with the principal men of the city in clamouring for His crucifixion. It appears much too unsafe to an unscrupulous man of the world to go against an entire city; and yet, with his ideas of Roman dignity proper to a Roman official of high rank, Pilate is not prepared all at once to degrade a Roman tribunal in his person into a mere instrument of gratifying the malice of Jews; but still something must be done. There has, it is true, been no notification of any assent on the part of the Jews to the proposed compromise, but Pilate thinks that the "scourging" may very possibly satisfy them; at least he will risk the experiment on his own responsibility, in hope of being able to set Him at liberty after He has been scourged. And, accordingly, in the plan of Divine providence, it is to Pilate's act that we owe the accomplishment of the Second Sorrowful Mystery—

THE SCOURGING OF JESUS AT THE PILLAR.

Nothing whatever has been brought to pass by the will of the Eternal Father, in the work of our redemption, for which there do not exist wise reasons known to God; and as nothing can be more certain than that it could have been for no mere superfluity of humiliation that the Manhood of the Eternal Word was subjected to the open indignity of a public scourging before the eyes of men, we therefore reverently ask and seek to know the reason why a public scourging, brought about by such a remarkable chain of providential circumstances, is chosen as so conspicuous a stage in the progress of our Lord's Passion, as to have its knowledge specially promulgated, and its memory perpetuated, among the whole multitude of the faithful as a Mystery of the Holy Rosary?

Public scourging, by the Roman law, was the punishment restricted exclusively to the slave, who had no citizen rights, or was inflicted on the criminal under sentence of death, who had forfeited his rights as citizen by his crime. The world, for the redemption of which the Eternal Word became man, was precisely in the

THE II. SORROWFUL MYSTERY.

The Rainbow and the Covenant made with Noe.

LEGE EZ IN PROPHETIS

ECUM FILIUM

THE OLD TESTAMENT TYPES OF

Job is struck by Satan.

ROSA MYSTICA PASSIM IN

UMBRA ORA PRO NOBIS

predicament of the latter. It had forfeited its right of citizenship in the eternal city, in the person of Adam, who in his transgression had become the bondservant of the devil, and had ever since been lying under sentence of death as a condemned criminal, waiting for the hour of his execution to come. In the Divine Passion, therefore, through which the bondsmen of the devil, under sentence of death, were to recover their forfeited rights as free citizens in the eternal city, it became the Man of Sorrows, who was sent to redeem them, that one of the solemn stages of His Passion should be His suffering publicly in the eyes of men the very penalty of a public scourging, which human law was wont to inflict in the case of the slave who was condemned to death, as the conjoint just due of his condition of bondage, coupled with the fact of his crime. The Restorer, therefore, of the liberty of the sons of God, fitly suffers the public scourging, the penalty reserved for the crime of a bondsman, that we may all learn to see reflected in this stage of His Passion our own lost state of bondage and condemnation to death, from which He is become our one sole merciful Deliverer; "there being," as the apostle says, "none other Name given under heaven whereby we may be saved, except His Name" (Acts iv. 12).

Moreover, there is a special healing power that flows from the wounds of Jesus. Isaias says, "Cujus livore sanati sumus,"—" by whose livid sores we are healed" (Isa. liii. 5). "We thought Him," continues Isaias, "to be as one smitten with leprosy, stricken of God, and humbled." "See," says St Chrysostom, "the Lord is made ready for the scourge. See it now descends upon Him. That sacred skin is torn by the fury of the rods; the cruel might of repeated blows lacerates His shoulders. Ah, me! God is stretched before man; and He in whom not one trace of sin can be discerned, suffers punishment as an evildoer."

"The Lord Himself so willed it," writes Ludolph of Saxony, "that He should suffer a scourging, in order that, as it is written, 'Many are the scourges of the sinner,' we might be spared, and that He might deliver us from an everlasting scourging by His own suffering; as a loving mother, who sees the father about to smite his son, will sometimes run with outstretched arms, and screen her child by exposing herself in his place to the blows. Man had offended God, and had, therefore, deserved to suffer. Christ, therefore, willed to submit Himself to the scourgers, in order to appease the anger of God, and hence it is written, 'The discipline of our peace fell upon Him' (Isa. liii. 5). And if He who was innocent was thus grievously scourged for the sins of others, with what scourges do you not think those who are guilty will be scourged for their own crimes, except they correct themselves" (Life of Christ, part ii. ch. lxii.)

"And that godless man, Pilate," writes St Anselm, "was far from not knowing that all things were done against Thee through envy, and yet he did not keep his rash hands from Thee, but filled Thy soul with bitterness without a cause. He sent Thee to Herod to be mocked; he received Thee back again from the hands of Herod after Thou hadst been mocked; He commanded Thee to stand naked in the midst of Thy scorners, and spared not to tear Thy virgin flesh with scourges, inflicting blows upon blows, and wounds upon wounds. O Elect Child of my Lord! what hadst Thou done that deserved such bitterness and such shame? Alas, nothing! I, lost man that I am, was the cause of all this suffering and all this shame. It was I, Lord, 'that had eaten the sour grapes, and Thy teeth were set on edge;' and 'for that which Thou didst not seize Thou didst pay the forfeit.' Thy love and our injustice hath made Thee thus infirm. Cursed be the injustice that hath caused Thee thus to suffer! And yet, by all this, the impiety of the faithless Jews remained unsatisfied" (St Anselm, Meditation ix.)

"From this flagellation of Christ," writes Ludolph of Saxony, "we learn two things—First, That we ought at all times willingly to submit ourselves to the scourges of God, that each one of us may say with the Psalmist, 'For I am prepared for being scourged' (Ps. xxxvii. 18). And with the best of reasons; for if the only Son of God was ready to submit Himself to the scourges which are our portion, out of obedience to the Father, why should not we, who are sons by adoption, submit ourselves to the scourging which the same Father deigns to inflict upon us, either directly or by His ministers, as so many instruments intended in mercy for our correction ; for according to both the wise man and the apostle, 'Whom God loveth He reproveth, and He chastiseth the son whom He receives' (Prov. iii. 11 ; Heb. xii. 6). The second is that we should diligently beware how we renew the scourging of Christ, which we do whenever we fall into grievous sin. For as Christ was stricken with scourges on account of our sins, whenever we sin, as far as in us lies we inflict by each sin a blow of the scourge upon Him; as the apostle says of some, 'Crucifying the Son of God afresh in themselves, and making Him a mockery' (Heb. vi. 6)." (Life of Christ, part ii. ch. lxii.)

CHAPTER V.

THE SCRIPTURE TYPES OF THE SECOND SORROWFUL MYSTERY.

I. JOB SMITTEN BY SATAN.
II. THE RAINBOW OF MANY COLOURS THE SIGN OF MERCY.

1. *Job struck by Satan with an ulcer all over his body.*

THE narrative of Job's suffering occurs in the Sacred Scripture as follows :—

"And it came to pass, when on a certain day the sons of God came and stood before the Lord, and Satan came among them, and stood in His sight, that the Lord said to Satan : Whence comest thou? And he answered and said : I have gone round about the earth and walked through it. And the Lord said to Satan : Hast thou considered my servant Job, that there is none like him in the earth, a man simple and upright, and fearing God and avoiding evil, and still keeping his innocence? But thou hast moved me against him, that I should afflict him without cause. And Satan answered, and said : Skin for skin, and all that a man hath he will give for his life ; but put forth thy hand, and touch his bone and his flesh, and then thou shalt see that he will bless thee to thy face. And the Lord said to Satan : Behold he is in thy hand, but yet save his life. So Satan went forth from the presence of the Lord, and struck Job with a very grievous ulcer, from the sole of the foot even to the top of his head : and he took a potsherd and scraped the corrupt matter, sitting on a dunghill" (Job ii. 1–8).

The better to appreciate the proofs of Divine forethought which will appear in the foreshadowing of the humiliation which Jesus underwent in His public scourging at the pillar, by the person of the holy patriarch Job struck by Satan with a grievous ulcer, an introductory word or two on the general bearing of the parallel between the great example of patience in the old law and the Man of Sorrows of the new law will not be thrown away.

Job, then, has Satan in person for his adversary, and Jesus is pursued by the more than Satanic malice of the Jews, for they are His own people who have turned against Him. Satan, again, has no direct power in his own hands to maltreat Job, but is obliged to appear as a suitor before the higher court to obtain the requisite power to act against him;

and the Jews in like manner are without the power to wreak their malice against Jesus, and are obliged to appear as suitors before the court of Pontius Pilate. For when Pilate says to them, "Take ye Him and judge Him according to your law," they reply, "We have not the power to put any man to death." Satan, moreover, is moved to pursue Job for exactly the same reason for which the Jews hate Jesus, because He is a just and upright man. "Hast thou considered my servant Job," said the Lord to him, "that there is none like him in the earth, a simple and upright man, fearing God and avoiding evil?" The Jews, in like manner, were continually in the habit of observing Jesus to see what He would do (Mark iii. 2), and finding Him to be a Man to whom none was like on the earth, they hated Him and sought how they might put Him to death.

Satan, also, it is further to be observed, at the particular time in which we are to look for our parallel, is by no means described as being just at the commencement of his persecutions against Job; on the contrary, he has had his eye upon him for some considerable time, and at the moment that our parallel begins, he has actually succeeded in depriving him of all his substance; he has broken up his family, and has driven all his friends and acquaintances away from him, so that Job is now desolate and forsaken, and he is waiting to be as it were the helpless victim of the next turn or assault of Satan's malice. In the same way, the Jews are by no means now for the first time venting their hatred and rage against Jesus. They have long ago spread evil reports of Him, and sought occasion against Him; and they have now so far actually succeeded, that they have dispersed all His followers and adherents, and driven away from Him all His chosen friends. He is in consequence now bodily in their hands, desolate and alone, waiting patiently to know what the next turn of their malice will be able to do against Him.

At the moment, then, that our parallel with the subject of the Second Mystery of the Holy Rosary begins, Satan has now gone to the utmost extent of the power that had been given to him against Job, and his malice being still unsatisfied, he appears, as we learn from the scripture narrative above quoted, before the Lord and His court to sue for further powers to torment him. The chief priests and the principal Jews appear with precisely the same end in view before the court of the Roman Governor, to sue for the grant of further powers to proceed against Jesus in order to put Him to death.

Satan having succeeded in obtaining a hearing, proceeds to press his petition for the grant of further powers against Job, but his suit does not find favour. The Lord answers him, "Hast thou not seen that he still keepeth his innocence? Thou hast moved me against him that I should afflict him without a cause." The Jews, in a precisely similar manner press their suit before Pontius Pilate and his court, and it fails to find favour. They are met by a perfectly similar remonstrance, "Why, what evil hath He done? I find no cause in Him."

However, notwithstanding all Job's exemplary patience under his former trials, by which he has merited the testimony "that he still keepeth his innocence," he is nevertheless to be called upon to give a further proof of his patient endurance of evil. Jesus, in like manner, is to be called upon to give a further proof of His patient endurance, which is, moreover, to be proclaimed to all generations of the faithful as the Second Sorrowful Mystery of the Rosary. Satan pleads in reply to the Lord's remonstrance, "Skin for skin, all that a man hath he will give for his life; but put forth Thy hand and touch his bone and his flesh, and then Thou shalt see that he will bless Thee to Thy face." The Lord answers Satan's suit by granting him the power he asked, but with the limitation annexed "not to touch Job's life. "Behold he is in thy hand, yet save his life." This is precisely Pilate's answer to the importunity of the Jews, "I will not give you His life, but I will chastise Him, and then I will let Him go free."

Satan, on receiving the power he had sued for, immediately goes forth from the presence of the Lord, and loses no time "in striking Job with a very grievous ulcer from the sole of his foot even to the crown of his head." Jesus in like manner is forthwith hurried away to the pillar, and subjected to the scourges of the Roman soldiers; the Jews, according to the revelations made to St Bridget, giving them money to inflict the scourging in the most cruel manner they were able; and in the words of the prophet Isaias we have the parallel of the two sufferers completed, "From the sole of the foot to the top of the head there is no soundness in Him, wounds and bruises and swelling sores; they are not bound up or dressed or fomented with oil" (Isa. i. 6).

Job remains perfectly patient, as previously, under this fresh infliction of the wrath of his relentless adversary; and Jesus, in like manner, in the hands of his tormentors, fulfils the Scripture which says of Him, "He shall not cry nor strive, neither shall His voice be heard in the streets" (Isa. xlii. 2). Job retires from the tents of the people to a dunghill, where his wife comes to him and says, "Dost thou still continue in thy simplicity? bless God and die." Job justifies his patience by an appeal to God: "Shall we not also receive evil from the hand of the Lord?" Pilate comes to Jesus after He has suffered the scourging, and says to Him, "Knowest thou not that I have power to crucify Thee and have power to release Thee?" and Jesus in a similar manner justifies His own patience by the appeal to God, "Thou couldest have no power at all against Me, except it were given thee from above." Jesus had before said, "The chalice which My Father hath given Me, shall I not drink it?" as Job, the wonderful figure of His patience and endurance, had said, "Shall we not also receive evil from the hand of the Lord?" Such, then, is the remarkable correspondence between the great sufferer of the old law and the Man of Sorrows of the new.

2. The rainbow of many colours the sign of God's mercy to a guilty world.

Every type or shadow, by an imperfection inherent in its nature, cannot fail to fall short of the Divine original which it prefigures. Wonderful, then, as we have found the parallel to be between the sufferings of Job with those of Jesus, there is a healing virtue for the whole world in the wounds of Jesus, which no one has ever thought of claiming for those of Job. Jesus "was wounded for our iniquities," says the prophet, "and was bruised for our sins. The chastisement of our peace fell upon Him, and by His bruises we are healed" (Isa. liii. 5).

We have now briefly to study another type, in which Jesus, submitting Himself to be scourged at the pillar, is foreshadowed as the sign of the mercy and reconciliation of God with a guilty world. This figure is the rainbow of many colours—the sign of His covenant which God Himself has set in the heavens: "And God said, This is the sign of the covenant which I will give between Me and you, and to every living soul that is with you for perpetual generations; I will set my bow in the clouds, and it shall be the sign of a covenant between Me and the earth. And when I shall cover the sky with clouds, My bow shall appear in the clouds, and My bow shall be in the clouds and I shall see it, and shall remember the everlasting covenant which was made between God and every living soul of all flesh which is on the earth" (Gen. ix. 12).

The true sign of the everlasting covenant between God and every living soul of all flesh is Jesus Christ, in whom God is well pleased. In Him alone has the Eternal Father found the acceptable sacrifice of a sweet smelling savour. Look at Jesus, bent down to the pillar, livid with blows, the fresh blood streaming under the lashes of the soldiers over the delicate hue of His virgin flesh; and behold, the bow of many colours, the sign of the Son of Man, in the Christian heavens, the token of the everlasting covenant between God and all flesh, when "it is in a cloud on a rainy day" (Ezech. i. 28).

"Look at the rainbow," says the son of Sirach, and "bless Him that made it. It is very beautiful in its brightness. It

THE THIRD SOR-ROWFUL MYS--TERY.

Ave~ Maria~ Gratia~ Plena~ Dominus~ Tecum~

Quoniam die
ac nocte gra-
vata est super
me manus tua;
conversus sum
in aerumnâ
meâ dum con-
figitur spina.
(*Psalm* xxxi. 4.)

In laboribus
comedes ex eâ
cunctis diebus
vitæ tuæ;
spinas et tribu-
los germinabit
TIBI.
(*Gen.* iii. 5.)

~Benedicta~ ~Tu in mulieribus et Benedictus fructus ventris~ ~tui Jesus~

JESUS IS CROWNED WITH THORNS.

In labours shalt
thou eat of it all
the days of thy life.
Thorns and thistles it shall bring forth

For day and night
Thy hand has lain
heavy upon me. I
have been turned in my anguish, whilst the

encompasseth the heaven about with the circle of its glory; the hands of the Most High have displayed it (Ecclus. xlviii. 12). Look at Jesus bent down to the pillar, and bless Him who hath made Him thus to suffer for us. He is very lovely in His humiliation, for He suffers out of love for those who are to be healed by His wounds. Though He is in the hands of men, yet He encompasses the heavens in the brightness of His glory, and the hands of the Eternal Father have thus displayed Him."

Ezechiel, in his vision, saw the likeness of a throne, and upon it the appearance of a man, "From his loins upward and from his loins downward," the prophet says, "I saw as it were the resemblance of fire shining round about, as the appearance of the rainbow when it appears in a cloud on a rainy day" (Ezech. i. 48). In Jesus, in the hands of men, bent down to the pillar and scourged for our sins, from his loins upward and from his loins downward there stream forth the many coloured signs of the everlasting covenant, "as the appearance of the rainbow when it is in a cloud on a rainy day."

The Third Sorrowful Mystery of the Rosary.

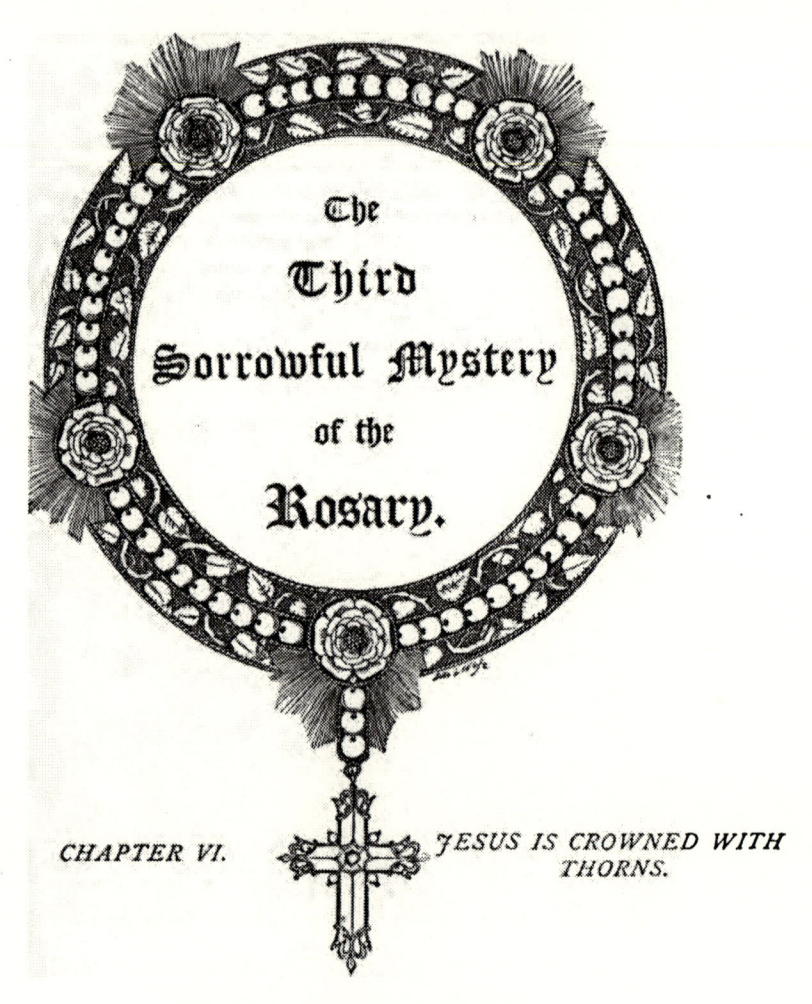

CHAPTER VI.   *JESUS IS CROWNED WITH THORNS.*

THE HOLY SCRIPTURE NARRATIVE.

"Then Pilate, having taken Jesus and scourged Him, the soldiers plaiting a crown of thorns, put it upon His head; and they put on Him a purple garment. And they came to Him and said: Hail, King of the Jews; and they gave Him blows. Pilate therefore went forth again, and said to them: Behold, I bring Him forth unto you, that you may know that I find no cause in Him. Jesus therefore came forth, bearing the crown of thorns and the purple garment. And he said to them: Behold the Man" (St John xix.)

Pilate has now found that his hope of being able to appease the hatred and bloodthirsty animosity of the enemies of Jesus, by the attempt to put them off with the compromise of inflicting a public scourging, in the place of passing the judgment of death for which they were clamouring, has failed. The enemies of Jesus are not satisfied, and not disposed to abate in any degree their clamorous demand for His being put to death. What is Pilate to do? Is he to allow himself to be driven forward against his will to pass the sentence of death, when he has publicly said that, after having scourged his prisoner, he would then let Him go free? This would be a manifest humiliation of Roman power before Israelite clamour, to put the injustice of the judgment out of the question. But, on the other hand, Pilate is a man of the world, and he must, above all things, look to it that he allows no handle to be taken against himself by reason of any love of justice which he may show. The weak point in Pilate's case, and the one which the adversaries do not fail to press relentlessly, is that his Prisoner is accused of making Himself a King. And if Pilate is as good as his word and lets Him go after the scourging, all the malignant malice of the Jews, enraged at being disappointed of their Victim, will turn its fury upon Pilate, and pursue him to the uttermost, as the betrayer of Cæsar's interests, in letting a man go who had made Himself a King. The dilemma, therefore, is not a small one. He is publicly pledged to let his Prisoner go free, and yet by it he must not turn the whole city against himself. Pilate is a man of expedients, and he has one ready for the emergency, and it is to this expedient of Pilate that we owe the Third Sorrowful Mystery of the Rosary—

THE CROWNING OF JESUS WITH THORNS.

Pilate, then, up to the present moment, has no intention whatever of surrendering his pledged word to the clamour of the Jews; but he sees quite clearly that, whatever happens, the infuriated rage which the people and their leaders now show against Jesus must not be turned against himself, particularly with such a plausible handle against him as his enemies would be sure to make out of the accusation of his having let a man go that had made Himself a King. He must therefore take the best care to be beforehand with the accusation if it should come to be made, and make sure of having reliable evidence to bring forward to prove that the character of King attributed to his prisoner, was, in a political point of view, nothing but a perfectly harmless hallucination. The reputed King must be exposed to a public mockery and ridicule of His pretensions as King. He must be dressed in a mock purple robe, He must receive mock homage on bended knee, He must have a reed put in His hand for a mock sceptre, and lastly, He must have a crown of thorns put on His head for a mock crown; and after all this has been done, Pilate will come and exhibit Him in this mock guise to the people, saying, "Ecce homo," "Behold the Man,"—as if adding, behold the man whom you say makes Himself the King, who contests the right to reign against Cæsar. Accuse me to Cæsar, then, if you can or dare, of being Cæsar's enemy, for letting such a mock King as this Man is go free.

Such, then, was the chain of natural circumstances which were overruled, according to the counsels of God, to bring about this remarkable stage in the Divine Sufferer's Passion, that constitutes the Third Sorrowful Mystery of the Rosary, and in which the Victim for the sins of the world is exhibited to the eyes of men crowned according to the established usage of sacrifices, and wearing for His crown the very thorns which the earth, when laid under a curse for the sin of Adam, was commanded to bear in punishment of the crime that had been committed. As it is written, "cursed is the earth in thy labour, thorns and thistles shall it bring forth to thee" (Gen. iii. 17).

"Behold the Man," says the Eternal Father, to all generations of the children of Adam in this Mystery of the Rosary. "Behold the Man" whom I have sent to you, to be your ransom from death, and to make you citizens of the celestial city, the Heavenly Jerusalem which is above.

Like the prophet of old in the desert, who saw the fire bursting forth from the bush which was not consumed, and who said, "I will turn aside to see this great sight," can we resist turning aside to see this fire of Divine love bursting out from the midst of the thorns? and beholding, can we do otherwise than, like Moses, fall down and adore?

This is He of whom St Jerome says, "He has been crowned with thorns that

He might earn for us a royal diadem in the kingdom of His Father."

This is He who is given to us for a testimony of the power of God, that we should seek, as Tertullian says, "the crown which afterwards came to Him," for He ate of the honeycomb after He had tasted of the gall, and He was not saluted King of glory by the hosts of heaven before He had been crowned with thorns King of the Jews, and at their suit condemned to the death of the Cross, being, as St Paul writes, made a little lower than the angels, that He might be crowned with honour and glory (Heb. i.)" (Tertullian, De Corona).

This is He of whom St Augustine says "that He is our King. The King of a kingdom which, though not of this world, nevertheless has overcome this world, not by the fierceness of fighting, but by the humility of suffering, wearing the crown of thorns and the purple robe, not exhibiting the magnificence of power, but overwhelmed with mockery and insult" (Tract. 116 on St John).

This is He who is given to us as an example of patience. "Not one member only of His body," says St Chrysostom, "but His whole body suffered these atrocious injuries. His head was pierced with thorns, and struck with a reed, His face was besmeared with spittle, and His cheeks were deformed with blows; the rest of His body was tortured with stripes and nakedness, the buffoonery of the purple robe and the simulated homage. His hands were mocked with the reed which they made Him hold in the place of a sceptre; His lips and His tongue were tortured with the vinegar and gall that was given Him to drink" (Chrysostom, Homily lxxxviii. on St Matthew).

"From this crowning of Christ," writes Ludolph of Saxony, "there are three lessons which we may derive. First, that we should bear our sins in mind, as Christ bore the thorns of our sins on His head; for, according to Bede, His taking our sins upon Himself is shown in the crown of thorns which He wore. For it was said to the first man concerning these thorns, 'the earth shall bear thorns and thistles to thee,' for our earthly body brings forth sins which inflict their sharp wounds on our consciences after the manner of thorns. These thorns, then, Christ took to Himself to wear them as a crown of victory; for it is the wont of conquerors to carry the arms of their conquered enemies as a trophy of their victory. The arms of the devil are our sins, with which he is armed against us, and these the Lord has taken away from him through His Passion, for 'He is the Lamb of God, who hath taken away the sins of the world.' Therefore, He deigned to wear the crown of thorns on His head as a token of His victory; and it is delightful to every loving soul to see our King in this crown; and consonant with this are the words of the spouse of the Canticles, 'Come forth, ye daughters of Sion, and behold the King Solomon in the diadem with which His mother (the synagogue) has crowned Him in the day of His espousals' (Cant. iii. 11). The second, according to Theophilus, recommends us to seek the crown of a disciplined and abstemious life in honour of the crown of thorns. And in the third, we are exhorted to study how to gain a crown by the victory over our temptations; for each temptation is, as it were, a thorn in the mind, which, on the temptation being overcome, is changed into a crown; and in proportion as a man is able to bear up under the thorns of the temptations that come across his path in this life, and to overcome them, he thereby gains so many precious jewels for his crown" (Life of Christ, part ii. ch. lxii.)

THE III. SORROWFUL MYSTERY.

Daniel cast into the Den of Lions.

LEGE · ET · IN · PROPHETIS

JESUM · ET · FILIUM · SUUM

THE SUFFERER FROM THE MALICE OF OTHERS GIVEN
UP TO THEIR WILL BY HIS FRIEND.

THE OLD TESTAMENT TYPES OF

The Ram held fast in the Thorns.

ROSA · MYSTICA · PASSIM · IN

UMBRA · ET · ORA · PRO · NOBIS

THE SUBSTITUTE VICTIM CAUGHT IN THE THORNS,
WHICH GOD PREPARED TO TAKE THE PLACE OF
THE ONE DESTINED FOR SACRIFICE.

CHAPTER VII.

THE SCRIPTURE TYPES OF THE THIRD SORROWFUL MYSTERY.

I. THE VICTIM PROVIDED BY GOD CAUGHT IN THE THORNS.
II. THE PROPHET CAST INTO THE DEN OF LIONS AT THE COMMAND OF HIS FRIEND.

1. *The Victim of the sacrifice caught in the thorns.*

ACCORDING to the ideas and customs prevalent throughout all nations of the world, there were two well-known public and sacred uses of the crown—as the acknowledged sacred symbol of royalty, and the religious adornment of the victim destined for sacrifice. Thus Evander, in the eighth book of the Æneid of Virgil, relates in what way the crown and sceptre of the kingdom had been sent to him:

"Regnique coronam,
Cum sceptro misit, mandatque insignia Tarcho."
Lib. viii. 505.

And the same poet, describing the mortality liable to be caused by a murrain among cattle, says, it is such that even the very victim when it is standing at the altar may fall down in a dying state, as the ministers of the sacrifice are tardy in putting the crown of white wool round its head (Georgics, iii. 486). And when the people of Lystra thought that Paul and Barnabas could be no less than the gods come down in the likeness of men, the priest of Jupiter came out with his bulls and their "crowns," to offer sacrifice (Acts xiv. 12). And so prevalent was the custom of associating the symbol of the crown with that which was offered on an altar in sacrifice, that it was extended to inanimate offerings, as Virgil describes even the goblet of wine being encircled with a crown previous to its being offered.

"Tum Pater Anchises magnum cratera corona,
Induit, implevitque mero, Divosque vocavit."
Æneid, iii. 525.

In civil life, the crown had its place as the natural mark of distinction for the victor in any kind of public game or contest of skill. Thus, the victors in the Olympic games of Greece were crowned with laurels, and in the races described in the fifth book of the Æneid, Æneas promises to the three first in the race, a crown of olive to each ; while in private life crowns were worn by guests at banquets, as the unbelievers say in the Book of Wisdom, "Come, let us crown ourselves with roses before they fade, let no meadow escape our riot" (Wisd. ii. 8). But in public or political life, the crown ranked as a sacred emblem, when it was the distinctive mark of royalty (the person of the king being always regarded as "sacrosanct," that is, bound under a divine sanction to the duties of his office) ; or as the sacred ornament of the victim dedicated to God and about to be put to death in the presence of the altar of sacrifice, as a fitting preparation to its being offered upon it. With the above brief remarks in the way of introduction, we proceed to the figure which typifies the Divine Victim of sacrifice provided by God, as He stands before all the people crowned for His sacrifice, with His crown of thorns.

Jesus, then, to proceed with the explanation of our figure, is the Victim preordained of God from all eternity to be offered up as the Ransom for the life of all whom the Eternal Father has called to be the heirs of His promised salvation ; and it becomes Him, according to that which we have seen to be the universally accepted custom of all people, to receive and wear on His head the sacrificial crown which denotes Him to be a Victim solemnly destined for sacrifice to God. Jesus then receives this sacrificial crown, and it proves to be a garland of thorns ; and to be convinced how appropriate such a crown is to the Victim who offers Himself of His own free will to pay the price of redemption for the sin of Adam, it needs but to be remembered that His crown of sacrifice is a garland woven from that which the earth was sentenced to produce in consequence of Adam's sin. "Cursed is the earth in thy work," said God to Adam, "thorns and thistles shall it bear to thee" (Gen. iii. 18). The first Adam finds the work of raising his subsistence from the soil beset with the thorns which the earth produced in consequence of his sin, and the second Adam finds the work of His atoning sacrifice equally beset with the same thorns. He is solemnly crowned as the Victim of sacrifice with a crown of thorns, and we shall shortly see Him go forth to the consummation of His sacrifice, wearing for His sacrificial crown the selfsame thorns that were the fruit of the transgression which His sacrifice was to redeem.

The Roman soldiers, then, having plaited a crown of thorns, placed it upon the head of the Lamb which was prepared before the foundations of the world. And thus it came to pass that the earth furnished its redeeming Victim with a crown of sacrifice, woven from those very thorns which itself bore as the participant in the sin of Adam. "And the angel said to Abraham, Lay not thy hand upon the boy, neither do thou anything to him. And Abraham," continues the Book of Genesis, "saw behind his back a ram amongst the thorns, sticking fast by the horns, which he took and offered for a holocaust instead of his son" (Gen. xxii. 13). Adam and all his children, notwithstanding that they were heirs of the promises of God, had fallen by transgression, so that their life had become forfeit to the justice of God. In this Mystery of the Crowning with Thorns, we contemplate the Angel of the New Testament, who says to the Eternal Father, "Lay not Thy hand upon the heirs of Thy promises, neither do Thou anything to them, notwithstanding that their life is forfeit. Behold here is a Victim, who is caught in the thorns, and who is bound so fast that He cannot escape. See, He offers Himself for their life. Take Thou Him, then, O Eternal Father, and offer Him for a holocaust, and spare the forfeit life of those who are the predestined heirs of Thy promises."

O true Lamb of God, caught in the thorns, and bound fast by the bands of Thy love, have mercy upon us, and let the light of Thy countenance shine upon us!

2. *The prophet who was cast into the den of lions by the friend who sought to save him.*

What is so remarkable in the various acts of our Lord's Passion, from the moment that He is brought before the court of Pontius Pilate, is the hand of God overruling the course of events. For everything which Pilate does as an act of friendliness towards the accused, and with a view to consult for His eventually being set free, only issues in the infliction of a new intermediate suffering, preparatory to the consummation of His sacrifice on the Cross, fulfilling thereby the words of the prophet, "With these wounds have I been wounded in the house of them who loved Me" (Zach. xiii. 6).

It was Pilate's desire to satisfy the passions of the Jews with something short of the death clamoured for by His enemies which caused him reluctantly to say, "I will scourge Him and then let Him go." It was the same desire to save Him from death that extorted from him reluctantly His exposure to the mockery of the purple robe, and the crown of thorns, and the derisive maltreatment of the soldiery. But so intense was the hatred of Christ's fellow-citizens against Him on account of His being a Man of God, contrary to their ways, and filled with the Spirit of God above them, that Pilate's reluctance was forced in the end to yield to their importunity, and to trust Him to the protection of His God, leaving Him to say with the Psalmist, "They mocked Me with mockery, they gnashed upon Me with their teeth; Lord, when wilt Thou look upon Me? restore My soul from their malignity, My only one from the lions" (Ps. xxxiv. 17).

Of this we have a striking and instructive figure in the parallel history of the prophet Daniel, who incurred the bitter

THE FOURTH SORROWFUL MYSTERY.

JESUS CARRIES HIS CROSS.

Ave — Maria — Gratia — Plena — Dominus — Tecum

Benedicta — Tu in mulieribus et Benedictus fructus ventris — tui Jesus.

Verumtamen servire me fecisti in peccatis tuis; præbuisti mihi laborem in iniquitatibus tuis. (*Isaias* xliii. 24.)

Of very truth, thou hast made me to serve by thy sins. Thou hast caused labour to me in thy evil doings. (*Isaias* xliii. 24.)

... et imposita colla neo. Infirmata est virtus mea; dedit me Dominus in manu de qua non potero surgere. (*Lam.* i. 14.)

... and have been laid upon my neck. My strength hath turned to weakness: the Lord hath delivered me up to a hand from which I shall not escape (*Lament.* i. 14.)

and malignant hatred of his fellow-citizens for the same reason as Jesus Christ—his fidelity to the law and worship of his God, and because the Spirit of God was greater in him than in them (Dan. vi. 3). They said then to one another, "We shall not find any cause against him except perchance in the law of his God." They therefore came to the king and asked that an imperial decree should go forth, in virtue of which "any one who should make any petition to any god or man except to the king, should be cast into the den of lions." This was meant as a snare against Daniel, just as the Jews came to Christ with the question, "Is it lawful to give tribute to Cæsar or not?" in order that they might have an occasion against Him with the Roman power. Daniel went to his regular hours of prayer regardless of the edict, and was presently accused to the king of setting himself above the edict of the empire, as the Jews accused Christ of setting Himself above the Roman empire, by making Himself a king. "Then the king was made very sad on account of Daniel, and set his heart upon letting him go, and laboured till the setting of the sun to save him." But the men, perceiving this, came and said to the king, "Know, O king, that the law of the Medes and Persians is, that every decree which the king hath made may not be changed. Then the king commanded, and they brought Daniel and cast him into the den of lions" (Dan. vi. 14). "Whosoever," said the Jews, "maketh himself a king, setteth himself up against Cæsar;" and Pilate, overcome by their remonstrances, gave Jesus into the hands of the soldiers, worse than the lions.

The sequel is equally remarkable. "When Daniel came out safe from the den of lions, at the command of the king, they brought the men who had accused Daniel, and they cast them, themselves, their wives, and their little ones, into the den of lions; and they did not reach the pavement before the lions seized them, and broke all their bones" (Dan. vi. 24). Some years after the resurrection of Christ from the dead, the same Roman soldiery, into whose midst Jesus had been cast by the command of Pilate, surrounded the city of His accusers, and as the lions had done to the accusers of Daniel, tore all before them in pieces, and destroyed the city to the ground.

The Fourth Sorrowful Mystery of the Rosary.

CHAPTER VIII.   *JESUS CARRIES HIS CROSS.*

THE HOLY SCRIPTURE NARRATIVE.

"And bearing His own Cross, He went forth to the place which is called Calvary, but in Hebrew, Golgotha; and there followed Him a great multitude of people, and of women, who bewailed and lamented Him; but Jesus turning to them said: Daughters of Jerusalem, weep not over me, but weep for yourselves and for your children, for behold the days shall come wherein they will say, Blessed are the barren and the wombs that have not borne, and the paps that have not given suck; then shall they begin to say to the mountains: Fall upon us; and to the hills, Cover us. For if in the green wood they do these things, what shall be done in the dry?" (John xix.; Luke xxiii.)

"A marvellous spectacle," writes St Augustine. "As seen with impious eyes, an object to be mocked at; as seen by piety, a great mystery. Is the looker-on an impious man, he will say, 'What an exhibition of ignominy!' is he a pious man, he will say, 'What a tower of strength for the defence of faith!' If he is the former, he sees a King carrying the instrument of His execution, in place of the sceptre of His kingdom; if the latter, he sees a King carrying that to which He is about to affix Himself, and which He is hereafter to stamp on the foreheads of kings. That which makes Him an object of contempt to the impious is the very thing itself which will make the joy and boast of the hearts of the saints. In carrying His Cross on His shoulders, he commends it to the Paul who is hereafter to say, 'God forbid that I should glory, except in the Cross of my Lord Jesus Christ;' and to the candle which is about to be lighted to give light to all that are in the house, and which may not be set under a bushel, He Himself carries the candlestick" (Tract. cxvii. on St John).

"Till the day break and the shadows flee away," says the bride of the Canticles, in answer to the King's invitation, "I will go the mountain of myrrh and the hill of frankincense." We have seen in the preceding Mystery the Victim chosen of God crowned for the consummation of His sacrifice with the thorns which the earth has produced as its offering to Him whose precious blood is about to remove the curse under which it has so long lain. We now see the same Divine Victim in the Fourth Mystery toiling along the streets of Jerusalem, bearing on His shoulders the wood of the Cross on which He is soon to die.

"He had but short time since," writes Father Camphausen, "been cruelly scourged, crowned with thorns, spit upon, mocked, and condemned to death. The purple robe is now taken from Him, and He is again covered with His own garments, so that all can now recognise Him as One who is found guilty of being a public malefactor of the worst kind. See the ignominious Cross is laid upon His shoulders, and He embraces it with both His arms, though scarce able to keep from falling! See how He is hurried and dragged by the lictors through the streets of Jerusalem to the Mount of Calvary!" (Matt. Camphausen, S. J. Jesu, Christi Passio Adumbrata, vol. ii. p. 90.)

What are the words which He utters on this most dolorous of ways? "Daughters of Jerusalem," He says to certain women who wept and lamented for His sufferings, "weep not for Me, but weep for yourselves and for your children."

Such are the words that our Lord utters outwardly with His voice on His way to Mount Calvary, but inwardly and in the depth of His mind I seem to hear nothing else except the words above cited, "I will go to the mountain of myrrh. Oh, how bitter, how painful to Me will this mountain of myrrh prove! Nevertheless, I will go thither, I will take courage and go to the mountain of myrrh,—the mountain of death. I will go thither out of love to My Father, that I may be a Son obedient even unto death, like another Isaac. I will go thither for the love of men, that I may be offered up as a Victim for the sins of the whole world on the altar of the Cross. I will go to the mountain of myrrh, be the way thither never so bitter and never so beset with pain. I will go to the bitterest and most ignominious of all deaths. Behold I go!"

Here on His way to Calvary, laden with His heavy Cross, there are not wanting other words which He utters besides those of "I will go to the mountain of myrrh." He not only invites us in these words to accompany Him and to follow Him, as Solomon invited the Sunnamite, but He constrains us to follow Him that we may suffer something for His sake; hence His words, Luke ix., "*If any one will come after Me, that is, to heaven, to eternal blessedness, let him deny himself and take up his cross daily, and follow Me to the mountain of myrrh*"—to the Mount of Calvary. For by this royal way of the Cross, and by no other, can faithful people journey on their way to heaven. Yes, He even threatens, saying, "He that taketh not up His cross and followeth Me, is not worthy of Me." I acknowledge him not as Mine, He is not worthy of My name, to be called a Christian,—I reject, I refuse, I disown him. Oh no, Lord! Let each of us take up our cross daily, and let us bear patiently and willingly all that may befall us in the way of suffering. And thus let us follow, and say to our Lord, with even more earnestness than the Sunnamite said to Solomon, with deeds rather than with words, " With Thee, my Jesus, will I go to the mountain of myrrh."

"It is sufficient," says our Divine Saviour, " for the disciple if he be as his Master." These words alone ought to be sufficient for those who in this Fourth Mystery contemplate Jesus Christ bearing His Cross to make them shudder at the false doctrine on which the great falling away of the people in Europe in the sixteenth century was based. Jesus, it was then said, had borne the Cross not as an example for us to follow, but as a substitute for us. The root of the error is not difficult to see. The antipathy of the old Adam to find himself hedged in and controlled by the commandments of God, is something extremely old and well known in the world. "The flesh," says Christ, "lusteth against the spirit," and does not of itself embrace the Cross willingly. "If it be possible," were our Divine Saviour's own words in His agony, " let this chalice pass from Me." Simon of Cyrene bore the Cross after Jesus only because He was compelled to do so. Thomas à Kempis says, " Jesus has many lovers of His heavenly kingdom, but few bearers of His Cross; for all wish," he continues, " to rejoice with Him but few wish to bear anything for Him" (Book ii. ch. xi.) All the antipathy which the old Adam has to be hedged in and controlled by the commandments of God offers more than a mere passive resistance to the doctrine in which the new Adam calls us to deny ourselves, to take up our Cross, and to follow Him. Thus Dr Faust complains in Goethe's celebrated drama—

" Deny thyself, deny thyself;
   This is the old, the everlasting chime,
Which dins unceasingly upon the ear of man,
Which, through the whole of our most weary course,
Each hour repeats with more and more of force.*

Yet we cannot eliminate from His Gospel the words which Jesus Christ has

* " Entbehren sollst du, sollst entbehren;
   Das ist der ewige Gesang
   Der jedem an die Ohren klingt;
   Den unser ganzes Leben lang
   Uns heisser jede Stunde singt."
                 Goethe's Faust, Part i. Act i.

spoken, for " heaven and earth," He says, " shall pass away, but My words shall not pass away." The new Adam calls upon the old Adam to deny himself, to take up His Cross, and to follow Him.

Let us hear what Thomas à Kempis says on this point.

"These words, 'Deny thyself, take up thy Cross and follow Jesus,' seem to many to be a hard saying. But it will be much harder to hear at the last the words, ' Depart from Me, ye cursed, into the everlasting fire' (Matt. xxv. 41).

"For they who now willingly hear and follow the word of the Cross, shall not at that time labour under the fear of eternal damnation. This sign of the Cross shall be in heaven when the Lord shall come to judgment. Then shall all the servants of the Cross, who in this life shall have conformed themselves to the pattern of Him who was nailed upon it, draw near to their Judge with great boldness. Wherefore, then, dost thou fear to take up thy Cross, seeing that by it is the way to a kingdom? There is no salvation for the soul, neither hope of everlasting life, except in the Cross.

"Take up, therefore, thy Cross and follow Jesus, and thou shalt go to everlasting life. He hath gone before thee carrying His Cross, and has died for thee on the Cross, that thou mightest bear thy Cross, and learn to desire to die upon the Cross. For if thou shalt die together with Him, thou shalt also live with Him; and if thou sharest His humiliation, thou shalt be partaker of His glory" (Imitation of Christ, book ii. ch. xii., on the Royal Way of the Holy Cross).

"And now," writes St Anselm, " O Lord Jesus my Redeemer, I adore Thee as very and true God. I believe in Thee, I hope in Thee, and I long with all possible longing for Thee. Help Thou my infirmity, while I incline myself before all the glorious signs of Thy Passion, by which Thou hast worked out my salvation. There breathes to me the sweet savour of life in all these things. Raise up, O Lord, my spirit by their life-giving savour from the death of sin; guard me through the virtue that comes forth from them, from the deceits of Satan; strengthen

The Old Testament Types of The IV. Sorrowful Mystery.

Isaac carries the Wood of his own Sacrifice.

The Shepherd David encounters Goliath.

ROSA · MYSTICA · PASSIM · IN · LEGE · ET · IN · PROPHETIS

UMBRA · ET · ORA · PRO · NOBIS · DEUM · ET · FILIUM · TUUM

THE VICTIM GOING WILLINGLY TO HIS DEATH

THE VICTORY OF THE SHEPHERD CARRYING HIS SHEPHERD'S STAFF OVER THE ADVERSARY OF HIS PEOPLE.

me that the yoke of Thy commandments may become sweet to me, and that the burden of Thy Cross, which Thou commandest me to bear after Thee, may become light and tolerable to the shoulders of my soul. For what is my strength that I should be able, as Thou commandest, to bear with an unbroken spirit so many and so various troubles of this life? Are my feet as it were the feet of stags that I should be able to follow Thee as Thou passest swiftly along the rugged path of Thy Passion? Hear, I beseech Thee, my prayer, and lay, I pray Thee, on Thy servant that sweet Cross of Thine, which becomes the Tree of Life to all that lay hold of it, in order that, as I hope, I may run cheerfully under it. I will bear after Thee, without growing faint. The Cross which comes from enemies lay on my shoulders. I beseech Thee lay on them the burden of that most Divine Cross, whose breadth is the charity that extends itself to all that lives, whose length is eternity, whose height is Omnipotence, whose depth is the Inscrutable Wisdom" (St Anselm, Meditation ix.)

By the grace of God, then, even the way of the Cross may come to abound in sweetness and in spiritual joys. And the Church sings of the Apostle St Andrew in words capable of encouraging the most timid and faint-hearted of her disciples. When the blessed Andrew reached the place where the Cross stood ready for him, he cried out, and said, "O good Cross, so many years desired, and now at length granted to my longing soul! with confidence and great joy I come unto thee; and do thou, in like manner, rejoice and be glad at receiving a disciple of Him who hung upon thee, my Master Christ" (Vespers of the Feast of St Andrew).

CHAPTER IX.

THE SCRIPTURE TYPES OF THE FOURTH SORROWFUL MYSTERY.

I. ISAAC CARRYING THE WOOD OF THE SACRIFICE.
II. DAVID GOING FORTH WITH HIS SHEPHERD'S STAFF TO MEET GOLIATH.

1. *Isaac carrying the wood of the sacrifice up Mount Moria.*

"BEFORE Isaac comes to the place where he is to be sacrificed," St Augustine says, "he carries the wood of the sacrifice on which he is to be lifted up, and something is herein signified. Jesus went to the place where He was to be crucified, carrying His Cross. O most wonderful sight! as seen by the eyes of the wicked, an object to be mocked at; as seen by the eyes of faith, a deep mystery."

The narrative from the Holy Scripture occurs in the Book of Genesis:—

"After these things God tempted Abraham, and said to him: Abraham, Abraham. And he answered: Here I am. He said to him: Take thy only-begotten son Isaac, whom thou lovest, and go into the land of vision; and there thou shalt offer him for an holocaust upon one of the mountains which I will show thee. So Abraham rising up in the night, saddled his ass; and took with him two young men, and Isaac his son; and when he had cut wood for the holocaust, he went his way to the place which God had commanded him. And on the third day, lifting up his eyes, he saw the place afar off. And he said to his young men: Stay you here with the ass; I and the boy will go with speed as far as yonder, and after we have worshipped will return to you. And he took the wood for the holocaust, and laid it upon Isaac his son; and he himself carried in his hands fire and a sword. And as they two went on together, Isaac said to his father: My father. And he answered: What wilt thou, my son? Behold, saith he, fire and wood: where is the victim for the holocaust? And Abraham said: God will provide Himself a victim for an holocaust, my son. So they went on together" (Gen. xxii. 1–8).*

Isaac, in bearing the wood of the sacrifice on his shoulders, as St Augustine explains, bore the burden that was properly that of the ass, which was the beast of burden by nature; yet Abraham took the wood for the sacrifice, and laid it upon Isaac his son. Thus Isaias says of Christ,

"Surely He hath borne our infirmities, and carried our sorrows, ... and the Lord hath laid upon Him the iniquity of us all" (Isa. liii. 6). Jesus carries His Cross, the proper burden of the condemned malefactor, that the Scriptures might be fulfilled. "He was reputed with the wicked." His Eternal Father lays upon His shoulders the burden of the malefactor, and He, like Isaac, obedient to His Eternal Father, says, "I will go to the mountain, to the mountain of myrrh, till the day break and the shadows retire" (Cant. iv. 6).

2. *David goes out against the enemy of the armies of the Living God, with his shepherd's staff that he always carried in his hands.*

In the reign of Saul, the Holy Scripture relates, the armies of Israel and of the Philistines were gathered together to fight; and a certain Philistine, Goliath, of the sons of the giants, came forth, and defied the army of Israel. And the Philistine said, "I have defied the bands of Israel this day: give me a man, and let him fight with me hand to hand." And Saul and all the Israelites, hearing these words of the Philistine, were dismayed and greatly afraid.

As the Philistine continued to defy Israel for forty days, David came into the camp to inquire after his brethren's welfare; and hearing the Philistine's challenge, he asked to be led to Saul. When he was brought before Saul, he said to him, "Let not any man's heart be dismayed in him; I, thy servant, will go and fight against the Philistine." After giving a patient hearing to him, Saul said to David, "Go, and the Lord be with thee." And David took his staff, which he had always in his hand, and choosing five smooth stones from the brook, took a sling in his hand, and went against the Philistine. And the Philistine, seeing David, a stripling, of a ruddy countenance, despised him, and said to David, "Am I a dog, that thou comest to me with a staff?" And the Philistine cursed David by his gods. And he said to David, "Come to me, and I will give thy flesh to the birds of the air, and to the beasts of the earth." And David said to the Philistine, "Thou comest to me with a sword, and with a spear, and with a shield; but I come to thee in the name of the Lord of hosts, the God of the armies of Israel, which thou hast defied. This day the Lord will deliver thee into

---

* It will be instructive to see a specimen of the lively interest with which this touching history was treated as a popular Christian heirloom in the ages of faith.

It is thus paraphased in the "Coventry Plays." The spelling of the words has been somewhat modernised.

Abraham.—" Now son, on thy neck this faggot thou take,
And this fyre bear in thy honde (hand);
For we must now sacrifice go make,
Even after the wylle of Goddy's sonde (providence).
Take this brenning bronde,
My swete chylde, and lete us go;
There may no man that levyth in londe
Have more sorrow than I have wo."

Isaac.—" Fair fadyr, ye go right stylle;
I pray you, fadyr, speke unto me."

Abraham.—"My good chylde, what is thy wylle?
Tell me thyne hert, I pray to thee."

Isaac.—" Fadyr, fyre and wood here is plentye,
But I kan se no sacryfice;
What ye xulde offer fayn wold I se,
That it were done to the best avyse."

Abraham.—" God xal that ordeyn, that sytt in hevynne,
My swete son; ffor this offryng,
A dearer may no man nempne (name)
Than this xal be, my dere derlyng."
—*Coventry Plays: Abraham's Sacrifice.*

THE FIFTH SORROWFUL MYSTERY.

Ave Maria Gratia Plena Dominus Tecum

Foderunt manus meas et pedes meos. Ipsi vero consideraverunt, et inspexerunt me; diviserunt sibi vestimenta mea et super vestem meam miserunt sortem. (*Psalm xxi. 17.*)

Invenerunt me custodes qui circumeunt civitatem, percusserunt me et vulneraverunt me, tulerunt pallium meum custodes murorum. (*Cant. v. 7.*)

Benedicta tu in mulieribus et Benedictus fructus ventris tui Jesus.

They have pierced my hands and my feet. They have looked upon me, and have gazed at me. They have parted my garments among them, and for

The watchmen that go about the city found me and struck me; they wounded me, and the keepers of the walls took away my

THE CRUCIFIXION AND DEATH OF JESUS ON THE CROSS.

my hand, and I will slay thee, and take away thy head from thee: and I will give the carcasses of the army of the Philistines this day to the birds of the air, and to the beasts of the earth; that all the earth may know that there is a God in Israel. And all this assembly shall know that the Lord saveth not with sword and spear; for it is His battle, and He will deliver you into our hands."

Jesus bearing His Cross on His way to Mount Calvary is the true David, the Champion of the armies of the living God, who rejects the armour of the kings of this world, and who is going out to fight against the prince of darkness with His Cross, "*the staff that He always has in His hands,*" and to deliver them from him who up to this time had the power of death, "and to whose servitude they were all their lifetime subject through the fear of death" (Heb. ii. 15). The prince of darkness, in the beginning, prevailed by the wood of the fatal tree in Paradise, but One stronger than himself now comes against him, with the "*staff that He always had in His hands,*" to destroy him, and to spoil him of his goods. "Jesus went forth carrying His Cross," as the Church sings—

"Forth comes the standard of the King!
All hail! Thou Mystery adored!
Hail, Cross! on which the Life Himself
Died, and by death our life restored."
— *Vexilla Regis,* Caswall's Version.

Jesus had seen the serpent under the branches of the fatal tree in the Garden of Eden. He had seen the hand stretched out to take of the fruit at the insidious words of the deceiver, when Eve fell a victim to his deceit; and in the language of the Church hymn, He now comes, according to the will of the Eternal Father, against the arch-deceiver, to defeat him with his own weapon. As the Church sings—

" Eating of the tree forbidden,
Man had sunk in Satan's snare,
When our pitying Creator
Did the second tree prepare,
Destined, many ages later,
That first evil to repair.

" Such the order God appointed
When for sin He would atone,
To the serpent thus opposing
Schemes yet deeper than his own;
Thence the remedy procuring
Whence the fatal wound had come."
— *Office of Passion-Sunday,* Caswall's Version.

On the tree of the Cross Jesus was to repair the fall that was brought about through the tree of the knowledge of good and evil; and now, in the sight of all the people, He goes against the enemy of the armies of the living God, with His staff of victory in His hand. "Jesus went forth bearing His Cross."

"The children of Israel," writes St Augustine, "stood over against their adversaries forty days; which signify the present life, in which the Christian people cease not to fight against Goliath and his army—that is, against the devil and his angels. Nor would they have prevailed had not the Christ, the true David, come down amongst them with His staff in His hands; that is, with the mystery of the Cross. David, therefore, came and found the people of the Jews in battle-array against the devil; and when not one of them dared to come forward to a single combat, he, who was the figure of Christ, went forth to fight, carried his staff in his hands, and went out against Goliath. And thus, in him, there was shown in a figure that which was afterwards accomplished in our Lord Jesus Christ. For Christ, the true David, came forth, and when He was about to fight with the spiritual Goliath, He carried His own Cross. Observe, my brethren, where David wounded Goliath; in his forehead, where he was not marked with the sign of the Cross. For as the staff he carried was the figure of the Cross, so the stone with which Goliath was slain was the figure of Christ the Lord" (Augustine, Sermon cxcvii., De Tempore).

The Fifth Sorrowful Mystery of the Rosary.

CHAPTER X.

THE CRUCIFIXION AND DEATH OF JESUS ON THE CROSS.

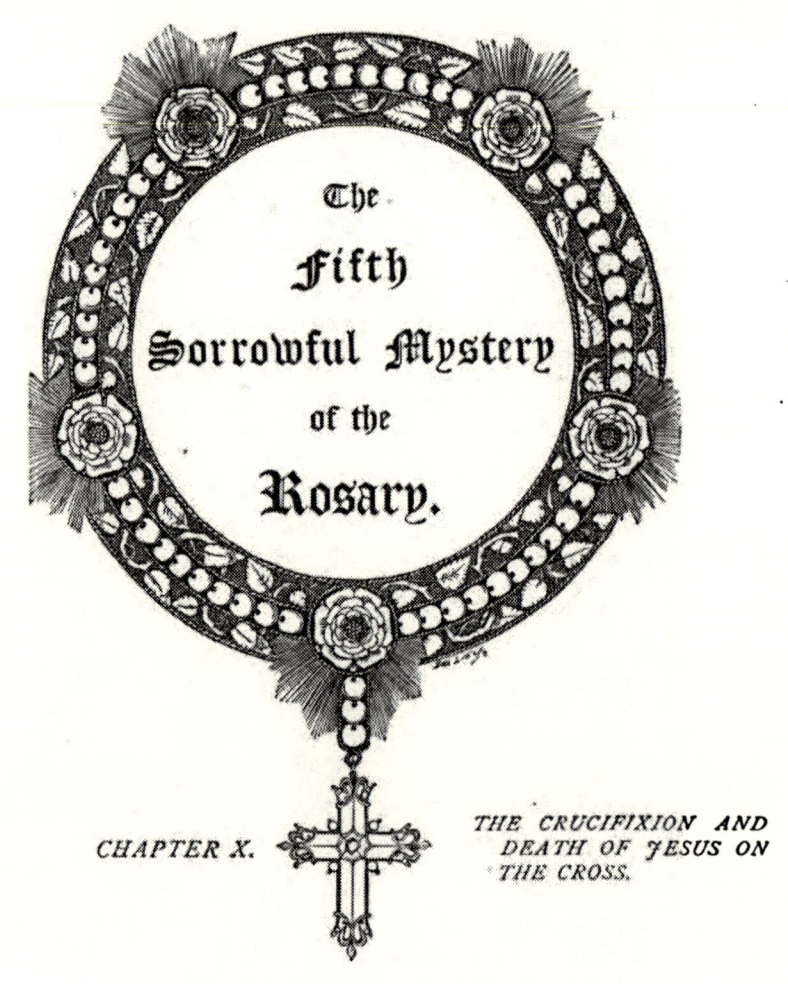

THE HOLY SCRIPTURE NARRATIVE.

"And when they were come to the place which is called Calvary, they crucified Him there, and the robbers, the one on the right hand, and the other on the left. And Jesus said: Father, forgive them, they know not what they do. . . . And it was almost the sixth hour, and there was darkness over all the earth until the ninth hour; and the sun was darkened, and the veil of the Temple was rent in the midst.' And Jesus cried with a loud voice, saying: Father, unto Thy hands I commend My spirit. And saying this, He gave up the ghost" (Luke xxiii. 33, 34, 44, 46).

The following commentary of the great St Augustine will briefly explain the principal circumstances of the crucifixion and death of Jesus Christ:—

"That two thieves were crucified, the one on His right and the other on His left, shows that some would suffer, as it were, on His right hand, and others on His left—those on the right being they of whom it is said, 'Blessed are those that suffer persecution for the sake of justice;' and those on the left, to whom the Apostle's words apply, 'And though I should give my body to be burned, and have not charity, it profiteth me nothing' (1 Cor. xiii. 3).

"That a title was placed over His Cross, on which it was written, 'The King of the Jews,' shows, notwithstanding that the Jews were putting Him to death, they could not help themselves from having Him for King over them, hereafter to manifest His power, and to render to them according to their works. As it is written in the Psalm, 'I am set up by Him to be King over His holy mountain Sion' (Ps. ii. 6).

"By the title being written in the three languages, Hebrew, Greek, and Latin, it is signified that He was to reign not only over the Jews, but also over the Gentiles. In the same Psalm where it is said, 'I am set up by Him to be King over Sion, His holy mountain,' that is, where the Hebrew language prevailed, there is immediately added, as if subjoining the Greek and Latin title, 'The Lord said unto Me, Thou art my Son; this day have I begotten Thee. Ask of Me, and I will give Thee nations for Thine inheritance, and the uttermost parts of the earth for Thy possession' (Ps. ii.) Not that the Greek and Latin languages are the only languages known to the nations, but they are more excellent than any of the others—the Greek on account of its literature, and the Latin on account of the superior intelligence of the Romans. But although in these three languages the future subjugation to Christ of the whole body of the nations is shown, it is not any the more on this account written on His title, 'King of the Gentiles,' but 'King of the Jews.' 'For the law,' it is written, 'shall go forth from Sion, and the word of the Lord from Jerusalem' (Isa. ii. 3). And who are the speakers in the Psalm who say, 'He hath subdued the people to us, and the nations under our feet" (Ps. xlvi. 4), except they of whom the Apostle says, 'For if the nations have been partakers with them in spiritual things, they ought also to minister to them in carnal things' (Rom. xv. 27).

"In that His garments, which the soldiers carried off, were divided into four parts, by this are signified the four quarters of the globe, into which His sacraments were to find their way.

"By their casting lots for His vesture, which was woven without seam from the top downwards, rather than part it among themselves, is very clearly shown that some might come to have the visible sacraments, which are the garments of Christ, without their being possessed of an entirely sincere faith, which works through love a perfect union with God. 'For the love of God is shed abroad in our hearts by the Holy Spirit which is given to us.' This perfect union being imparted by the secret grace of God as it were by lot. Hence St Peter said to Simon Magus, who had obtained baptism without the grace of which we are speaking, 'Thou hast neither part nor lot in this faith.'

"In that, when hanging on the Cross, He recognised His Mother, and commended her to the care of His beloved disciple, in this He suitably showed His human affections at the time when He was about to die as Man. His hour was not then come, at the time when He said to His Mother, as He was about to turn the water into wine, 'Lady, what is there between thee and Me? My hour is not yet come.' For He did not take from Mary that which He had as being God, but He took from her that which hung upon the Cross.

"When He said 'I thirst,' He was seeking for faith in His own people; but because He came to His own, and His own received Him not, for the sweetness of faith they gave Him the vinegar of treachery, and this upon a sponge—like sponges as they were themselves, swollen up, without solidity, full of the tortuous openings and lurking crevices of snares and deceits.

"In that He said, 'It is finished, and bowing His head, He gave up the ghost,' He showed not the compulsory, but the voluntary character of His death, by waiting until all things were fulfilled which had been foretold of Him in prophecy. For this also was written, 'And in My thirst they gave Me vinegar to drink' (Ps. lxxviii. 22). As one who possessed, as He had Himself testified, the power to lay down His life, He gave up His life by an act of humility, that is, 'bowing down His head,' to receive His life again in His resurrection, with His head lifted up. The patriarch Jacob showed in a figure the great power of this death and the bowing down His head in the benediction of Juda, 'Lying down thou hast ascended up,' 'As a lion thou hast fallen asleep;' by the 'lying down' signifying His death, and by the lion, His power.

"In that the legs of the two thieves were broken, while no bone of His was touched on account of His being already dead, the Gospels explain the reason. For it was necessary that the figure of the Pasch of the Jews should be fulfilled, it being a precept of the law as regards the Pasch, 'that no bone of the lamb should be broken.'

"In that His side was pierced with a spear, and that there flowed forth from it both water and blood, are signified beyond doubt the sacraments from which the Church is formed, as Eve was taken from the side of Adam when he was thrown into a deep sleep, Adam being the figure of Him who was to come" (Augustine, Sermon ccxviii., Sermon to the People on the Passion and Death of Jesus).

In the preceding commentary of the great St Augustine, the devout reader will find perhaps the most concise, and at the same the most complete, commentary on the prominent events of our Lord's Passion. "The well is here very deep," and since volumes have been written, and may be written, in order not to be lost in the multitude of pious meditations that press in upon the mind, we will endeavour to concentrate our thoughts on the three following truths :—

1. That Jesus Christ, according to the purpose of God, known from all eternity, by His own will died on the Cross in the sight of all the people, a true and real death, inflicted upon Him from His own choice, by the hands of His enemies.

2. That the death of Jesus Christ has satisfied, and alone could satisfy, for the sin of Adam.

3. That by His death the way of salvation has been truly purchased for all men.

On the first of these truths, St Athanasius, the great Doctor of the Eastern Church, writes as follows :—

"Our Divine Redeemer did not come to be the Author of His own death, but to receive death at the hands of man. For He who is the Life itself is not the Author of death. He did not therefore put off the body by a death of which He was Himself the cause, but He endured a death inflicted by the hands of men. For, notwithstanding that His body had been afflicted and had suffered in the sight of men, it was not becoming that He who was to heal the sins of others should suffer sickness in His own person. And even if, without submitting to any disease, He had put off His body apart in some remote place, He would not have been believed when speaking of His resurrection. For with what kind of reason could He have openly proclaimed His resurrection, if He had chosen to die in secret? What calumnies would not His unbelieving adversaries have invented and propagated, if His death had been in private? And, how else was it possible that the victory of Christ over death should have been made manifest, otherwise than by His being seen to undergo death in public in the sight of all men, He should thereby prove death to have been swallowed up in the incorruptibility of His body? But you will say, at least, He ought to have devised for Himself a more glorious death, and to have avoided the death of the Cross. But if He had done this, He would have made Himself suspected of not having power over every kind of death. In the same manner, then, as the combatant who overcomes everything that is opposed to him, thereby proves himself to be superior to all, so the Life itself who gives life to all men, chose the manner of His death for the express reason that, both in itself and in being inflicted by His enemies, it might be the most dreadful and shameful of all possible deaths. Such, then, was the abominable death of the Cross, and He chose it in order that, having destroyed it, the dominion of death might be thereby absolutely and entirely overthrown; for which reason His head was not cut off, as was that of John the Baptist, He was not sawn asunder, as Isaias, that He might preserve His body entire and indivisible in death, and not become a pretext for those who would divide the Church. For He desired to bear the curse of sin, which we had incurred, by taking upon Himself the accursed death of the Cross. As it is written, 'Cursed is he that hangeth upon a tree.' He dies also upon the Cross with outstretched hands, that with one He may draw to Himself the ancient people, and with the other the Gentiles, thus making both one in Himself. Dying also upon the Cross, He purges the air of evil spirits, and prepares for us the ascent to heaven" (St Athanasius, Treatise of the Incarnation).

2. *That the death of Jesus Christ has satisfied, and alone could satisfy, for the sin of Adam.*

We shall not be able to do better here than attentively to listen to the words of Christian wisdom, in exposition of the above truth, which are uttered by St Anselm, the great Doctor of the medieval Church. They occur in his treatise on the question, "Why God became Man?" which is written in the form of a dialogue between Anselm and his disciple.

"*Disciple.* Infidels," says the disciple, "object to us, in derision of our simplicity, that we offer an injury and an insult to God by saying that He has come down into the womb of a female, was born of a woman, and grew up from being fed with milk and other articles of human diet; not to mention other things which appear not at all becoming in God, viz., that He should have to endure weariness, hunger, thirst, scourging, crucifixion between thieves, and lastly, death.

"*Anselm.* We offer neither injury nor insult to God, but, with hearts full of the warmest gratitude, we praise and magnify Him for the unspeakable depths of His mercies. For the more marvellous and unexpected is the way in which He delivered us from the great and justly due evil plight into which we had fallen, restoring us to all the glorious and wonderful good things to which we had forfeited every claim, so much the more in this has He shown His love and tenderness towards us. For if these unhappy unbelievers would only give their minds to consider in how suitable a manner the restoration of man has been thus procured, so far from deriding our simplicity, they would join with us in praising the wisdom and the goodness of God. For it was most fitting that as death entered into the world through the disobedience of one man, so life should be restored through the obedience of one Man; and as the transgression which was the cause of our condemnation had its beginning from a woman, so the Author of our justice and salvation should be born of a woman; and seeing that the devil overcame man by his tasting of the fruit of a tree, to which act he persuaded him, it was in the highest degree fitting that he should be overcome by a Man through the very suffering on a tree which the devil inflicted upon him. And there are besides innumerable other things which, carefully considered, show the unspeakable beauty of the salvation that has been in this way procured for us."

St Anselm, proceeding in due order, gives us the following clear definition of sin : "If angels and men were always to render to God what is due to Him, there would be no sin. To sin, therefore, is nothing else than not to render to God that which is His due. And the debt which is due to God is that the will of every reasonable creature should be subject to His will. This is the debt which angels and men both owe to God; which if it be paid there can be no sin, and which every one who does not pay, sins. This is the justice or rectitude of will, which makes men just and upright of heart, that is of will, and this is the whole and sole honour which we owe to God, and which God exacts from us. He, therefore, who does not give to God the honour that is His due, takes away from God that which belongs to Him, and robs God of His honour, to do which is to sin ; and as long as he does not repay what he has taken away, he remains in guilt. Nor does it suffice merely to restore what he has taken away, but, on account of the insult which has been offered, he is bound to restore more than he has taken away."

The Doctor then proceeds to show that God cannot from mercy alone forego to exact the repayment of what is due to Him on the score of injury done to His honour. For that thus to remit sin would be merely to suffer sin to go unpunished; and on these terms both the man who sins and the man who keeps himself from sin would stand upon an equality before God, and if mere mercy brought about remission of sin, injustice would then possess greater freedom than justice, and there would be no law to which injustice would be amenable. "All of which," he says, "are repugnant to the nature and subversive of the sovereignty of God." He then leads his disciple through a train of reasoning to show that Adam by his transgression had incurred a debt to the justice of God which it was wholly out of his power to discharge.

"Man," reasons St Anselm, "created without sin, was placed in Paradise as it were for God, between God and the devil, that he should overcome the devil by not consenting to his solicitations to sin, for the double motive of the honour of God and the confusion of the devil, who, although the stronger of the two, nevertheless himself sinned in heaven, no one thereto persuading him. And man, when he could easily have resisted, by the mere persuasion of the devil, without the least compulsion, and entirely of his own free will, suffered himself to be overcome so as that he followed the will of the devil, greatly to the dishonour of God and to the despite of His sovereign will. Judge, therefore, if it be not wholly contrary to the honour of God, that man should be reconciled to God with the guilt of this injury to God resting upon him, except he were first to honour God by conquering the devil in the same manner as he dishonoured Him by letting the devil gain the upper-hand. And, moreover, the victory is bound to be such, that, in like manner as he easily consented to the devil when he was in his strength and the heir of immortality (from which act of consent to the devil he has justly incurred the penalty of death), so in his weakness and subjection to death (into which condition he brought himself by his own act), he should, through the hardship of death, overcome the devil in such a manner as to be free from sin; a thing which it is impossible for him to do, so long as he is conceived subject to the wound of original sin, and is born in sins.

"And further, consider what it was that man took away from God when he suffered himself to be overcome by the devil. Did he not take away from God all that He proposed to do with His human creature? Man therefore lies under the guilt of injustice, because he does not render to God what he owes Him; and he is not excused by reason of his inability, for it was solely his own doing by which he came into his inability; his inability therefore does but add to his fault.

"How, then," asks the disciple, "can man be saved, if he cannot possibly pay the debt that he owes, and still ought not to be saved except he does pay it?

"*Anselm.* Ask those to explain how, who think that man can be saved without Christ; and if they are unable in any sort of way to explain how, let them then cease to laugh at what they call our simplicity, and come over to our side, who do not in the least doubt but that man can be saved by Christ.

"God must either have fruitlessly made so sublime a nature for so great a good, or He will certainly perfect His own work; and yet this cannot be except such a full and entire satisfaction is offered for the sin of man as it is out of the power of any sinner to offer. Who therefore is to offer this satisfaction? It cannot be offered except there be some one found who will offer for satisfaction of the sin of man something which is greater than everything which exists external to God Himself. But he who is able to give of his own something which is greater than everything which is under God must himself be greater than everything which is not God, and this can be true of nothing besides God Himself. No one, therefore, has the power to offer this satisfaction except God alone. And no one ought to offer it except man, for otherwise *man does not satisfy.*

"*Disciple.* Nothing can be more just.

"*Anselm.* Since, therefore, it is clear, as we have said, that the vacancies in the celestial city must be filled up from the ranks of men,* and this cannot be except the satisfaction be offered which none but God has the power to offer, and none but man is under debt to offer, it becomes necessary that it be done by one who is GOD AND MAN.

"*Disciple.* Blessed be God! we have lighted upon an immense truth in our investigation. Only proceed as you have begun, and may God come to our aid!"

St Anselm then proceeds to show that liability to death appertains to the nature of man not necessarily, but only as corrupted by sin, and that God, by becoming Man, incurred no necessity of dying, but retained the power, either not to die, if such were His will, or, if He willed, to die and to rise again; and that whether He laid down His life directly by an act of His own, or whether another took away His life by His permission, this would make no difference as regards His power.

Of what kind, therefore, was the gift to be which He was to give in satisfaction for the sin of man? Something proper to Himself it must be, for anything merely external or inferior to Him would be clearly insufficient. Were we then to say that He should give Himself up to obey God, and to persevere in a life of submission to His will in the fulfilment of all justice, it is obvious this would not be to give to God that which is not already His due, for every intelligent and rational creature already owes this obedience to God. There must, therefore, be some other mode in which He is to give, either Himself, or something proper to Himself, to God. Let us see if this be not to give or to lay down His life, or to deliver himself up to death for the honour of God. For this God will not exact from Him as His due, inasmuch as, from never having sinned, He has not incurred the debt of death. Let us consider whether this is not highly agreeable to reason.

"*Disciple.* Speak, and I will willingly listen.

"*Anselm.* If man sinned in the way of luxury, is it not most fitting that he should make his satisfaction for sin in the way of hardship? And if he was drawn to dishonour God, in his disobedience at the persuasion of the devil, with such an extreme ease and facility that it is impossible to see how he could have been more easily persuaded, is it not altogether just that man, in satisfying for his sin, should overcome the devil to the honour of God, in a manner so difficult that it is impossible to conceive any manner of obedience more difficult? And is it not most agreeable to reason that he who by his sin removed himself from God, in such a way that he could not remove himself more, should give himself up to God so unreservedly, that he should be unable to do this more unreservedly?

"*Disciple.* Nothing, as you say, can be more agreeable to reason.

"*Anselm.* But there is nothing harder and more difficult, which it is in the power of a man to suffer, for the honour of God, of his own free-will, and not in the way of a debt, than death; and there is no degree in which a man can more unreservedly give himself up to God than when he delivers himself up to death for the honour of God.

"*Disciple.* This is quite true.

"*Anselm.* He, therefore, who undertakes to satisfy for the sin of man, must consequently be one who has the power to die, if such be his will?

"*Disciple.* I see clearly that the man whom we are seeking for must be one who is not under the necessity of death by reason of His omnipotence, and who is not under the debt of death by reason of His immunity from sin, and who is notwithstanding a person able to die of His own free will, because His death is needed.

"Thinkest thou then," continues St

---

* It is St Anselm's doctrine, following St Augustine, that God created man lower than the angels, intending to promote a lower creation to the places of honour left vacant by the fall of the rebel angels.

Anselm, " that the gift of that which is so inestimably precious as His life is not able to satisfy for all that is due for the sins of the whole world?

" *Disciple.* Undoubtedly, it is infinitely more than able.

" *Anselm.* Then you see how this life, if it be given for them, more than counterbalances all the sins of the world?

" *Disciple.* I see it clearly.

" *Anselm.* If, therefore, to give away life be the same thing as to accept death, in the same manner as the gift of His life outweighs all the sins of men, so also does this acceptance of death.

3. *That by the death of Jesus Christ the way to salvation has been truly purchased for all men.*

This proposition, which forms the appropriate transition to the glorious Mysteries that are to follow, may be suitably continued in the words of St Anselm, which fortunately here do not require the same degree of abbreviation as the foregoing, and may be simply quoted directly from the text.

" *Anselm.* Let us now endeavour to see in how extremely reasonable a manner human salvation follows upon His death.

" *Disciple.* This is what my heart longs for. And though I seem as if I understood it, still I wish to hear the reasons at length from you.

" *Anselm.* There is no further need to explain the greatness of that which God the Son has given of His own free will.

" *Disciple.* This is quite clear enough.

" *Anselm.* But you will not judge it to be by any means fitting that He who gives so great a gift should go without reward?

" *Disciple.* I quite see the propriety of this, that the Father should give a reward to the Son, otherwise He must appear to be unjust if He be unwilling, or else impotent if He be unable to give it, both of which are repugnant to the nature of God.

" *Anselm.* He who rewards a second person, either gives that which the second person does not possess, or remits to him something which might with justice be exacted from him. But before the Son accomplished His great work, all that belonged to His Father was His, and He was never in debt for anything that could be remitted to Him. What, therefore, can be given to Him who is in need of nothing, and who is One to whom nothing can be either given or remitted?

" *Disciple.* On the one hand I see the necessity of a reward being given, and on the other its impossibility. For it is necessary that God should pay what He owes, and yet there is no one to whom to pay it.

" *Anselm.* If so great and so justly due a reward is not given, either to Him, or to some one else, the Son will appear to have accomplished His great work in vain.

" *Disciple.* This is inconceivable.

" *Anselm.* The reward, then, must be given to some one else, since it cannot be given to Him.

" *Disciple.* The consequence is inevitable.

" *Anselm.* If the Son were to will to give His reward to another, could the Father justly prohibit Him, or deny it to the third person to whom the Son should desire to give it?

" *Disciple.* Certainly, I understand it to be just and fitting that the reward should be given by the Father to the persons to whom the Son should desire to give it, inasmuch as it is lawful for the Son to give that which is His own, and the Father cannot give that which He owes except to some third party.

" *Anselm.* To whom shall the Son more fittingly make over the fruit and the reward of His death, than to those for whose salvation (as the scheme of truth teaches us) He made Himself man, and to whom by His death He gave an example of dying for justice' sake? For it will be entirely in vain that men imitate His example if they are not to be partakers in His merits. Or whom shall He make with greater justice the heirs of that which is due to Him, and which He does not want by reason of the abundance of His own fulness, than His parents and His brethren, whom He sees pining away in want and in the depth of misery, weighed down with heavy and innumerable debts, so that what they owe on account of their sins may be remitted to them, and that of

THE V. SORROWFUL MYSTERY.

THE OLD TESTAMENT TYPES OF
The Fountain of the River in Paradise.
The Paschal Lamb.

LEGE · ET · IN · PROPHETIS

MEUM · FILIUM

THE VICTIM OF WHICH A BONE WAS NOT TO BE BROKEN.

ROSA · MYSTICA · PASSIM · IN

SIBON · ORTO

AQUMBR · T · A · RUMR

THE SPRING OF WATER FROM PLACE OF PLEASURE THAT WATERED ALL THE EARTH.

which they are deprived on account of their sins may be given to them?

"*Disciple.* There is nothing that the world can hear, which is more agreeable to reason, more delightful, and more to be desired. I, for my part, conceive such courage from this, that I cannot tell with what joy my heart exults. For it seems to me that God will reject no man whatever who comes to Him in the name of this Man.

"*Anselm.* It is indeed so, if he come as he should come. As to the manner in which we should present ourselves to be partakers of such great grace, and in what manner we ought to live under it, the Sacred Scriptures everywhere teach. And further, the mercy of God, which seemed to you to perish when we were considering the justice of God and the sin of man, we have found to be so great and so entirely in harmony with His justice, that we cannot conceive how it could be more in harmony. For what can be understood as more merciful than when God the Father says to the sinner, who is condemned to eternal torments, and who has nothing wherewith to redeem himself, 'Take My only-begotten Son, and give Him for thyself;' while the Son says, 'Take Me, and redeem thyself?' For this is, as it were, what they say when they call and draw us to the Christian faith. For what can be more just than that he to whom a thing is given of greater price than the debt which is owed, should, provided it be given with due dispositions, remit the entire debt?"

The following touching words, with which St Anselm concludes his "Meditation on the Sufferings of Jesus Christ," may serve as our appropriate passage to the glory and triumph of the glorious Mysteries:—

"I beseech Thee, therefore, most merciful Father, as in the beginning Thou didst create me, and afterwards restoredst me to life by the Passion of Thy only-begotten Son, so Thou wouldst make me to think of and to love everything that appertains to Thy praise. But for the reason that I am weak, and cannot perform what I desire, grant to me, by the diligent confession of my faults, ever to study to obtain the grace of Thy redemption and salvation. And whatsoever work I may undertake out of, by, and in Thy grace, cause it to turn entirely to Thy praise; and preserve me from sins for the time to come, and teach me to be more vigorous in good works, that as long as I may live in this body, I may be always doing some service for Thee. And grant that after the departure of my soul from the body, I may obtain the pardon of my sins and the gift of eternal life, through Him who liveth and reigneth with Thee world without end" (St Anselm, Meditation ix.)

CHAPTER XI.

THE SCRIPTURE TYPES OF THE FIFTH SORROWFUL MYSTERY.

**I. THE FOUNTAIN IN PARADISE WHICH WATERED THE WHOLE EARTH.
II. THE PASCHAL LAMB. III. THE PASSAGE OF THE RED SEA.
IV. THE PRAYER OF MOSES ON THE MOUNT. V. THE BRAZEN SERPENT.
VI. THE ROCK WHICH YIELDED A STREAM OF WATER.**

1. *The fountain springing up in the place of pleasure in Paradise, which, being divided into four streams, watered the whole earth.*

THERE can be no part of the work of the Eternal Son for the redemption of man, which antecedently we should be prepared to believe would be more richly prefigured in the previous Covenants of God with man, than His supreme act of the laying down His life on the Cross, when He uttered the words, "It is consummated." And the fifth sorrowful mystery is shadowed forth, in fact, in an endless variety of ways; nevertheless, because the well is deep, we must be satisfied to draw from it, not what we could wish, and what it contains, but what space and opportunity permit.

> In figuris præsignatur (*sings the Church*),
> Cum Isaac immolatur,
> Agnus Paschæ deputatur,
> Datur manna Patribus.
> —*Hymn,* "*Lauda*"

The figure of "Isaac" and of the "manna" have already occupied our attention, and with that of the "Paschal lamb" we will associate those above enumerated, each in their own way, reflecting their particular portion of light upon the sacred mystery.

"There was not a man to till the earth," says the Book of Genesis, "but a spring rose up out of the earth, watering all the surface of the earth. And the Lord had planted a paradise of pleasure from the beginning, wherein He placed man whom He had formed. And a river went out from the place of pleasure, which from thence is divided into four heads" (Gen. ii. 5–10).

Let us briefly study the particulars of the parallel, and see if the resemblance is not almost minute. "*But there was not a man to till the earth when this fountain sprang up in paradise.*" When Jesus came into the world, there was not a man to remedy its disorders, nor to heal its wounds. Isaias, in the spirit of prophecy, foresaw the state of the world at His coming, and has thus described it:— "And the truth had become forgotten, and he that departed from evil lay open to be a prey. And the Lord saw it, and it appeared evil in His eyes, for judgment had failed. And He saw that there was no man, and He was astonished that there was not one to oppose himself. Therefore, His own arm wrought salvation, and His justice it strengthened Him" (Isaias lix. 15).

"*And the river went out from the place of pleasure, which from thence is divided into four heads.*" Let us contemplate Jesus attentively as He lies stretched out on the Cross. He is beautiful above the sons of men, yet His head flows with blood from the wounds of the thorns. His hands flow with blood at each extremity of the transverse beam of the Cross. His feet flow with blood at the foot of the Cross. And here we behold the healing stream which gives life to the world, flowing from the fountain of salvation, and which from thence is divided into four heads.

"*But the spring rose up out of the earth, watering all the surface of the earth.*" As the waters of the river of paradise, which went forth from the place of pleasure, after being divided into four heads, spread themselves over the earth, watering its surface, so the doctrines of the gospel, which went forth from Mount Sion, "the city of perfect beauty, the joy of the whole earth" (Lam. ii. 15), and "the city which the Lord hath built" (Ps. ci. 17), having been sent east and west, north and south, are spreading themselves daily over the earth, ever covering its surface with fresh falls of the heavenly dew of the Word of Life.

The V. Sorrowful Mystery.

The miraculous Passage of the Red Sea.

LEGE EZ IN PROPHETIS

CUM EO FILIUM SUUM

THE ROD WHICH CAUSED THE WATER OF THE SEA TO DESTROY THE ENEMIES OF GOD.

The Old Testament Types of

The Stream of Water from the Rock.

ROSA MYSTICA PASSIM IN

TUMBRIS OR PRO NOBIS

THE ROCK WHICH, BEING STRUCK BY THE ROD, YIELDED A STREAM OF WATER FOR THE LIFE OF THE PEOPLE.

2. The Paschal Lamb; and 3. The Passage of the Red Sea.

For these things were done, says the Evangelist, that the Scriptures might be fulfilled. "You shall not break a bone of Him." There exists no other prophecy in the Sacred Scriptures to this effect, except the typical history of the Paschal lamb, which the Israelites were commanded to kill and eat the night of their sudden departure from the land of Egypt, having first sprinkled the door-posts of their houses with the blood of the lamb, that the destroying angel, who was sent to strike the first-born of the Egyptians, might see the sign of salvation on their dwellings, and pass them over. The Paschal lamb is thus placed by the Evangelist as among the figures of Christ, and the allegory, or figure, hardly needs explanation. "Christ our Pasch is slain," says the apostle, "therefore let us keep the feast" (1 Cor. v. 7). Again, Christ, our atoning sacrifice, is called in the Book of Revelations, "The Lamb slain before the foundations of the world." And the Church sings—

" As the avenging angel passed
   Of old, the blood-besprinkled door ;
As the cleft sea a passage gave,
   Then closed to whelm the Egyptians o'er ;
" So Christ, our Paschal Sacrifice,
   Has brought us safe all perils through :
While for unleavened bread we need
   But heart sincere and purpose true."
—*Hymn, Ad Regias Agni*, Caswall's version.

The miraculous passage of the Red Sea, in the same manner, is also recognised by St Paul as a figure of the salvation of the Cross : " I would not have you ignorant, brethren," he writes, " how our fathers all passed through the sea, and all in Moses were baptized in the cloud and in the sea." Now, all these things happened to them in a figure, and they are written for our correction, upon whom the ends of the world are come (1 Cor. x. 1). After these things, as St Augustine also writes, " Moses is commanded to strike the sea with his rod. Behold in this rod the mystery of the Holy Cross. Observe, and see, that except the rod be lifted up over the sea, the people of God are not delivered out of the hands of Pharao. And, in the same manner, if the Holy Cross also had not been lifted up, the Christian people would have perished for ever. But when the rod is raised up, that is, when the Cross is placed erect, then the sea gives way, and its waves yield. Let us, my brethren, pray to our Lord to perform in our hearts and persons the same work which He accomplished on the Egyptians, that we may receive the gift of the Holy Spirit to destroy in ourselves the spiritual Egyptians, for he does this who destroys in himself the works of darkness " (Sermon XXIV.)

4. The Prayer of Moses on the Mount.

Scarcely were the people fairly advanced into the wilderness, the Scripture relates, when an enemy comes against them to dispute their further progress. This is the people of Amalec. And Moses said to Josue, " Choose out men, and go and fight against Amalec, and I will stand on the top of the hill, having the rod of God in my hand." Moses went up into the mount with Aaron and Hur, and the battle began. As long as Moses lifted up his hands to pray, Israel overcame, but if he let them down even a little, Amalec overcame. Moses' hands, however, became heavy, and at length Aaron and Hur, taking a stone, placed it under him, so that he sat upon it, and they stayed up his hands on both sides. And thus it came to pass that his hands were not weary until sunset. And Josue prevailed against Amalec, and put them to flight by the edge of the sword (Exod. xvii. 12).

" Herein, my brother," writes St John Chrysostom, "thou seest the blessed Moses pointing to the Cross by another figure. And if you desire to know in what manner, listen, for those who discourse of the Cross should be prepared with every variety of figure and mystery. 'And it came to pass, as long as Moses lifted up his hands to pray, Israel overcame, but if he let them down even a little, Amalec overcame.' What is the meaning of this figure? A Jew, alarmed lest the glory of the Cross should be seen shining through it, will say, " This figure has no reference whatever to what you are dreaming about. It was no more than a mere mode of prayer, and not the figure of what you imagine. But, against this, it is to be answered, if the victory were the fruit of nothing but the prayer of Moses, how comes the Scripture not to ascribe the victory to his prayer. For the language of the Scripture is not 'when Moses prayed,' but it ascribes the victory simply to the holding out his hands. 'For when Moses,' says the Scripture, 'let his hands drop down even a little, Israel was overcome, and when he stretched them out, Amalec was put to flight.' If this is solely to be ascribed to his prayer, the words certainly should have been, ' When Moses prayed.' But, as I have said, the Scripture, omitting all direct mention of his prayer, not indeed as if it were useless, but as being second in importance to the figure of the cross, ascribes the victory solely to the type and to the sign ; ' for when Moses stretched out his hands, Israel conquered.' What does this stretching out of his hands signify? Picture to yourself these stretched-out hands, and behold in them a resplendent figure of the adorable Cross " (Homily on the Brazen Serpent).

5. *The Brazen Serpent.*

In the next figure we shall see foreshadowed the power of the Cross over the confusion and suffering brought about by the sins of the people. This is the brazen serpent of the wilderness, the history of which may be narrated briefly as follows from the Book of Numbers :—" The forty years of wandering were drawing to an end, but the murmuring and discontented spirit of the people remained unchanged. The children of Edom had refused them the right of passage through their territory, and this refusal made it necessary to return back southward, and pass to the east of Mount Seir, where Edom dwelt. This increase of marching drew from them complaints and murmurs ; they quarrelled with the manna, and asked Moses why he had brought them up out of Egypt, and complained that they had neither bread nor water. To punish them, God sent serpents among them, which bit and killed many of them. The people came at length, and said that they had sinned, and prayed Moses to take away the serpents from them. Moses prayed for the people ; and the Lord said to him, "Make a brazen serpent, and set it up for a sign ; whosoever, being struck, shall look upon it, shall live." Moses did so, and when they who were bitten looked upon it, they were healed" (Num. xxi.).

Jesus, in His discourse by night with Nicodemus, declares this brazen serpent to be a figure of His passion on the Cross, saying, " For as Moses lifted up the serpent in the wilderness, so the Son of man must be lifted up, that every one who believeth in Him may not perish, but have everlasting life" (John iii. 14).

" Brethren," says St John Chrysostom, above quoted, " this figure of the serpent was an image of the Cross. And if it be asked in what way, we may reply, that as this image of the serpent had all the shape and form of a serpent, without its venom and stealthiness, so our divine Redeemer, according to the apostle, appeared in the likeness of sinful flesh, yet was without sin. 'Who did no sin,' as St Peter says, ' neither was deceit found in His mouth.' Behold the truth shining through the figures of the Scripture. Serpents bit the children of Israel when the people rushed into transgression. Moses prays God to show him some healing remedy, and God shows to His servant the remedy he asks for. 'Make a brazen serpent,' He says, ' and set it up before the tabernacle of the testimony.' What can be the meaning of such a sign as this? The serpents which inflict the bites are one thing, and another serpent is crucified for them. What can this riddle mean? What can be the mystery of which it is the shadow and figure? In the same way as another

The Victory of Jesus and the Joy of Mary over the vanquished Prince of the Power of Darkness

are prefigured by

The Song of Triumph of the Three Children when they were cast into the Fiery Furnace by the King of Babylon.

serpent which does not bite is in this figure nailed to the Cross for the serpents inflicting the bites, so the innocent Jesus is about to suffer for all those who have sinned. For the serpents which bit the people, the serpent which is harmless is crucified; and for us, who are subject to death, He is nailed to the Cross, over whom death hath of right no dominion: as the prophet says, 'The Lord hath delivered Himself up for our sins' (Isa. liii. 12). And again we ask, why is a serpent made of brass fixed to the cross? and the answer is, that the bites of the serpents might be removed. One thing is raised on the cross, and another thing is done away with by means of it. As in this case, it was the image of the serpent which was publicly exposed that removed the bites of the other serpents, so it is the death of Christ which has taken away death, and which has routed the assaults of the demons" (Homily on the Brazen Serpent).

6. The rock in the wilderness which yielded a stream of water upon being struck.

The narrative in the Holy Scripture runs as follows:—" And the people wanting water, came together against Moses and Aaron. And making a sedition, they said: Would God we had perished among our brethren before the Lord. Why have you brought out the Church of the Lord into the wilderness, that both we and our cattle should die? And Moses and Aaron leaving the multitude, went into the tabernacle of the covenant, and fell flat upon the ground, and cried to the Lord, and said: O Lord God, hear the cry of this people, and open to them Thy treasure, a fountain of living water, that being satisfied, they may cease to murmur. And the Lord spoke to Moses, saying: Take the rod, and assemble the people together, thou and Aaron thy brother, and speak to the rock before them, and it shall yield waters. And when thou hast brought forth water out of the rock, all the multitude and their cattle shall drink. Moses therefore took the rod, which was before the Lord, as He had commanded him. And having gathered together the multitude before the rock, he said to them: Hear, ye rebellious and incredulous: Can we bring you forth water out of this rock? And when Moses had lifted up his hand, and struck the rock twice with the rod, there came forth water in great abundance, so that the people and their cattle drank" (Numb. xx.)

"On this subject," writes St Augustine, "we have the clearest and most reliable testimony of the Apostle, who says, 'And they drank of the Spiritual Rock which followed them, and the rock was Christ' (1 Cor. x. 4). For as it is the custom with the Divine mysteries, contained in the Sacred Scriptures, that the same person should, according to the thing which is to be signified at one time, wear one character, and at another a different one, Moses, at the present moment, represents the character of the people of the Jews under the law. For as Moses, striking the rock with his rod, doubted the power of God, so the people which was under the law given by Moses, when they nailed Him to the wood of the Cross, did not believe Him to be the Power of God. But, nevertheless, just as the rock when struck yielded a stream of water for those who were athirst, so the wound inflicted upon Jesus in His Passion, became the source of life to all that believe" (Contra Faust., lib. xvi.)

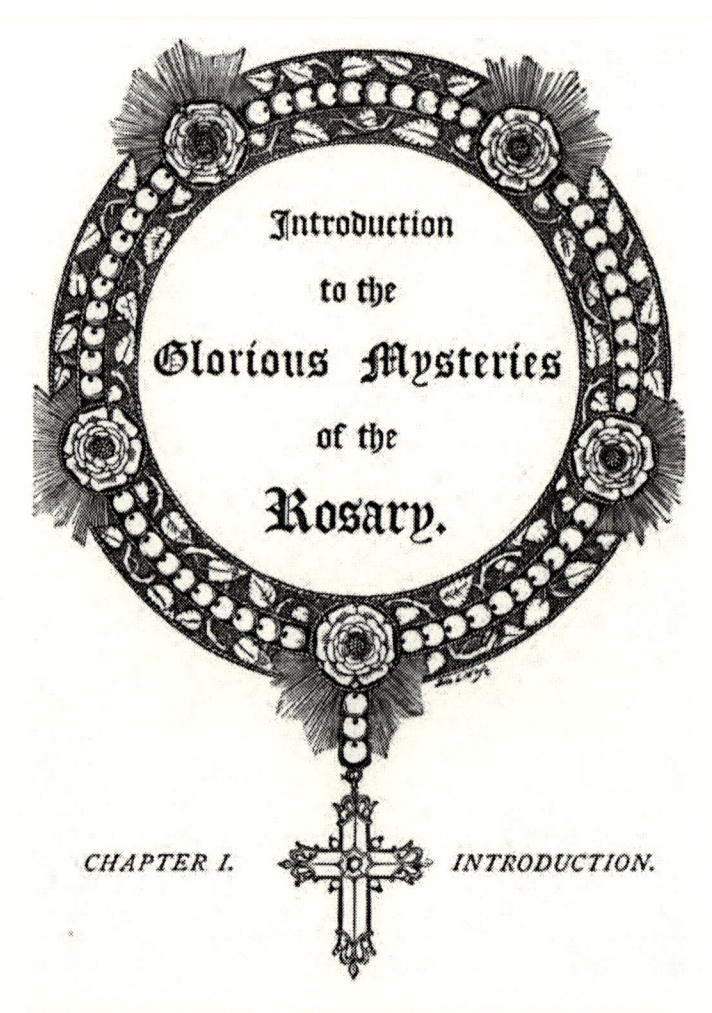

Introduction to the Glorious Mysteries of the Rosary.

CHAPTER I.   INTRODUCTION.

THE SONG OF TRIUMPH FROM THE MIDST OF THE FIERY FURNACE.

"In the evening sorrow shall have place," says holy David, "but in the morning cometh gladness" (Ps. xxix. 6). "You shall weep and lament," says Jesus to His disciples, "but your sorrow shall be turned into joy. For you now indeed have sorrow," He continues, "but I will see you again, and your heart shall rejoice, and your joy no man shall take from you" (John xvi.)

The Five Sorrowful Mysteries, recording the sufferings and death at the cost of which Jesus has rebuilt the city of God, are now past; and agreeably to the inspired promise, we naturally expect in the Mysteries that are to follow that after "the evening of sorrow, in the morning there will come gladness." And, indeed, no sooner do these Mysteries present themselves in view, than the expectation gains in strength. The finding again of Jesus at the age of twelve years, by His blessed Mother, after a sorrowing search of three days, throughout sustained by the natural hope of soon discovering Him, is, as we have seen, one of the Five Joyful Mysteries. But what must have been the joy of the first meeting of Mary with Jesus on the morning of His resurrection, after the three days of agonising participation in His Passion, from which the concluding scenes of His death and burial appeared to shut out to all but the supernatural light of faith the last glimmer of the hope of ever meeting Him again! In the Mystery of the Ascension, we are filled with joy at remembering how Jesus said, "I go to prepare a place for you." In the Mystery of the Mission of the Holy Spirit, we learn the coming of One who fills the hearts of the faithful with joy and gladness. In the Assumption of the Blessed Virgin, we are invited to rejoice with the holy angels, because Mary, their Queen, is assumed into heaven. And, again, in the Fifth Mystery, we are called upon to rejoice with all the saints in the Coronation of their Queen. "In the evening sorrow has had place, but in the morning cometh gladness."

Thus, the result of even the most rapid and cursory glance at the Mysteries which follow, suffices to leave us in possession of the conviction that they might with perfect fitness have borne the designation of a second series of Joyful Mysteries. And yet, the universal sense of all the faithful, in the place of "Joyful Mysteries," has accepted the title of "Glorious Mysteries." Let us then pause for a moment to try to seize upon the particular import and meaning conveyed in the designation " GLORIOUS."

The joy of an intelligent creature, in its primary sense, would seem to consist in the response of the intelligent soul to that which is intrinsically beautiful and lovely. Such, for example, we may suppose, to have been the joy which the first sight of Eve must have conveyed to Adam. What words, for example, can easily describe Adam's sense of delight on first beholding the bright and lovely creature whom God had given to him to be the partner of his life and sovereignty in Paradise? Here must have been a heart simply overflowing with joy at the bounty and goodness of his Maker, in the gift of his beautiful and amiable helpmate.

"Awake!
My fairest, my espoused, my latest found,
Heaven's last, best gift, my ever new delight!
Awake! the morning shines, and the fresh fields call us."
—Milton's *Paradise Lost*, Book V.

Here there had been no symptom of anything like previous sorrow or suffering. Here there had been "no evening of lamentation to which gladness had succeeded in the morning." Adam's rejoicing was pure joy that had never known so much as the name of grief. Again, when the angels of God were for the first time admitted to see His work of creation, the Book of Job says, "The morning stars praised Him, and all the sons of God made a joyful melody" (Job xxxviii. 7). This universal jubilee of all intelligent creation, in like manner, had been preceded by no previous sorrow or affliction; all was pure rejoicing and overflowing joy. They praised the wise and merciful, the good and glorious Creator of the universe which they surveyed, and sang together—

"Praise the Lord of Heaven, praise Him in the highest;
Praise Him, all ye angels; praise Him, all ye hosts of His:
He spoke the word, and all was made; He gave command, and they were created."
—*Ps.* cxlviii.

Next in degree to the joy of intelligent creation on beholding the wonders of the works of God, and on seeing the good gifts with which their Creator has surrounded their own life, would seem to be the joy of those who have fallen into ruin and misery, and who hail with delight the approach of a Deliverer, and gladly welcome the advent of a Saviour. If the first is the joy which renders its glad homage to the beauties and wonders of work of God the Creator, this, on the other hand, is the joy which greets the coming of God the Redeemer, and overflows with gladness at the drawing near of His redemption. It is this latter joy which is the subject of the Five Joyful Mysteries of the Rosary, and it is a joy, as we have seen, which the depth of the fall of man only heightens instead of impairs; and which it is not in the power of any present misery or wretchedness, however great, to obliterate or even to diminish. As the prophet says, "Though the fig-tree blossom not, and the vine put not forth her shoots; though the fruit of the olive fail, and the land yield not her increase; though the sheep be cut off from the fold, and no herd be found in the stalls; yet I will rejoice in the Lord, I will joy in God my Saviour" (Habacuc iii.)

Even the very angels in Heaven who had never fallen, when they beheld the joyful salvation of God for fallen men, in the Infant Saviour lying in the arms of Mary in Bethlehem, so far partook of the joys of men, that by permission of God they came to this earth to testify their joy in hymns of praise, saying, "Glory to God in the highest, and on earth peace to men of good will."

But as God the Redeemer Himself came into the world to suffer, and as He has said to all whom He intends to save, "Take up your Cross and follow Me;" there is yet a further and third form of joy to be noticed, which is that of the Deliverer and His ransomed ones who, have themselves passed through the fire of great tribulations, and now enjoy either the possession or else the near prospect of the glory and triumph of their victory; according to David's words, "In the evening sorrow shall have place, but in the morning gladness." Here it is to be observed, that there is more than one entirely new element which enters into this joy of the redeemed. There is not only joy and thanksgiving for the mercy of their redemption and deliverance; there is not only the most joyful thought that "tears are now wiped away from every eye, and that mourning, crying, and sorrow shall be no more;" but there is also what is more than all, the exultation over an enemy that is laid low—there is the glory and triumph of the conqueror over a fierce and merciless adversary who is confounded for ever. Such is the Christian joy of the "Glorious Mysteries."

And we may see this exemplified in the way of figure in many striking events of the old law. Thus in the delivery of Israel out of the hands of the Egyptians, by the closing in of the waters of the Red Sea over the Egyptian host, the song of triumph which Moses sang on the shores of the sea, brings out in the strongest relief this feeling of a conqueror's exultation over the fallen foe, and the triumph and jubilee of the victor over the defeated pride of the adversary.

The enemy said: "I will pursue after and overtake, I will divide the spoils, and my soul shall have its fill. I will draw my sword, and my hand shall slay them.

"Thy breath went forth, and the sea covered them. They sank like lead in the mighty waters.

"Lord, who is like unto Thee among the strong? who is like unto Thee, glorious in holiness, doing wondrous things?" (Exod. xv. 9).

Exactly the same character of exultation marks the song of Debbora the prophetess, on the occasion of the defeat of Sisara. The prophetess glories and rejoices over the fallen Sisara, and says:

"At her feet he fell, he fainted and he died, he rolled before her feet, and he lay lifeless and wretched.

"His mother looked out of a window and howled, she spoke from her inner chamber, and said, Why is his chariot so long in coming back? why are the feet of his horses so slow? So let all Thine enemies perish, O Lord, but let them that love Thee shine as the sun shineth in his rising" (Judges v. 27).

Judith's inspired song of victory runs in quite a similar strain of exultation over the fallen adversary:

"The Assyrian came out of the mountains of the north in the multitude of his strength, his multitudes stopped up the torrents, and their horses covered the valleys.

"He boasted that he would set my

Introduction to the Glorious Mysteries. 97

borders on fire, and kill my young men with the sword; that he would make my infants a prey and my virgins captives. "But the Almighty hath struck him, and hath delivered him into the hands of a woman, and hath slain him" (Judith xvi.)

The prophet Isaias, under the figure of the fallen empire of Babylon, describes a kind of forlorn jubilee of exultation, extending even to the lost themselves, who take up their parable to rejoice over the fall of the prince of pride that sought to exalt himself above God: "How art thou fallen from heaven, O Lucifer, thou son of the morning! how art thou fallen to the earth that didst wound the nations! And thou saidst in thy heart, I will ascend into heaven, I will exalt my throne above the stars of God, I will sit in the mountain of the covenant, I will ascend above the height of the clouds, I will be like unto the Most High. Is this then he that troubled the earth, that shook kingdoms, that made the world a wilderness and destroyed the cities? How art thou fallen!" (Isa. xiv.)

But if the fall of defeated pride is a just cause of such a forlorn kind of congratulation as, at the best, that must be which can be supposed possible to those who have fallen into the same condemnation, with how much more of truth and justice is the same fall of the adversary not a cause of joy and triumph to those who were marked out to be the very victims of his pride and malice, and who are now delivered from the cruel gripe that sought to seize them! "He boasted," sings Judith, "that he would set my borders on fire, and kill my young men with the sword; that he would make my infants a prey, and lead my virgins captive. But the Almighty hath slain him, and hath delivered him into the hand of a woman."

Such, to the Christian, is the joy of the Glorious Mysteries. The devil, who boasted that he would lead the whole race of Adam captive, has been slain by Jesus through the Cross of Calvary, and the Almighty has delivered his spoils into the hand of a woman, the Blessed Virgin, Mother of God, whom Jesus her Son has assumed into heaven and whom has crowned Queen over the whole blessed company of angels and saints. As heirs of redemption, then, in the Glorious Mysteries we glory over the fall of our great adversary, we take up the parable of the partners of his condemnation, and we re-echo their cry—"O Lucifer, thou son of the morning! how art thou fallen! thou that saidst I will be like unto the Most High, how art thou fallen to the depths of hell!"

As redeemed by the blood of Jesus, we say to our Lord and Deliverer, "How hast Thou humbled Thyself for us, and hast become obedient to death, even the death of the Cross! and how hath God highly exalted Thee, and given Thee a name which is above every name, that at the name of Jesus every knee should bow, of things on earth and things under the earth!" (Phil. ii. 8). Children of Mary, by the deed of gift spoken from the Cross in the gracious words, "Lady, behold thy son," we say to our Mother, in these Glorious Mysteries, "How hath God had respect unto the lowliness of His handmaiden, and hath exalted thee above angels and archangels, above thrones and dominions, and above all the host of heaven, and hath set upon thy head the royal diadem, as Queen of all creation!"

For these things we will indeed rejoice; but we have nevertheless to remember that the Christian's joy must still be the joy of those who have yet to pass through the fire of the tribulations of this present life. Jesus, from the throne of His glory, bids us who are upon earth take up His Cross and so follow Him to His glory. "Ought not Christ to suffer," He says, "and so to enter into His glory?" and "Is it not sufficient," He says, "for the disciple to be as His Master?" In the midst of our joy, therefore, we take up our Cross and follow Him, for we bear in mind His glory; "and for this cause," as says St Paul, "we faint not at that which is at present momentary and light in our tribulation, which worketh for us above measure an eternal weight of glory; for we look not at the things which are seen, but at the things which are not seen, for the things which are seen

G

are temporal, but the things which are not seen are eternal" (2 Cor. iv. 17).

This joy in the glorious Mysteries of the Rosary of the soldier of the Christian army, who glories in the victory of the Captain of his salvation, and in the fall of his merciless adversary, and who is, notwithstanding, in his own person, being still tried and proved in the furnace of affliction, "as gold is tried seven times in the fire," is prefigured in the old law in a beautiful manner by the song of triumph of the three children from the midst of the fiery furnace in Babylon.

Nabuchodonosor, who is a figure of the devil, had set up a golden image in the plains of Doura, in the province of Babylon, and had issued a royal decree by a herald, "To you it is commanded, O nations, tribes, and languages, that what hour soever you shall hear the sound of the trumpet, of the flute, the harp, the sackbut, psaltery, dulcimer, and all kinds of music, ye fall down and adore the golden statue that Nabuchodonosor the king hath set up; but if any man shall not fall down and adore, he shall be cast the same hour into a furnace of burning fire." Sidrach, Misach, and Abdenago refused to fall down and adore, and by the king's command they were cast into the furnace, which, to satisfy the king's rage, was heated seven times more than it was accustomed to be heated. Then these three men, that is, Sidrach, Misach, and Abdenago, fell down bound in the midst of the furnace of burning fire. And they walked in the midst of the flame, praising God and blessing the Lord. For the angel of the Lord went down with Sidrach and his companions into the furnace, and drove away the flame, and made the midst of the furnace like the blowing of a wind bringing dew, and the fire touched them not at all, nor troubled them, nor did them any harm. Then the three, with one mouth, praised, glorified, and blessed God in the furnace, saying:

(THE SONG OF PRAISE OF THE THREE CHILDREN IN THE MIDST OF THE FURNACE.)

"Blessed art Thou, O Lord, the God of our fathers, worthy to be praised and glorified and exalted above all for ever; and blessed is the holy name of Thy glory, and worthy to be praised and exalted above all in all ages. Blessed art Thou in the holy temple of Thy glory, and exceedingly to be praised, and exceeding glorious for ever. Blessed art Thou on the throne of Thy kingdom, and exceedingly to be praised, and exalted above all for ever. Blessed art Thou, that beholdest the depths, and sittest upon the cherubims, and worthy to be praised and exalted above all for ever. Blessed art Thou in the firmament of heaven, and worthy of praise, and glorious for ever" (Dan. iii.)

Such was the joy and exultation of the three children over the defeated pride of the king of Babylon, in the very midst of the fiery furnace, and such is also the joy of the Christian in the glorious Mysteries of the Rosary in which, from the midst of the fiery furnace of the afflictions and sorrows of this present life, he glories over the fallen pride of his adversary the devil, and rejoices in walking in the midst of the flames, praising and giving thanks to God, who is blessed for ever, and who by His death and resurrection has opened the way for him, notwithstanding his fall, to a more exceeding weight of glory in the heavens.

THE FIRST GLORIOUS MYSTERY.

Ave — Maria — Gratia — Plena — Dominus — Tecum

Terra tremuit et quievit dum exurgeret in judicio Deus, ut salvos faceret omnes mansuetos terrae. (*Psalm* lxxv. 9.)

Habebitis autem hunc diem in monumentum; et celebrabitis eam solemnem Domino cultu sempiterno. (*Exod.* xii. 14.)

Benedicta — Tu in mulieribus et Benedictus fructus ventris — tui Jesus.

The earth trembled and was still, while God arose in judgement to save all the meek of the earth. (*Psalm* lxxv. 9.)

You shall keep this day for a memorial, and you shall celebrate it a solemn day to the LORD with a perpetual worship. (*Exod.* xii. 14.)

THE RESURRECTION.

The First Glorious Mystery of the Rosary.

CHAPTER II.   THE RESURRECTION.

THE HOLY SCRIPTURE NARRATIVE.

"And in the end of the Sabbath, when it began to dawn, towards the first day of the week, came Mary Magdalen and the other Mary, to see the sepulchre. And behold there was a great earthquake. For an angel of the Lord descended from heaven, and coming, rolled back the stone, and sat upon it. And his countenance was as lightning, and his raiment as snow. And for fear of him, the guards were struck with terror, and became as dead men. And the angel answering, said to the women: Fear not you; for I know that you seek Jesus who was crucified. He is not here, for He is risen, as He said. Come and see the place where the Lord was laid. And going quickly, tell ye His disciples that He is risen: and behold He will go before you into Galilee; there you shall see Him. Lo, I have foretold it to you" (Matt. xxviii.)

"But Mary stood at the sepulchre without, weeping. Now as she was "weeping, she stooped down, and looked into the sepulchre, and she saw two angels in white, sitting, one at the head, and one at the feet, where the body of Jesus had been laid. They say to her: Woman, why weepest thou? She saith to them: Because they have taken away my Lord; and I know not where they have laid Him. When she had thus said, she turned herself back, and saw Jesus standing; and she knew not that it was Jesus. Jesus saith to her: Woman, why weepest thou? whom seekest thou? She, thinking that it was the gardener, saith to Him: Sir, if thou has taken Him hence, tell me where thou hast laid Him, and I will take Him away. Jesus saith to her: Mary. She turning, saith to Him: Rabboni (which is to say, Master). Jesus saith to her: Do not touch Me, for I am not yet ascended to My Father. But go to My brethren, and say to them: I ascend to My Father, and to your Father, to My God and your God" (St John xx.).

The angel of the Lord has descended from heaven, the stone has been rolled away from the sepulchre, the soldiers of the watch are fallen to the ground, and are become as dead men for fear. And thus the great mystery of our salvation is accomplished. JESUS RISES AGAIN FROM THE DEAD.

"Oh, how great troubles hast Thou showed Me," says David, in a figure of Christ, "many and grievous, and turning Thou hast brought Me to life, and hast brought Me back again from the depths of the earth" (Ps. lxx. 20).

It is the constant tradition of the Church, that before Jesus is seen by any other human eye, after His resurrection from the dead, He goes first of all to console His Blessed Mother. Thus St Ignatius Loyola writes in his "Spiritual Exercises," "That there can be no doubt but that the Lord after His resurrection first appeared to His Mother, as the Scripture says that He appeared to many. Although it does not mention her by name, it leaves the fact nevertheless to us for certain, as being supposed to have a right understanding, lest, otherwise, we should justly hear it said, 'Are ye also without understanding?'" (Spiritual Exercises).

The Patriarch of Nicomedia adds the following reason why the Blessed Virgin is never adduced by the holy Apostles as a witness of the resurrection:—"For although," he says, "they were informed by her of the fact of His resurrection with so much greater certainty than by the other holy women who carried ointments to the tomb, they notwithstanding never make any mention of her when they are speaking of the resurrection, and in so doing they act with a very wise and becoming prudence, doubtless under the direction of the Holy Spirit. For had they brought a person forward as a witness of the resurrection who might be supposed to have had the motive of seeking her own glory, they would have incurred the blame of throwing a suspicion on the truth of the fact, justly calculated to discredit it with unbelievers. On this account, they omit all mention, and observe a very proper silence respecting the Blessed Virgin in connection with her Son's resurrection" (George, Patriarch of Nicomedia, Sermon on the Resurrection).

How gloriously then are the holy David's inspired words now fulfilled to this most sorrowing of mothers: "Sorrow may endure for a season, but joy cometh in the morning." Her lost son, Jesus, as this Mystery shows us, is once more embraced in the arms of His Mother Mary. "Death hath no more dominion over Him." What the thoughts were which passed through the mind of the Blessed Virgin Mother at this august moment of her joy and triumph, can never be fully known to us; but there will be no presumption in our attempting to form for ourselves some faint picture of what they may have been, when we remember that, by the precious grace of our adoption as children of God, Mary is become our mother, and that we have consequently a full right and title to share in her joy in the Resurrection of Jesus.

Mary has, then, as we learned from the Fourth Joyful Mystery, given her unreserved assent as Mother, to her Divine Son's submitting to the death of

The First Glorious Mystery.

the Cross. She knew that the ransom of the world depended on the consummation of His most precious sacrifice, and as Mother, she has allowed the offering up of the sacrifice of Her Son. Mary thus became a participant as Mother in the work of redemption; and as the Eternal Father so loved the world that He gave His only-begotten Son for the life of the world, so the daughter of Eve, the earthly parent, has also ratified the decree of the Eternal Father, by her maternal assent to the consummation of the sacrifice.

In the same manner, then, that Mary fully knew the value of that which was to be effected by the sacrifice of Jesus upon the Cross, so the full value of that which is now accomplished by the resurrection of Jesus from the dead will be equally present to her mind; and as she clasps Jesus in her arms, she doubtless exclaims in spirit with the Apostle, "Now is Christ risen from the dead, the First-fruits of them that sleep. For as by man came death, by Man came also the resurrection from the dead: and as in Adam all die, so in Christ shall all be made alive" (1 Cor. xv. 20). Again, as Mary hears the familiar voice of her beloved Son telling her of His victory over death, can she fail to rejoice over the downfall of the power of Satan over men, which he exercised over them through their fear of death, and to exclaim with the Apostle, "Now is death swallowed up in victory. O death! where is now thy sting? O grave! where is now thy victory?" (1 Cor. xv.)

As Mary contemplates the kingdom of heaven, now from henceforward open to all believers, will she not say to herself, in the words of Josue, "Now you know with all your mind, that of all the words the Lord promised to perform for you, not one hath failed" (Jos. xxiii. 14).

As Mary foresees in spirit how the word of her Divine Son is soon to go forth from Jerusalem to "cover the earth with the knowledge of the Lord as the waters cover the sea," the words of the holy Archangel cannot fail to return to her memory, in which he said to her, "He shall be great, and shall be called the Son of the Most High, and the Lord God shall give unto Him the throne of David His father, and he shall reign in the house of Jacob for ever, and of His kingdom there shall be no end."

In Thy resurrection, O Lord, "sings the Church, "the heavens and the earth rejoice." Mary's joy as she clasps Jesus again in her arms is the first-fruits of the universal rejoicing of all creation in the resurrection of God its Redeemer from the dead. "Behold, I create a new heavens and a new earth, saith the Lord, and the former things shall not be in remembrance" (Isa. lxv. 17). The earth has been sprinkled with the blood of the Just One, which speaketh better things than the blood of Abel. And Mary rejoices to see in spirit the fulfilment of His promise, "If He shall lay down His life for sin, He shall see a long-lived seed, and the will of the Lord shall be prosperous in His hand" (Isa. liii. 10). In the glorified presence of her Divine Son, she has an earnest of the fulfilment of these words, "For as the new heavens and the new earth which I make to stand before Me," saith the Lord, "so shall your seed stand before Me, and your name" (Isa. lxvi. 22).

Mary's joy as she clasps Jesus in her arms is a joy that succeeds to an intensity of grief. A moment ago, and she was the Mother of Sorrows, now the first-fruits of the rejoicing of all creation at its restoration to justice are hers. Can she then fail to call to mind the words of consolation addressed in a figure to the holy Job, "Thou shalt forget misery, and remember it only as waters that are passed away, and brightness like that of noonday shall arise to thee in the evening, and when thou shalt think thyself consumed, thou shalt rise as the daystar" (Job xi. 16). "According to the multitude of the sorrows that were in my heart," exclaims holy David in a figure of Mary, "Thy comforts have given joy to my soul" (Ps. xciii. 19).

If only some such thoughts as these may have passed through the mind of Mary on the morning of the resurrection, can they fail to commend themselves to the heart of the pious Christian who shall stop to contemplate this great mystery of His faith—the Resurrection of Jesus from the dead, the victory of creation over death!

"Death is swallowed up in victory," each one who names the name of Christ may now say. And he who had the power of death, to whom all by reason of their fear of death were subject, that is the devil, is now overcome by One stronger than himself. Can any thought be more full of consolation for one who knows that it is appointed to him once to die? The devil, who before this held men subject to him by the fear of death, has, thanks be to God! had this power of the terror of death taken out of his hands. Jesus, by submitting Himself to death, and by rising from the dead, has shown us that death is no longer to be feared. "Glory be to God!" therefore is the Christian's cry: "The net is broken, and we are delivered" (Ps. cxxiii. 7).

"Thou hast opened the kingdom of heaven to all believers." Before this, not the wisest of men knew for certain for what he lived or for what he was required to toil. "Vanity of vanities, vanity of vanities, all is vanity," said the wisest of men. Now that Jesus is risen, thanks be to God! every Christian knows for what he has to live, to toil, and to suffer. He is seeking a place in the kingdom of heaven, which will be given only to those who, in this present life, fear and love God, and by His grace strive to keep His commandments. In this mystery He learns to know the real prize of His calling, which is to be won by a Christian life and to be lost by an unchristian life.

Mary foresaw in spirit the kingdom of her Son spreading east and west, north and south, over the whole world. The Christian, as St Augustine remarks, since the resurrection of Jesus, sees the fact before his eyes, that the faith of the Church has spread east and west, north and south, over the world, and derives from this the greatest confirmation of his own faith.

When Jesus, in His resurrection from the dead, stood again in the presence of His Blessed Mother, in the midst of her unspeakable joy Mary still looked upon Him with the print of the nails in His hands and feet, and with the wound of the spear in His side; and the Christian also, in the midst of his joy at the victory of Jesus, cannot too often thus contemplate Him. For the life which leads to the earning a seat in the kingdom of heaven is not, and, in the midst of the sin of this present world, cannot, be free from pain and suffering. Hence St Paul earnestly calls every Christian to this frequent contemplation of Jesus: "Let us run," he says, "by patience the race that is set before us, looking on Jesus, the Author and Finisher of our faith, who, for the joy that was set before Him, endured the Cross, despising the shame, and now sitteth at the right hand of the throne of God. For think diligently upon Him that endured such opposition from sinners against Himself, that you be not wearied, fainting in your minds" (Heb. xii. 3).

The practical fruit of this great Mystery, as St Augustine sets forth at some length, is to teach us to disregard the things of the earth, and to "seek the things which are above." "Let us hear the Apostle saying to us," writes St Augustine, "'If ye are risen again with Christ?' Ah! what? How comes he to speak to us who are not yet dead of rising again? What could the apostle have meant by the words, 'If ye are risen again with Christ?' Could Christ have risen again if He had not died? Yet he is speaking to those who are alive, not to those who were just lately dead, and are now rising again from the dead. What is he bringing us to? Observe carefully what it is that he says: 'If ye are risen again with Christ, seek those things that are above, where Christ sitteth at the right hand of God. Mind the things which are above, not the things which are upon the earth, *for ye are dead*' (Col. iii. 1-4). These are words that the Apostle speaks, and not words of mine, and yet they are true; and therefore I say so also. Why do I say so also? 'I have believed, and therefore do I speak.' If we are living well, we have died and have risen again. He who has not as yet died, neither risen again, is living ill, and if he be living ill, he is not living at all. Such a one ought to die that he may escape death. What do you mean by 'he ought to die, in order that he may escape death?' I mean, let him change his life that he be not damned. I repeat the words of the Apostle: 'Seek those things which are above, where Christ sitteth at the right hand of God. Mind the things that are above, not the things that are upon the earth, for ye are dead, and your life is hidden with Christ in God. When Christ, who is your life, shall appear, then shall ye appear also with Him in glory.' Such are the words of the Apostle. To him, therefore, who has not yet died, I say, Let him die; and to him who still lives a bad life, I say, Let him change; for if once he lived a bad life, and does so now no longer, then he has died, and if he is now living a good life, he is risen again.

"But what does 'living a good' life' mean? It means, 'minding the things that are above, and not the things that are upon the earth.' 'How long will you be earth, and creep upon the earth? How long will you lick the earth?' For if you love the earth, be certain that you lick the earth, and you become an enemy of Him of whom the Psalm says, '*His enemies shall lick the earth*' (Ps. lxxi. 9). What were you formerly? 'Children of men.' What are you now? 'Sons of God.' 'O ye children of men, how long will you be so sluggish of heart? Why do ye so love vanity and seek a lie?' (Ps. iv. 3). What the lie is that you seek I will tell you by and by. You all wish to be happy. I know this very well. Show me the thief, or the evil-doer, the adulterer, the sorcerer, the perpetrator of sacrilege, the wretch stained with every vice, and sunk in every sort of crime and wickedness, who does not wish to be happy. I know very well you all wish to be happy, but what it is that makes a man happy, that you are not willing to seek out and learn. You hunt after gold, because you think gold will make you happy. But gold does not make you happy. Why do you seek after a lie? What is it that makes you desire to raise yourself in the world? Because you think that you will be made happy by the honour of men, and the pomp of the world. But the pomp of the world does not make you happy. Why do you seek after a lie? And whatever else you seek after, as long as you seek after it in a worldly spirit, loving the earth, and licking the earth, you seek after it expecting it to make you happy, but no earthly thing can make you happy. Why, then, do you not give over seeking a lie? Wishing all the while to be happy, you seek those things that are sure to make you miserable. You are deceived in what you seek, for what you seek is a lie.

"You wish to be happy; I will show you, if you desire it, how you can become happy. Follow the words of the Psalm: '*How long will ye be so dull of heart? Why will ye be in love with vanity, and seek a lie? Know ye!*' What? '*That the Lord hath magnified His Holy One.*' Christ has come to share our miseries. He hungered, suffered thirst, weariness, He slept, He worked miracles, He suffered ill-treatment, He was scourged, He was crowned with thorns, He was disfigured with spittle, He was buffeted, nailed to the Cross, pierced with a spear, laid in His sepulchre, but on the third day, His work being finished, He rose again, and swallowed up death in His victory. Fix your attention on His resurrection, and behold how He has so magnified His Holy One as to raise Him again from the dead, and to give to Him the honour of sitting at His right hand in the heavens. He hath in this shown to you on what you ought to set your mind if you wish to be happy, for you cannot be so here. In this life you cannot be happy, nor can any one. You seek a thing that is beyond doubt very good, but this earth is not the place for obtaining it. What is it that you are seeking? A happy life! well, but it is not here. If you were seeking for gold in a place where there was no gold, any one who happened to know that there was no gold to be found in it, would he not say to you, 'What are you digging for? Why do you turn up the ground, and sink a shaft into it, to make yourself a way to where you will find nothing when you have got there?' What would you answer any one who might speak to you in this way? 'I am seeking for gold;' and would not he reply, 'I did not say that what you were seeking for is not good, but that, in the place where you are searching, it is not there to be found.' Just in the same manner when you say, 'I wish to be happy,' undoubtedly you are seeking for a very good thing, only it is not to be found here. If Christ had found it here, then you might find it too. Listen, and attend to what He found here. And, indeed, what else should He have found here, besides such things as abound and are plentiful. He partook with you of all that is to be found in the abode of your misery. Here He drank vinegar with you, and tasted gall. See what it was that He found in your abode! And now He has invited you to His royal table, the table of the angels, where He is Himself the food of His guests. Coming down, and finding all these evil things in your abode, He has not disdained to share your table with you, and to promise you His own in return. And what is it that He says to us? 'Have faith, and believe that you will come to the good things of My table; for you see that I have not disdained to taste the evil things of yours.' Has He borne your evil, and will He not give you His own good? Certainly He will give it you. He has promised to us the gift of the life which He has to give, but He has done something besides that far more surpasses belief. He has given us the preliminary gift of His death, as if He thereby said to us, 'I invite you to My life, where none die, where life is truly happy, where food does not perish, but both refreshes and fails not. Behold, that to which I invite you! the abode of the angels, the friendship of the Father and of the Holy Ghost, to a feast that never ends, and to brotherhood with Me. Lastly, I invite you to Myself, to My life. If ye will not believe that I will give you My life, take My death for your security.' Only, therefore, let us, while we are living in this corruptible flesh, die with Christ by the change of our ways of life, that we may live with Christ in the love of justice, being certain that we shall not attain to a happy life until we shall have come to Him, who has come to us, and until we shall have begun to be with Him who died for us" (Sermon ccxxxi. in the Paschal Season).

On the resurrection of Jesus Christ from the dead depends the great Christian doctrine of the resurrection of our bodies from the dead. Let us hear, in the words of the great Doctor of the Church St Thomas Aquinas, the extent of the benefit conferred upon us by the resurrection of Jesus Christ from the dead:—

"It has been shown in the preceding pages," says St Thomas, "that it is through Christ that we have been liberated from all that we have incurred through the sin of the first man. For through the sin of the first man not only do we derive the stain of sin, but also death, which is the penalty of sin; according to the words of the Apostle, 'By one man sin entered into the world, and death through sin' (Rom. v. 12). It is necessary, therefore, that we should be delivered by Christ from both; that is to say, from our guilt, and also from death. Whence the Apostle adds, 'For if by the sin of one man death reigned through one, much more shall they who receive the abundance of the gift of grace and of justice reign in life through One, Jesus Christ' (v. 17). In order, therefore, that He might show both to us in His own person, He willed both to die and to rise again. It was His will to die that He might cleanse us from sin; as the Apostle says, 'As it is appointed to all men once to die, so Christ was offered once to take away the sins of many' (Heb. ix. 27). It was His will to rise again that He might deliver us from death; hence the Apostle says, 'Christ has risen from the dead, the First-fruits of them that sleep; for as by man came death, by Man also is the resurrection from the dead' (1 Cor. xv. 20). We obtain, therefore, the effect of the death of Christ in the sacraments, in respect of the remission of our sin; for it has been said above that the sacraments derive their efficacy from the Passion of Christ; and the effect of the resurrection of Christ we shall obtain, in respect of our liberation from death, at the end of the world, when we shall all

THE I. GLORIOUS MYSTERY.

Samson bursts the bands which bound him.

LEGE · ET · IN · PROPHETIS

BEUM · ET · FILIUM

THE STRONG MAN WHO COULD NOT BE BOUND BY HIS ENEMIES.

THE OLD TESTAMENT TYPES OF

The fish casts Jonas on the dry land.

ROSA · MYSTICA · PASSIM · IN

TENEBRAS · ORA · PRO · NOBIS

THE PROPHET WHOM THE DEPTHS COULD NOT RESTRAIN FROM HIS MISSION.

am seeking for gold;' and would not he reply, 'I did not say that what you were seeking for is not good, but that, in the place where you are searching, it is not there to be found.' Just in the same manner when you say, 'I wish to be happy,' undoubtedly you are seeking for a very good thing, only it is not to be found here. If Christ had found it here, then you might find it too. Listen, and attend to what He found here. And, indeed, what else should He have found here, besides such things as abound and are plentiful. He partook with you of all that is to be found in the abode of your misery. Here He drank vinegar with you, and tasted gall. See what it was that He found in your abode! And now He has invited you to His royal table, the table of the angels, where He is Himself the food of His guests. Coming down, and finding all these evil things in your abode, He has not disdained to share your table with you, and to promise you His own in return. And what is it that He says to us? 'Have faith, and believe that you will come to the good things of My table; for you see that I have not disdained to taste the evil things of yours.' Has He borne your evil, and will He not give you His own good? Certainly He will give it you. He has promised to us the gift of the life which He has to give, but He has done something besides that far more surpasses belief. He has given us the preliminary gift of His death, as if He thereby said to us, 'I invite you to My life, where none die, where life is truly happy, where food does not perish, but both refreshes and fails not. Behold, that to which I invite you! the abode of the angels, the friendship of the Father and of the Holy Ghost, to a feast that never ends, and to brotherhood with Me. Lastly, I invite you to Myself, to My life. If ye will not believe that I will give you My life, take My death for your security.' Only, therefore, let us, while we are living in this corruptible flesh, die with Christ by the mortifying of our ways of sin, that we may live in Christ in the newness of justice, and obtain that we may attain to eternal life until we shall come to it when it

has come to us, and until we shall have begun to be with Him who died for us" (Sermon ccxxxi. in the Paschal Season).

On the resurrection of Jesus Christ from the dead depends the great Christian doctrine of the resurrection of our bodies from the dead. Let us hear, in the words of the great Doctor of the Church St Thomas Aquinas, the extent of the benefit conferred upon us by the resurrection of Jesus Christ from the dead:—

"It has been shown in the preceding pages," says St Thomas, "that it is through Christ that we have been liberated from all that we have incurred through the sin of the first man. For through the sin of the first man not only do we derive the stain of sin, but also death, which is the penalty of sin; according to the words of the Apostle, 'By one man sin entered into the world, and death through sin' (Rom. v. 12). It is necessary, therefore, that we should be delivered by Christ from both; that is to say, from our guilt, and also from death. Whence the Apostle adds, 'For if by the sin of one man death reigned through one, much more shall they who receive the abundance of the gift of grace and of justice reign in life through One, Jesus Christ' (v. 17). In order, therefore, that He might show both to us in His own person, He willed both to die and to rise again. It was His will to die that He might cleanse us from sin; as the Apostle says, 'As it is appointed to all men once to die, so Christ was offered once to take away the sins of many' (Heb. ix. 27). It was His will to rise again that He might deliver us from death; hence the Apostle says, 'Christ has risen from the dead, the First-fruits of them that sleep; for as by man came death, by Man also is the resurrection from the dead' (1 Cor. xv. 20). We obtain, therefore, the effect of the death of Christ in the sacraments, in respect of the remission of our sin; for it has been said above that the sacraments have their efficacy from the Passion of Christ, and the effect of the resurrection, we shall obtain, in respect of our rising from death, at the end of the world, when we shall

The Old Testament Types of the I. Glorious Mystery.

The fish casts Jonas on the dry land.   *Samson bursts the bands which bound him.*

ROSA · MYSTICA · PASSIM · IN · LEGE · ET · IN · PROPHETIS

UMBRÆ · ORE · PRO · NOBIS · EUM · FILIUM · TUUM

THE PROPHET WHOM THE DEPTHS COULD NOT RESTRAIN FROM HIS MISSION.

THE STRONG MAN WHO COULD NOT BE BOUND BY HIS ENEMIES.

am seeking for gold;' and would not he reply, 'I did not say that what you were seeking for is not good, but that, in the place where you are searching, it is not there to be found.' Just in the same manner when you say, 'I wish to be happy,' undoubtedly you are seeking for a very good thing, only it is not to be found here. If Christ had found it here, then you might find it too. Listen, and attend to what He found here. And, indeed, what else should He have found here, besides such things as abound and are plentiful. He partook with you of all that is to be found in the abode of your misery. Here He drank vinegar with you, and tasted gall. See what it was that He found in your abode! And now He has invited you to His royal table, the table of the angels, where He is Himself the food of His guests. Coming down, and finding all these evil things in your abode, He has not disdained to share your table with you, and to promise you His own in return. And what is it that He says to us? 'Have faith, and believe that you will come to the good things of My table; for you see that I have not disdained to taste the evil things of yours.' Has He borne your evil, and will He not give you His own good? Certainly He will give it you. He has promised to us the gift of the life which He has to give, but He has done something besides that far more surpasses belief. He has given us the preliminary gift of His death, as if He thereby said to us, 'I invite you to My life, where none die, where life is truly happy, where food does not perish, but both refreshes and fails not. Behold, that to which I invite you! the abode of the angels, the friendship of the Father and of the Holy Ghost, to a feast that never ends, and to brotherhood with Me. Lastly, I invite you to Myself, to My life. If ye will not believe that I will give you My life, take My death for your security.' Only, therefore, let us, while we are living in this corruptible flesh, die with Christ by the change of our ways of life, that we may live with Christ in the love of justice, being certain that we shall not attain to a happy life until we shall have come to Him, who has come to us, and until we shall have begun to be with Him who died for us" (Sermon ccxxxi. in the Paschal Season).

On the resurrection of Jesus Christ from the dead depends the great Christian doctrine of the resurrection of our bodies from the dead. Let us hear, in the words of the great Doctor of the Church St Thomas Aquinas, the extent of the benefit conferred upon us by the resurrection of Jesus Christ from the dead:—

"It has been shown in the preceding pages," says St Thomas, "that it is through Christ that we have been liberated from all that we have incurred through the sin of the first man. For through the sin of the first man not only do we derive the stain of sin, but also death, which is the penalty of sin; according to the words of the Apostle, 'By one man sin entered into the world, and death through sin' (Rom. v. 12). It is necessary, therefore, that we should be delivered by Christ from both; that is to say, from our guilt, and also from death. Whence the Apostle adds, 'For if by the sin of one man death reigned through one, much more shall they who receive the abundance of the gift of grace and of justice reign in life through One, Jesus Christ' (v. 17). In order, therefore, that He might show both to us in His own person, He willed both to die and to rise again. It was His will to die that He might cleanse us from sin; as the Apostle says, 'As it is appointed to all men once to die, so Christ was offered once to take away the sins of many' (Heb. ix. 27). It was His will to rise again that He might deliver us from death; hence the Apostle says, 'Christ has risen from the dead, the First-fruits of them that sleep; for as by man came death, by Man also is the resurrection from the dead' (1 Cor. xv. 20). We obtain, therefore, the effect of the death of Christ in the sacraments, in respect of the remission of our sin; for it has been said above that the sacraments derive their efficacy from the Passion of Christ; and the effect of the resurrection of Christ we shall obtain, in respect of our liberation from death, at the end of the world, when we shall all

THE OLD TESTAMENT TYPES OF THE I. GLORIOUS MYSTERY.

The fish casts Jonas on the dry land.
Samson bursts the bands which bound him.

ECCE ES IN PROPHETIS

SPECULUM · JUSTITIÆ

THE STRONG MAN WHO COULD NOT BE BOUND BY HIS ENEMIES.

ROSA · MYSTICA · PASSIM · IN

TURRIS · DAVIDICA · ORA

THE PROPHET WHOM THE DEPTHS COULD NOT RESTRAIN FROM HIS MISSION.

rise again through the power of Christ, according to the words of the Apostle, 'Now if Christ be preached that He rose again from the dead, how do some among you say that there is no resurrection from the dead, and that Christ has not risen again? But if Christ be not risen from the dead, our preaching is vain, and your faith is also vain' (1 Cor. xv. 12). It is, therefore, a necessary part of faith to believe in the future resurrection of the dead" (St Thomas, Contra Gentes, lib. iv. ch. lxxix.)

CHAPTER III.

SCRIPTURE TYPES OF THE FIRST GLORIOUS MYSTERY.

I. THE SIGN OF THE PROPHET JONAS.
II. SAMSON BURSTS THE BANDS BY WHICH HE WAS BOUND.

1. *Jonas the Prophet is vomited forth from the belly of the whale.*

THE foremost among all the figures of the resurrection of Jesus from the dead in the old law is that which our Divine Saviour Himself calls the "sign of the prophet Jonas." Certain of the scribes and Pharisees had said to Him, "Rabbi, we would see a sign from Thee?" To whom He replied, "An evil and an adulterous generation seeketh a sign, and no sign shall be given to it except the sign of the prophet Jonas. For as Jonas was in the belly of the whale three days and three nights, so the Son of Man shall be three days and three nights in the heart of the earth" (Matt. xii. 39).

. The history of Jonas may be briefly narrated from the book of the Holy Scripture which bears his name as follows: The word of the Lord came to Jonas, the son of Amath, saying, "Arise and go to Nineve, that great city, for the wickedness thereof is come up before Me." Jonas is jealous that a prophet should be sent to preach to a city of the Gentiles, and seeks to escape from before the face of the Lord by taking ship to sail in the opposite direction towards Tharsis; but the Lord sent a great wind upon the sea, and when all hope was lost, one sailor said to his neighbour, "Let us cast lots, and let us know wherefore this hath happened to us." And they cast lots, and the lot fell upon Jonas.

Jonas then said to the captain and the sailors, "Take me and cast me into the sea, and it shall be calm before your face, for I know that it is for me that this great tempest is come upon you." And the men rowed that they might get back to the land, but they could not, for the sea ran high and strong against them; and they cried to the Lord and said, "We beseech Thee, O Lord, let us not perish in the soul of this man, and lay not upon us the innocent blood, for as Thou hast willed, O Lord, so hast Thou done." And they took and cast Jonas into the sea, and the sea was stilled from its raging.

Now, the Lord had prepared a great fish to swallow Jonas, and Jonas was in the belly of the fish three days and three nights. And Jonas prayed to the Lord his God out of the belly of the fish, and said—

PRAYER OF JONAS IN THE BELLY OF THE FISH.

"I cried out of my affliction to the Lord, and He heard me: I cried out of the belly of hell, and Thou hast heard my voice. And Thou hast cast me forth into the deep in the heart of the sea, and a flood hath compassed me: all Thy billows, and Thy waves have passed over me. And I said: I am cast away out of the sight of Thy eyes: but yet I shall see Thy holy temple again. The waters compassed me about even to the soul: the deep hath closed me round about, the sea hath covered my head. I went down to the lowest parts of the mountains: the bars of the earth have shut me up for ever: and Thou wilt bring up my life from corruption, O Lord my God. When my soul was in distress within me, I remembered the Lord: that my prayer may come to Thee, unto Thy holy temple. They that in vain observe vanities, forsake their own mercy. But I with the voice of praise will sacrifice to thee: I will pay whatsoever I have vowed for my salvation to the Lord."

And God spoke and the fish vomited out Jonas upon the dry land.

"Jesus, the true Jonas," writes St Jerome, "may be understood to say to His apostles, who, in deserting Him in the hour of His Passion, in a manner took and cast Him into the sea, 'I know that this great tempest is come upon you for My sake. The world which lieth in wickedness rages, and its elements are in commotion. Death seeks to swallow Me up that it may destroy you likewise, and it does not understand that My death will be its own destruction. Take Me and cast Me into the sea. It is not for Me to throw Myself into the way of death, but to accept it joyfully at the hands of others. The tempest, which rages on My account against you, will be stilled from its raging on My death.' But the men would not, and rowed with all their might to get back to the land. These sailors strove against the raging elements with all their strength, that they might not have to lay violent hands on the prophet of God, although he had spoken against himself. O strange and marvellous perversion! The people who profess to be servants of God they cry out against their Prophet, 'Crucify Him! crucify Him!' and these men, when they are told to put him to death and the raging storm bids them comply, are more solicitous to save him than themselves. They thought that they should be able to save the ship without having to drown Jonas, and did not know that the drowning of Jonas would be the saving of the ship. When afterwards they say, 'Lay not the innocent blood upon us,' do not these words of the sailors appear to be identical with the confession of Pilate, who washes his hands and says, 'I am clean from the blood of this Man?' The Gentiles are unwilling that Christ should die, and protest that the innocent blood be not laid to their charge; while the Jews cry, 'His blood be upon us and upon our children;' and, therefore, even if they lift up their hands they shall not be heard, for they are full of blood: 'For as Thou hast willed, O Lord, so hast Thou done.' That we have taken Him on board, that the storm has arisen, that the sea runs high, that the Fugitive is betrayed by the lot falling upon Him, that He Himself directs us what is to be done, is all by Thy will, O Lord, for 'Thou hast done as Thou hast willed.' So Christ also speaks in the Psalm, 'I have willed to perform Thy will, O Lord' (Ps. xxxix. 9)."

"And further," continues St Augustine, "replying to the question of a heathen who represented himself as desiring to embrace the Christian faith if he could be satisfied upon it and some other points, as to what was prefigured by the monster who swallowed the prophet and vomited him forth alive on the third day, "there is scarcely room for inquiry, since Christ has Himself declared that His resurrection is signified by it. Therefore, just as Jonas was cast from the deck of the vessel, and was swallowed down into the belly of the whale, so Christ was taken from the wood of the Cross and laid in the sepulchre; and as this was done to Jonas for the benefit of those who were in danger of their lives on board the vessel, so Christ suffered for those who are tossed about upon the waves of this life. And as the command was in the first instance given that Jonas should go to preach to the Ninevites, but, notwithstanding his preaching, did not reach them until after the whale had vomited him up upon the shore, so the Word of prophecy had, in point of fact, long before been sent to the nations of the world, but it had never reached them until after the resurrection of Christ from the dead."

The sequel of St Augustine's explanation of the mysteries contained in the figure of Jonas will not need any apology, notwithstanding that the truths contained under it sómewhat pass beyond the strict limits of what the Mystery requires.

"When Jonas makes a dwelling-place for himself, and sits down opposite the city of Nineve, waiting to see what would happen, he assumes another character, and becomes another figurative personage, representing the people of Israel according to the flesh. For this people grudged the salvation of the Ninevites, that is, the liberation and redemption of the nations, though Christ came not to call just men but sinners to repentance. The shade of the gourd above his head were the promises of the old law, or its gifts themselves, in which beyond all doubt there was a shadow of what was to come, affording a kind of protection from the heat and burning of the evils which befell the people in the land of promise. The worm which God prepared in the morning and struck the gourd, so that it withered up and died, is the figure of Christ Himself, from whose mouth the Gospel has come, and who has caused all the things which possessed a temporary value among the people of the Jews, as shadows of what was to come, to wither up and to die. And this people having lost the kingdom of Jerusalem, the priesthood and the sacrifices of the temple, which were all shadows of things to come, are now scorched up with the burning heat of tribulation, just as Jonas, according to the narrative of the Scripture, was broiled in the heat, and suffered vehemently from it. And yet, notwithstanding, the salvation of the nations and of all who are penitent is held to be of more account than the sufferings of Jonas and the preservation of the shade which he so much loved.

"Unbelievers may laugh and babble in contemptuous derision of Christ being the worm here referred to, and indeed generally at all such figurative interpretation of the mysteries contained in the history of the prophets, until they find themselves consumed and destroyed. For of such as these Isaias prophesies, and by him God says to us, 'Hearken to Me, you that know what is just, My people, who have My law in your heart; fear ye not the reproach of men, and be not overcome by their calumnies, neither think anything of their despising you. For the worm shall eat them up as a garment, and the moth shall consume them, whereas My justice continueth for ever' (Isa. li. 7). Let us, therefore, acknowledge the worm of the morning, especially as He deigns to call Himself by this name in the Psalm which bears the title 'For the Morning Protection,' saying, 'But I am a worm and no man, the reproach of men, and the outcast of the people' (Ps. xxi.) This is one of those reproaches which we are commanded not to fear by Isaias when he says, 'Fear not the reproaches of men.'

"What can be clearer than the light which the sequel of events throws upon this prophecy? The same Psalm continues, 'They spoke against Me with their lips, and shook their heads at Me. He trusted in God, let Him then deliver Him; let Him save Him, seeing that He delighteth again in Him.' And when all was carried into execution which is there predicted, viz, 'They have pierced My hands and My feet;' 'They have numbered all My bones;' 'They have looked and stared upon Me;' 'They have parted My garment among them, and for My vesture did they cast lots;' the ancient prophecy does but describe everything as minutely and circumstantially when it is only about to come to pass, as it is afterward described in the words of the Evangelist who is narrating what has actually been done. If, therefore, in this His humiliation, this worm was an object of derision, does He continue an object of derision now that we see that the prediction which the Psalm continues is fulfilled, 'All the ends of the earth shall bethink themselves, and shall be converted to the Lord; and all the kindreds of the Gentiles shall adore in His sight. For the kingdom is the Lord's, and He shall have dominion over the nations.' The Ninevites thus bethought themselves and were converted to the Lord. This salvation, through the repentance of the nations, so long before prefigured in Jonas, Israel begrudged and still continues to begrudge, stripped of its shade and broiled with the heat. Any one, it is true, may most legitimately give a different interpretation to all the other Mysteries which are veiled under the figure of the prophet Jonas, provided his interpretation is conformable to the rule of faith; but as regards the fact of Jonas having been three days and three nights in the belly of the whale, no one may legitimately interpret this in any sense that is different from that which we have received from our Heavenly Master Himself" (Letter of St Augustine to the Priest Deogratias, cii. in the Benedictine edition).

2. *Figure of Samson bursting the bands with which, in his love for Delila, he had suffered himself to be bound.*

"Let us understand," writes St Augustine, "that great mysteries lie hid under this history. What does Samson himself prefigure? If I say that he is the type of Christ, I seem to myself to be saying nothing but the truth; and still, those who turn their thoughts to the subject will be sure to meet me with the question, Was Christ overcome by female blandishments? and what can there be in common between Christ and the yielding to the seductions of a harlot? Again, when had Christ His head shorn of its hair? when was He despoiled of His strength, bound, deprived of His eyes, and exposed to public derision? Let faith wake up and understand what Christ is, not merely what He did, but what He suffered. In all that He did, He was the Man of strength, in all that He suffered, He was the Man of infirmity. In Him I perceive both. I see the strength of the Son of God, and the infirmity of the Son of Man. And there is yet one thing more. For Christ in His entirety, as the Scripture represents Him, is both Head and Body. And as the Head of the Church is no other than Christ, so the Body of Christ is no other than the Church; for the Church has no existence in itself alone, but together with its Head forms the whole Christ. And in so far as Samson has worked prodigies of strength, he becomes the figure of Christ, the Head of the Church.

"And the woman of the Philistines whom Samson loved prefigures the Church, which, before the recovery of the knowledge of the one God, had committed adultery with idols, according to the words of the Apostle, who says, 'But God commendeth His love towards us, because when as yet we were sinners according to the time, Christ died for us' (Rom. v. 8)" (Augustine, Sermon ccclxiv., new order).

The particular passage in Samson's history which is figurative of the resurrection of Jesus from the dead is thus briefly narrated in the Holy Scripture: " And after these things, Samson loved a woman of the Philistines, who dwelt in the valley of Sorec, and who was called Delila. And the princes of the Philistines came to her and said: Beguile him, and learn where his great strength lies, and in what way we may prevail over him, and bind him to afflict him, and we will each of us give to thee one thousand one hundred pieces of silver. Delila therefore spake to Samson, and said: Tell me, I pray, wherein is thy great strength, and wherewith mayest thou be bound, so that thou canst not break loose. And Samson answered: If I shall be bound with seven withes, that are not yet dry, but still green, I shall become weak as other men. And the princes of the Philistines brought the seven green withes to her as he had said, and she bound him therewith. But as the princes of the Philistines lay in wait in her room, and hid themselves in ambush, she cried to him: The Philistines are upon thee, Samson! But he burst the bonds, as a man breaketh a thread of tow that is twisted on a distaff when it has been scorched by the fire, neither knew they where his great strength lay" (Judges xvi. 4, &c.)

"Samson loved," writes Father Camphausen, "and was deceived by his love. Love for a woman not deserving of his love sold him, betrayed him, bound him, and delivered him into the hands of his

THE SECOND GLORIOUS MYSTERY.

Ave — Maria — Gratia — Plena — Dominus — Tecum

Regna terrae
cantate Deo:
Psallite Do-
mino; Psallite
Deo qui ascen-
dit super
cœlum cœli,
ad Orientem.
(*Ps.* lxvii. 36.)

tui Jesus

O ye kingdoms of the earth, sing to God, sing psalms unto the Lord, to the God who hath ascended above the heaven of heavens, to the

Tu in mulieribus et Benedictus fructus ventris.

THE ASCENSION OF JESUS INTO HEAVEN.

Ascendisti in
altum, cepisti
captivitatem;
accepisti
dona in
hominibus.
(*Ps.* lxvii. 20.)

Benedicta

Thou hast ascended up on high: thou hast led captivity captive, and hast received gifts in men. (*Psalm* lxvii. 20.)

enemies. Why was he sold and betrayed?—he loved. Why was he caught and bound?—he loved. In all this, how truly is Samson the figure of Christ! Jesus Christ, the Son of God, loved. He loved the nations of the world, He loved the Jewish Synagogue. In the words of the prophet Isaias, He says, 'With an everlasting love have I loved thee. O man! for this cause have I been made Man; for this cause have I suffered such great things; for this cause have I been taken, bound, scourged, and crucified, because I have loved thee, O man!'" (Sermon iii. on Samson, Passio Christi Adumbrata.)

Samson suffers himself to be bound by Delila; Jesus suffers Himself to be nailed to the Cross by the officers of Pilate, though He had said to Peter, "Thinkest thou not that I could pray to My Father, and that He would presently give to Me more than twelve legions of angels. But how then should the Scriptures be fulfilled?" (Matt. xxvi. 53.)

Then when Samson is bound, and seems to be asleep in her arms, Delila cries, "The Philistines are upon thee, Samson." When Jesus, after having suffered Himself to be bound on the Cross, seems to be fallen asleep, and is laid in the tomb, Pilate says to those who had lain in wait to seize him, "Take ye the guard, go make the sepulchre sure as you know how?" But Samson is now no longer willing to be bound. He bursts the bands as a man would break a thread of tow twisted with the fingers, when it has smelt the fire. Jesus will now no longer submit to the dominion of death, and He bursts the bands with which He had suffered Himself to be bound. Behold the angel comes down from heaven, the stone is rolled away from the door of the sepulchre, and the keepers for fear become as dead men. Jesus, the true Samson, has now burst every band with which His enemies have sought to bind Him. Death hath no more dominion over Him; HE IS RISEN FROM THE DEAD.

The Second Glorious Mystery of the Rosary.

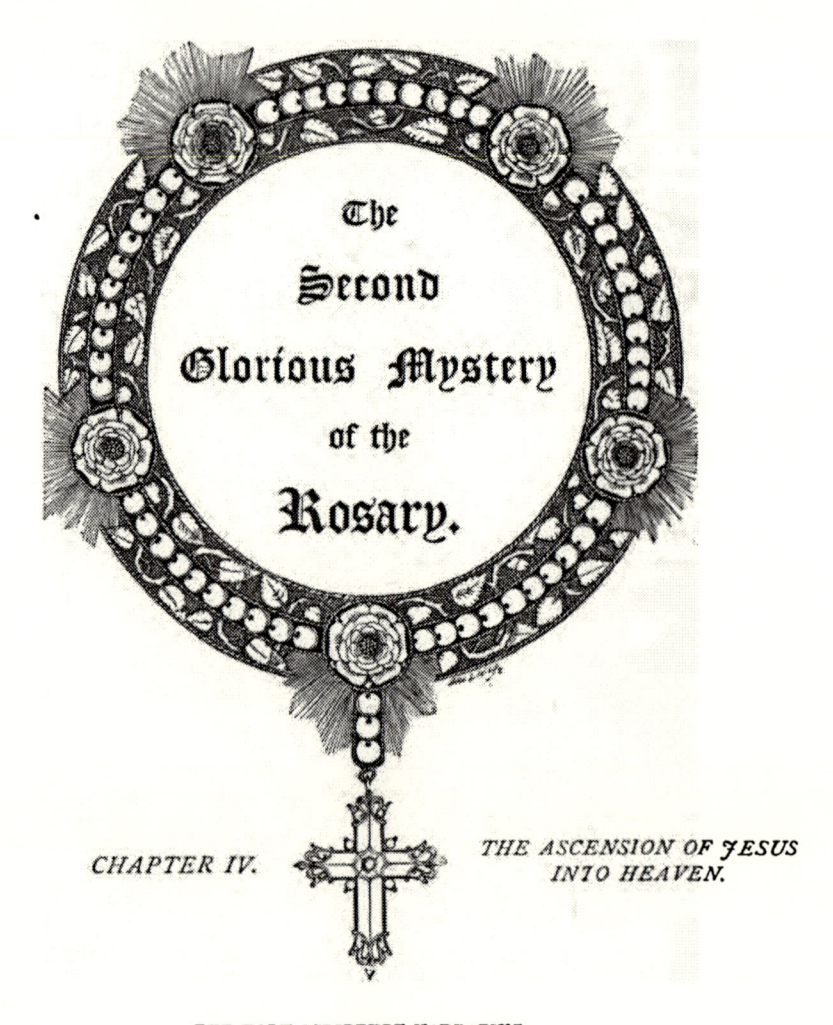

CHAPTER IV.   THE ASCENSION OF JESUS INTO HEAVEN.

THE HOLY SCRIPTURE NARRATIVE.

"And eating together with them, He commanded them that they should not depart from Jerusalem, but should wait for the promise of the Father, which you have heard (saith He) by My mouth. For John indeed baptized with water, but you shall be baptized with the Holy Ghost, not many days hence. And leading them out to Bethany, He blessed them.

"They therefore who were come together, asked Him, saying: Lord, wilt Thou at this time restore again the kingdom to Israel? But He said to them: It is not for you to know the times or moments which the Father hath put in His own power; but you shall receive the power of the Holy Ghost coming upon you, and you shall be witnesses unto Me in Jerusalem, and in all Judea and Samaria, and even to the uttermost part of the earth. And when

"He said these things, while they looked on, He was raised up; and a cloud received Him out of their sight. And while they were beholding Him going up to heaven, behold two men stood by them in white garments. Who also said: Ye men of Galilee, why stand you looking up to heaven? This Jesus who is taken up from you into heaven, shall so come as you have seen Him going into heaven" (Acts i.)

"Brethren," says St Augustine, "the last words of a parent about to go down into the grave are wont to be listened to with breathless attention, and the last words of the Lord Himself, who is about to ascend up to heaven, are not to be despised."

"In the spirit of His might," writes St Peter Damian, "Jesus, the Saviour, descending into hell, burst the brazen gates, and broke the iron bars (Cant. iii. 6; Ps. cvi. 16). At the acclamation of the angels crying out, 'Lift up your gates, ye princes,' the spirits that had fallen through pride answer with an ignorant disdain, 'Who is this King of glory?' Here are the beginnings of the one who said in his heart, 'There is no God;' 'I know not the Lord, and I will not let Israel go.' The angels of peace confidently answer, 'The Lord strong and mighty, the Lord mighty in battle,' as if they would have said, '*strong*' to confound your strength, '*mighty*' to destroy your might, '*in battle*,' in that battle, to wit, in which single-handed He put to flight all the powers of the air. Returning again from the prison with the standard of victory, He raised again His human body. And on appearing to present to His Father the sheep which had been lost, He hears again the alternate chant of the angels, 'Who is this King of glory?' and the reply from their united choirs, 'The Lord of hosts, He is the King of glory.' Of a truth the Lord of hosts had wrought a mighty work by His resurrection, such as He had not done before, in the redemption of a slave, and in the making him a son in the place of a slave. But on the great and most illustrious day of the Ascension, when, in the sight of His disciples, He was taken up into heaven, that most august and venerable company came to meet the Redeemer, and the whole host of the angels, as well they that do His bidding as they that stand by the throne, came to meet the Son, and, filled with wonder at His Ascension, exclaimed, 'Who is He that comes from Edom with dyed garments from Bosra, walking in the multitude 'of His strength?' (Isa. lxiii. 1). For seeing the crimson stains of blood still upon Him, they wonder at His patience and at the cruelty of the Jews, who were not afraid to condemn the Son of God to the ignominy of the Cross, and they add, 'walking in the multitude of His strength,' that is, not merely in His strength, but *in the multitude of His strength;* for what strength can be greater than that which has redeemed a servant to place him for ever at the right hand of God" (Sermon on the Ascension of the Son and the Assumption of the Mother).

If such be the acclamations of joy with which the whole august company of the holy angels greeted the Ascension of their Lord in His human nature, what, it will naturally be asked, will be the corresponding sentiments of the company of believers upon earth. For the thought can escape no one that the gain of the holy angels in having henceforward the presence of Jesus, the High Priest who was crucified in Jerusalem, among them, is, in a certain sense, the loss of the company of believers, among whom He ceases to be, in the same manner as before, visibly present—the bright cloud having now received Him out of their sight. How is it that the loss of the visible presence of Jesus from the company of the faithful comes to be esteemed by them a glorious mystery? St Augustine shall give the answer:—

"Attend, my brethren, to what St John says:—'If you loved me you would rejoice because I say I go to the Father, for the Father is greater than I; and because I have spoken these things sorrow hath filled your heart. Nevertheless I tell you the truth, it is expedient to you that I go away, for if I go not, the Paraclete will not come unto you; but if I go I will send Him unto you" (John xiv. 28, and xvi. 6).

"I speak somewhat plainly on account of

those of us who are rather slow of understanding, and all who do understand I entreat to have patience. 'If ye loved Me'— what does this mean? 'If ye loved Me ye would rejoice that I go to the Father.' What else can 'If ye loved Me' mean except that Ye do not love Me? What is it, then, that you do love? Clearly the body which you see! For you are not willing that it should depart out of your sight. If ye loved *Me?* What is properly meant by *Me?* 'In the beginning the Word was, and the Word was with God, and the Word was God,' as St John says. If, therefore, you loved Me in the way in which all things were made by Me, you would rejoice that I go to the Father. Why? Because the Father is greater than I. Whilst ye continue to see Me on earth, the Father is greater than I. I will depart out of your sight; your mortal flesh, which I assumed on account of your being subject to death, shall be taken out of your sight. Ye shall begin not to see the clothing which I have taken through humility, for it shall be raised up to heaven, that you may learn from thence what you have to hope for.' It was thus that He brought them to understand how Christ was the Word of God, very God of very God, by whom all things were made. For with this understanding they could not have been filled, except their love for His visible bodily presence had been taken away. And hence it was that He said to them, 'If ye loved Me ye would rejoice because I go to the Father, for the Father is greater than I.' In this respect is He less than the Father, because He became man that He might espouse the Church to Himself, but as being God He is equal to the Father. Wherefore, away with the desires of the flesh. As if He had said to His apostles, 'You are not willing to let Me go (just as a man is not disposed to let his friend go away from him, seeming as if he would say to him, 'Stay awhile with us, for it does us good to see you'), still it is notwithstanding better for you that you should cease to see the outward form, and that you should begin to meditate upon the invisible Godhead. Outwardly, then, I shall remove Myself away from you, but inwardly I shall fill you with Myself.' For, we may ask, is it according to the flesh, and with His flesh, that Christ enters into the heart? Clearly no; it is according to His Godhead that He holds possession of the heart. According to the flesh He speaks to the heart through the eyes, and His admonitions are from without; but He Himself dwells within, in order that we may be inwardly converted and restored to life by Him, and thus be moulded and formed by Him, for He is the indwelling Pattern that God has made inherent in all things" (Sermon cclxiv.)

The Ascension of Jesus into heaven is thus a glorious mystery to the company of believers upon earth, notwithstanding that it is in point of fact His reception into the bright cloud which hides Him from their sight. For if we love Him, we shall, as He Himself says to us, rejoice that He is gone to His Father, for His Ascension is the proof that in the Godhead He is, with the Holy Spirit, the co-equal of the Father.

St Paul, speaking of the Mystery of the Ascension, says, "Wherefore He saith, Ascending up on high, He hath led captivity captive, and hath given gifts to men" (Eph. iv. 8, and Ps. lxvii. 19). The saying of Jesus Himself, above quoted, explains these words of St Paul: "Nevertheless I tell you the truth; it is expedient for you that I go away, for if I go not away the Paraclete will not come unto you, but if I go I will send Him unto you." The mission of the Holy Ghost, which is the subject of the succeeding Mystery, follows from the Ascension of Jesus into heaven. He has not merely led captivity captive, as St Augustine says, and then cast off His captives. Mark the words: "He has given gifts to men." Do thou, then, O believer! open thy bosom and receive the gift of thy happiness (Sermon cclxi.) It is, then, manifestly very expedient for the company of believers on earth that Jesus should have ascended, as we shall have occasion to see more at length in considering the next Mystery— the mission of the Holy Ghost, which has followed from His going to the Father.

The Mystery of the Ascension possesses further essentially the character of glorious. "The form of a man, which Christ assumed to Himself," says St Augustine, "was glorified on two separate occasions

—the first when He rose again on the third day from the dead, and the second when He ascended into heaven in the sight of His disciples." The glorification of Jesus was completed by His Resurrection and Ascension; for He rose again to give us a proof that the dead shall rise, and He ascended that He might be our Protector from above." The Ascension of Jesus into heaven is also the joy and glory of the company of believers upon earth, because in it the nature of man is exalted above every creature. "God," says the Apostle, "who at sundry times and in divers manners spoke in times past to the fathers by His prophets, last of all in these days hath spoken to us by His Son, who, being the brightness of His glory, and the figure of His substance, and upholding all things by the word of His power, having made purgation of sins, sitteth on the right hand of the Majesty on high, being made so much better than the angels, as He hath inherited a more excellent name than they. For to which of the angels," continues St Paul, " said He at any time, Sit on my right hand until I make thy enemies thy footstool? For He took not on Him the nature of the angels, but of the seed of Abraham" (Heb. i.)

Hence, the whole company of believers is daily saying in the profession of its faith, " He ascended into heaven, and sitteth on the right hand of God the Father, from thence He shall come again to judge the living and the dead."

"Call to mind the Psalm" (Ps. lvi. 6), says St Augustine, "to whom are these words said, 'Be Thou exalted, O God, above the heavens?' Of whom can this be said?—of God the Father? But God the Father was never humbled. 'Be Thou exalted!' Thou who wast shut up in the womb; Thou who wast fashioned in that which Thou hadst made; Thou who wast laid in a manger; Thou who wast fed at the breast; Thou who sustainedst the world, and wast yet carried about by Thy Mother; Thou whose greatness the aged Simeon acknowledged while he held Thee an infant in his arms; Thou whom Anna saw suckled at the breast and confessed Thy omnipotence; Thou who sufferedst hunger and thirst for our sakes; Thou who wast weary and enduredst all things for us; Thou who wast subject to sleep, and yet never slumberedst in keeping watch over Israel; in a word, Thou whom the Jews bought but could not possess; Thou who wast seized, bound, scourged, crowned with thorns, suspended on the cross, pierced with a spear, wast dead and buried; be Thou exalted above the heavens, be Thou exalted because Thou art God. Thou that wast suspended upon the Cross, take Thy seat in the heavens."

The Mystery of the Ascension is also full of consolation to the company of believers in their pilgrimage over the desert of this life. "In My Father's house," says Jesus, "there are many mansions; if not, I would have told you; behold I go to prepare a place for you. And if I go to prepare a place for you, I will come again and will take you to Myself, that where I am, there you may be also" (John xiv. 2). Jesus is not merely raised to glory from His humiliation, but, in His state of glory, He is mindful of all those who are on their pilgrimage to Him, and is preparing a place for them. "Wherefore it behoved Him," says St Paul, "to be in all things like unto His brethren, that He might become a merciful and faithful High Priest before God" (Heb. ii. 17).

The Mystery of the Ascension, it should, however, also be remembered is full of the most striking warnings to the whole company of believers. "If the word spoken by angels," reasons St Paul, "held good, and every transgression and disobedience received a just recompense of reward, how shall we escape if we neglect so great a salvation? which, having begun to be declared by the Lord, was confirmed unto us by them that heard Him" (Heb. ii.) "Into the city whose light is the glory of God, and the Lamb the lamp thereof," it is expressly written, "That there shall not enter into it anything that defileth, or that worketh abomination, or maketh a lie" (Apoc. xxi. 27). We cannot carry our vices, or our worldly desires, or anything else which is of this world, into the kingdom where Jesus now sits at the right hand of God. Therefore, as St Paul says, "Let us learn betimes to set our hearts only on the things above, where Christ sitteth at the right hand of God."

CHAPTER V.

SCRIPTURE TYPES OF THE SECOND GLORIOUS MYSTERY.

I. THE HIGH PRIEST ENTERS INTO THE HOLY OF HOLIES.
II. ELIAS TAKEN UP FROM THE EARTH.

1. *The High Priest enters into the Holy of Holies to make atonement for the people.*

The figure of the Ascension of Jesus into heaven, which is contained in the entrance of the high priest into the holy of Holies, is so fully explained by St Paul in the Epistle to the Hebrews, that our purpose cannot be better served than by quoting his words in full :—

"Now of the things which we have spoken, this is the sum : We have such a High Priest, who is set on the right hand of the throne of majesty in the heavens, a minister of the Holies, and of the true tabernacle, which the Lord hath pitched, and not man. For every high priest is appointed to offer gifts and sacrifices : wherefore it is necessary that He also should have something to offer. If then He were on earth, He would not be a priest : seeing that there would be others to offer gifts according to the law, who serve unto the example and shadow of heavenly things. As it was answered to Moses, when he was to finish the tabernacle : See (says He) that thou make all things according to the pattern which was shown thee on the mount. For the former things, indeed, had also justifications of divine service, and a worldly sanctuary. For there was a tabernacle made the first, wherein were the candlesticks, and the table, and the setting forth of loaves, which is called the Holy. And after the second veil, the tabernacle, which is called the Holy of Holies : having a golden censer, and the ark of the testament covered about on every part with gold, in which was a golden pot that had manna, and the rod of Aaron that had blossomed, and the tables of the testament. And over it were the cherubims of glory overshadowing the mercy-seat : of which it is not needful to speak now particularly. Now these things being thus ordered, into the first tabernacle the priests indeed always entered, accomplishing the offices of the sacrifices. But into the second, the high priest alone, once a year : not without blood, which he offereth for his own, and the people's ignorance. The Holy Ghost signifying this, that the way into the Holies was not yet made manifest, whilst the former tabernacle was yet standing, which is a parable of the time present. But Christ being present a High Priest of the good things to come, by a greater and more perfect tabernacle not made with hands, that is, not of this creation : neither by the blood of goats, or of calves, but by His own blood, entered once into the Holies, having obtained eternal redemption."

St Paul then draws the consequence, and continues—" Having therefore, brethren, a High Priest over the house of God, let us draw near with a true heart in fulness of faith, having our hearts sprinkled from an evil conscience, and our bodies washed with clean water. Let us hold fast the confession of our hope without wavering (for He is faithful that hath promised). And let us consider one another, to provoke unto charity and to good works" (Heb. viii. ix.)

2. *Elias, taken from earth up into heaven, leaves his mantle to his successor, who works greater miracles than his master.*

"The sons of the prophets, that were at Bethel," the Scripture relates, "came forth to Eliseus, and said to him : Dost thou know that this day the Lord will

THE II. GLORIOUS MYSTERY.

The taking up of Elias.

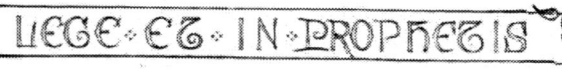

LEGE 29 IN PROPHECIS

CURRUS ET AURIGA EIUS

THE PROPHET WHO IS TO RETURN AGAIN LEAVES HIS MANTLE BEHIND HIM.

THE OLD TESTAMENT TYPES OF

The High Priest enters the Holy of Holies.

ROSA MYSTICA · RSSIM · IN MISSM

ADUMBRATA · ORA · PRO · NOBIS

THE SACRIFICE OF ATONEMENT IN THE PRESENCE OF GOD.

THE THIRD GLORIOUS MYSTERY.

THE MISSION OF THE HOLY GHOST.

Ave — Maria — Gratia — Plena — Dominus — Tecum

Benedicta tu in mulieribus et Benedictus fructus ventris tui Jesus

Spiritus Domini replevit orbem terrarum et hoc quod continet omnia scientiam habet vocis. (*Sap.* i. 7.)

The Spirit of the Lord hath filled the world, and that which containeth all things hath the science of speech. (*Wisd.* i. 7.)

Intonuit de coelo Dominus et Altissimus dedit vocem suam, et apparuerunt fontes aquarum. (*Ps.* xvii. 14.)

The Lord thundered from heaven; the Most High spake ... and the fountains of water broke forth. (*Psalm* xvii. 14.)

take away thy master from thee? And he answered: I also know it: hold your peace. And Elias said to him: Stay here, because the Lord hath sent me as far as the Jordan. And he said: As the Lord liveth, and as thy soul liveth, I will not leave thee: and they two went on together. And Elias took his mantle and folded it together, and struck the waters of the Jordan, and they were divided hither and thither, and they both passed over on dry ground. And when they were gone over, Elias said to Eliseus: Ask what thou wilt have me to do for thee, before I be taken away from thee. And Eliseus said: I beseech thee that in me may be a double portion of thy spirit. And he answered: Thou hast asked a hard thing: nevertheless if thou see me when I am taken from thee, thou shalt have what thou hast asked: but if thou see me not, thou shalt not have it." And as they went on, walking and talking together, behold a fiery chariot and fiery horses parted them both asunder: and Elias went up by a whirlwind into heaven. And Eliseus saw him, and cried: My father, my father! the chariot of Israel, and the driver thereof!" And he saw him no more: and he took hold of his own garments, and rent them in two pieces. And he took up the mantle of Elias, that fell from him" (4 Kings ii. 5).

"I call to mind," says St Bernard, "the holy Eliseus, who, when Elias spoke to him, that before he was taken away from him, he should ask what he would have him to do, answered, 'I pray thee that in me may be a double portion of thy spirit.' Elias answered, 'Thou hast asked a hard thing: nevertheless, if thou see me when I am taken from thee, thou shalt have what thou hast asked.' Does not Elias seem to you to prefigure the person of the Lord in His Ascension, while Eliseus is the figure of the company of the Apostles, who are anxiously looking up into heaven? For as Eliseus would on no account suffer himself to be separated from his master, so the Apostles in the same manner clung to the presence of Christ, and were with difficulty reconciled to part with Him. By the double portion of his spirit, we may certainly understand to be meant, that which Christ said to His disciples, 'He that believeth in Me, the works that I shall do, the same shall he do, and greater works shall he do.' Did not Peter through Christ do greater works than Christ Himself. For of Him we read that they laid the sick on couches in the streets, that the shadow of Peter passing by might overshadow them, and they were delivered from their diseases. The Lord Himself was never known to have healed sicknesses by His shadow" (Sermon iii. on the Ascension).

The Third Glorious Mystery of the Rosary.

CHAPTER VI.   THE MISSION OF **THE HOLY** GHOST.

THE HOLY SCRIPTURE NARRATIVE.

"And when the days of the Pentecost were accomplished, they were all together in one place: and suddenly there came a sound from heaven, as of a mighty wind coming, and it filled the whole house where they were sitting. And there appeared to them parted tongues as it were of fire, and it sat upon every one of them: and they were all filled with the Holy Ghost, and they began to speak with divers tongues, according as the Holy Ghost gave them to speak. Now there were dwelling at Jerusalem, Jews, devout men, out of every nation under heaven. And when this was noised abroad, the multitude came together, and were confounded in mind, because that every man heard them speak in his own tongue. And they were all amazed, and wondered, saying: Behold, are not all these that speak Galileans? And how have we heard, every man our own tongue wherein we were born? Parthi-

The Third Glorious Mystery.

"ans, and Medes, and Elamites, and inhabitants of Mesopotamia, Judea, and Cappadocia, Pontus and Asia; Phrygia, and Pamphilia, Egypt, and the parts of Lybia about Cyrene, and strangers of Rome; Jews also, and proselytes, Cretes, and Arabians: we have heard them speak in our own tongues the wonderful works of God. And they were all astonished, and wondered, saying one to another: What meaneth this? But others mocking said: These men are full of new wine. But Peter standing up with the eleven, lifted up his voice, and spoke to them: Ye men of Judea, and all you that dwell in Jerusalem, be this known to you, and with your ears receive my words. For these are not drunk, as you suppose, seeing it is but the third hour of the day: but this is that which was spoken of by the prophet Joel: *And it shall come to pass, in the last days (saith the Lord), I will pour out of My Spirit upon all flesh; and your sons and your daughters shall prophesy, and your young men shall see visions, and your old men shall dream dreams. And upon my servants indeed, and upon my handmaids, will I pour out in those days of My Spirit, and they shall prophesy*" (Acts ii.)

In the successive stages through which the scheme of God for compassing the end of human salvation unfolds itself to our view in the Fifteen Mysteries of the Rosary, the Third Glorious Mystery brings us to the Day of Pentecost; or, in other words, to the accomplishment of the promise given by the High Priest Himself on the day of His solemn entry into the Holy of Holies, that the Paraclete should come in His stead, to those whom He left on earth, and that they should be baptized by the Holy Spirit.

"See my brethren," says St Augustine, "what you ought to love, and what you ought to hold fast. Our Lord, when He rises again in glory, commends His Church to us; and again, when about to be still further glorified by His Ascension, He again commends His Church; and when He sends the Holy Spirit from heaven He once more commends His Church. For after His resurrection what does He say to His disciples: '*These things I said to you while I was yet with you, that all things must be fulfilled which are written in the Law, and the Prophets, and the Psalms concerning me.*' And then He opened their understandings that they should understand the Scriptures, and He said to them: '*Thus it was written, and thus it behoved Christ to suffer and to rise again from the dead on the third day.*' Where is the reference to the Church here? He goes on to say, '*That penance, and the remission of sins, should be preached in His name.*' We ask, where? '*Throughout all nations, beginning from Jerusalem.*' These were His words after His glorious Resurrection. And what does He say as He is about to be glorified by His Ascension into heaven? '*Ye shall be witnesses to Me in Jerusalem, and in all Judea and Samaria, even unto the ends of the world.*' What, again, does He say on the occasion of the Descent of the Holy Ghost? The Holy Ghost descends. They who are filled with the Holy Ghost are able to speak the languages of all nations. And each person is able thus to speak; what can this point to, except to the unity of all people and languages? Holding this truth fast, firmly built up in this, clinging to it with an unshaken charity, let us, who are His children, evermore praise the Lord, and say, 'Alleluia.' But is this to be done only here or there? or where? and how far? The prophet answers: '*From the rising up of the sun, to the going down of the same, praise the name of the Lord.*'"

Jesus had given to His disciples the commission, "Go ye into the whole world and preach the gospel to every creature;" but He had, notwithstanding, suspended the immediate effect of their commission, by bidding them wait in Jerusalem till they should be endued with power from on high; without which power it was in vain for them to attempt to go into the whole world to execute their mission. The sign and seal of the Third Person of the Ever-Blessed Trinity was thus needed to complete the work which had been begun; for the redemption of man is the joint work of the Three Persons of the Holy Trinity.

Here it will be fitting for us to observe in what way the Pentecostal gift of the Holy Ghost presents itself under a twofold aspect to the mind of the believer.

A man's life, even in his fallen condition, is twofold. He is both a little world in himself, the life of which he does not share in common with others, as Solomon says, "The heart knoweth its own bitterness, and a stranger intermeddleth not with its joy;" and he is, as both St Thomas and Aristotle say, also a social animal, both as member of a family, and as citizen of a state; in both of which respects, as St Paul says, "Men are members one of another, and we share our life with others." And even according to the dictates of natural wisdom, two things were held in the times before Christ to be wanted for the perfection of a happy life—namely, a sufficiency of personal gifts proper to the interior life of the man, and a sufficiency also of dignity and honour, in the way of social position. Hence it was a kind of sacred maxim of the old Roman empire to risk everything to insure the pre-eminent dignity of the rights of citizenship in the empire. The 'Civis Romanus' was one whom the whole power of the empire must protect in the possession of his rights. Divine grace, as the great Doctor of the schools teaches, does not overthrow the order of nature; and in the world before Christ, humanity has never been known to have attained to anything higher or better than what was exemplified in the choicest of the Roman citizens, who united in their persons the highest natural qualities, combined with the greatest external advantages of secure and dignified social position. So the Holy Trinity framed Its Divine plan for the restoration of the children of men in a way consonant to existing experience. There was to be the pouring out of the richest inward personal gifts and graces from the indwelling of the Holy Ghost, combined with the gift of an honourable citizenship in a city, not the perishable work of the political and legislative wisdom of man, as was the Roman empire, but an eternal city, whose maker and builder is God. This city is the Catholic Church, the work which Jesus Christ came into the world to gather together about Himself.

Man being made, not for solitude but for social life, cannot, ordinarily speaking, perfect himself otherwise than in social life, and it therefore became the wisdom and goodness of the Ever-Blessed Trinity, in Its plan for the restoration of fallen man, to found and extend over the world the Catholic Church, a visible society, in the bosom of which the Christian people might enjoy the best form of that social life, for which God, in His plan of creation, has formed them. It became, then, both the goodness and the wisdom of God to found His own society in the world, and so to throw it open to all believers, that all might receive from Him a place in it. And when any soul of man profits by the mercy of God, and receives from God what He freely offers to all, a place and a citizenship in the society of which He is Himself the founder and builder, God says to him, "Remain in the land, and thou shalt be fed with the riches of it" (Ps. xxxvi. 3). "As a bird which goes away from its nest, so is the man who leaves his place" (Prov. xxvii. 6). "I am the vine, ye are the branches; as the branches cannot bear fruit without the vine, so ye cannot bear fruit without Me" (John xv.) The work of the Ever-Blessed Trinity is one whole, and so long as you walk in humility before God, and remain in the place which He has given you, you will be to Him a dear son of His household, and all the riches of the household will be yours; but if you suffer yourself to be betrayed by the devil into the sin and folly of following the devil's example, by quitting your place, then you will cease to be fed with the riches of the land, and you will be in great danger of having your place with the fallen angels, "who did not preserve their principality, but left their abode, and are reserved in everlasting chains in darkness, for the judgment of the great day" (Jude).

As the doctrine of the necessity for accepting in due humility the duty of conforming to communion with the Catholic Church, is one that is found to be very galling and revolting to human pride, there is, consequently, the stronger reason on this account for taking pains to understand in what way the Third Glorious Mystery of the Holy Rosary teaches and inculcates this duty, as its own special and peculiar lesson.

The language of this Third Mystery, then, to all is, "Come into the Catholic Church, because its founder and builder is Jesus Christ; and when you are in it, walk humbly before God all your days in your place in the Catholic Church, that you may be fed with the riches of the land, that God, the Holy Ghost, may shed abroad in your hearts all His most excellent gifts." "The beginning of the pride of a man," says the Scripture, " is to turn away from God" (Ecclus. x. 14); and what sort of blindness and pride must it not be on the part of men, to think that they can substitute the work of their own hands for the city and the temple whose builder and maker is God? What kind of blindness must not that be which desires indeed to have the religion of Jesus Christ, for the sake of the spiritual riches and treasures of God the Holy Ghost in which it abounds, but insists upon having these outside the great society of the redeemed, which Jesus Christ has gathered together, and over which He is the Supreme Pastor, represented here below by the august person of His vicar, the Roman Pontiff? And who can fail to perceive how contrary the human pride that insists upon this must be to the design of the Holy and Ever-Blessed Trinity? As we have seen, there is in every man, by his creation, his interior life and his social life. A man is at once, by creation, a microcosm, or little world in himself, and a social being. The Ever-Blessed Trinity says to the creature of Its hands, "Your interior life shall be enriched and adorned by the graces of the Holy Ghost, and your social life shall be perfected in the place assigned to you in the great company of the redeemed, in which shall be given to you a far more honourable and enduring citizenship than ever was that of the Roman empire in its palmiest days;" and this creature, thus taken by an act of pure grace and Divine love once more into favour, answers either, "I do not believe and I value neither the graces nor the citizenship," or "I value indeed the graces that are offered, but I turn my back upon the citizenship, and prefer a society of my own making, free from all its shackles and restraints, which I neither relish, nor of which I can perceive either the utility or the advantage."

Thus it is that the pride of men is for ever cavilling and wrangling with God as to the terms of His salvation, and like Moses, in the very presence of the bush burning with fire, for ever disputing and bargaining with God over the very salvation of which man is alone to derive the profit. "My people," says the prophet Micheas, "I pray you remember what Balak, king of Moab, thought in his heart, and what Balaam the son of Beor answered him, that thou mayest know the justice of God. I will show thee, O man, what is good, and what the Lord requireth from thee, to do justice, to love mercy, and to walk humbly with Thy God" (Mich. vi. 7.)

If, then, the special lesson of the Third Glorious Mystery of the Rosary is to teach and inculcate upon us the duty of studying to remain humble, grateful, and contented in our place in the great company of the redeemed, the Catholic Church, ever on our watch lest the devil should tempt us through pride to take pattern by him and quit our domicile, it will also teach us to cultivate an overflowing charity and compassion towards all the unhappy souls who, victims of the multiplied scandals and disorders of this lower world, have hitherto failed to come into possession of the rightful place and citizenship in the Catholic Church to which the concluding words of the inspired volume invite them, "And the Spirit and the Bride say, Come; and he that heareth let him say, Come; and he that thirsteth let him come; and he that will, let him receive the water of life without price" (Apoc. xxii. 17).

And in this respect, the Third Mystery of the Rosary, while it inculcates this duty of an especial charity towards the multitudes who, scarcely so much through a fault of their own, as through the calamitous effect of sins and scandals anterior to the time of their coming into the world, are separated from the place in the Catholic Church which belongs to them, and would make their happiness, also puts in our hands a great power of helping them, of which in charity we should be studious to learn to understand and master the use.

The true city of God must plainly be one that is set on a hill, and that cannot be hid, except indeed to the eyes of those who, in their perverse hatred of the light which would guide them to its gates, resemble the blindness of the Jews, who can see in Jesus Christ nothing but the person of the disturber of public order, whom Pilate at their demand caused to be publicly executed upon the Cross. The same veil which is over the hearts of the Jews for so many generations, and which keeps them from acknowledging the true Son of David, may be also over the hearts and eyes of many among the nations, to keep them from acknowledging the Catholic Church, to whose citizenship all are invited. But the Scripture says to us, "He that heareth, let *him* say, Come;" and the Third Mystery of the Rosary certainly furnishes us with that which may enable us to say, "Come" with better effect. It is in this mystery, that we are presented with a remarkable note of the city of God that is set upon a hill and cannot be hid. The true company of believers, with whom are all the riches of the outpouring of the Holy Ghost, is one that on the day of Pentecost suddenly by miracle received the gift of speaking all the languages of the earth, and has continued ever since in possession of this gift, as a mark by which it may be always securely known. In the early times after the Flood, the Holy Trinity baffled the pride of men, when they thought to make a unity of their own, and perpetuate it in a stronghold of their own making: "And the Lord came down that He might see the city and the tower that the children of Adam were building. And He said, Behold the people is one, and there is one lip to them all. They have begun to do this, and they will not desist from their undertaking until they have completed it. Let Us come down and confuse their speech, so that no man may understand the speech of his neighbour. And in this way the Lord divided them from that place into all lands, and they ceased to build the city" (Gen. xi. 5). But that which the Holy Trinity brought upon men as the punishment designed to repress and to set limits to their pride, it is manifest that the same Holy Trinity alone can repeal and reverse. From the day of Pentecost to the present hour, there is only one Christian company in the world that is known by the token of speaking all the languages of the earth, that is, the Catholic Church. The unity of nations, which is the work of God, no power or wisdom that is of men can counterfeit. And whatever falls away from this unity becomes a separated fragment, broken off from the great body; like one of the tribes which the Lord, in the punishment of pride, divided off with a separate speech of its own, and sent to find its place in the general confusion of the world, "Behold, then," the Third Mystery of the Rosary teaches us to say to all, who are willing to hear, "the true city of God, speaking all the languages of the earth, restored by humility to the unity which was broken up through pride, 'The Spirit and the Bride say, Come, and let him that heareth say, Come.' Come to the inheritance which God has given to all the nations of the earth, acknowledge His Vicar the Holy Roman Pontiff, and come and rest yourselves under the shadow of the great tree which has spread its branches over the whole world, and whose leaves the Apostle says are for the healing of the nations (Apoc. xxii. 2). If you have any doubt which is the Church, the Bride of Christ and His mystical Body, ask the nations of the world, for Christ has received them for His inheritance,—not this or that one nation, for it may be blinded by its particular pride, but all the nations, for these are the inheritance of Christ, and see if they do not answer you with a voice that comes from the east and the west, from the north and the south,—the one true Church is the Roman Catholic Church. Roman, because Jesus Christ has established its centre of unity in the city and See of Rome. Catholic because it has all the nations of the earth for its inheritance."

Thus it is, then, that the Holy and Ever-Blessed Trinity perfect Its work by the double outpouring of the Holy Spirit into the heart of the believer and into the whole body of the Church. St John relates that "on the last day of the feast, Jesus stood and cried out, If any man thirst, let him come to Me. He that believeth in Me, as the scripture saith, out of his belly shall flow rivers of living water" (Deut. xviii. 15). "Now this He said of the Spirit, which they should receive who believed in Him; for as yet the Spirit was not given, for Jesus was not yet glorified" (John vii. 37). Here are the gifts that are promised to the believers individually. And, again, St Paul writes, "He hath given some to be apostles, some prophets, others to be evangelists, others pastors and teachers, for the perfecting of the saints, for the work of the ministry, for the building up of the body of Christ, until we all come together in the unity of faith and of the acknowledging the Son of God, to a perfect man, to the measure of the stature of the fulness of Christ" (Eph. iv. 11). Here is the outpouring of the Holy Spirit into the Body of Christ, the Church.

CHAPTER VII.

SCRIPTURE TYPES OF THE THIRD GLORIOUS MYSTERY.

I. THE LAW GIVEN TO MOSES ON THE HOLY MOUNTAIN.
II. THE SACRIFICE CONSUMED BY FIRE.

1. *The law given to Moses on the holy mountain.*

It was beyond doubt brought to pass by the special providence of God, by whose will the Mosaic covenant is in so many respects the shadow and figure of the new law which was to succeed to it, that the law of the Ten Commandments was solemnly proclaimed in the midst of the fires and thunderings of Mount Sinai, on the fiftieth day after the offering of the Paschal Lamb, and the sudden departure out of Egypt. The people were delivered out of the hands of the destroying angel and of the Egyptians by the blood of the Paschal Lamb, and through the terror caused by the death of the first-born of the Egyptians; and on the fiftieth day after this delivery, they who had been slaves and bondsmen in Egypt, receive the law of God from His own mouth, speaking in the midst of the thunders and fires with which the mountain burned, and are raised to the dignity of being a priestly kingdom and a holy people. In the New Covenant, the faithful were delivered out of their bondage by the blood of Jesus, the true Paschal Lamb, and by the destruction of the power of the devil; and exactly fifty days afterwards the Spirit of God descends upon them, giving them that Spirit of adoption as sons of God, "whereby," as the Apostle says, "we all cry, Abba, Father," and raising them to the dignity of free citizens of the celestial city, "for where the Spirit of God is, there," says St Paul, "is liberty."

We have, however, not selected the passage of the history in the old covenant which accurately coincides, in point of time, with the Pentecost of the new law, solely for the sake of bringing more to light the essential contrast between the two covenants, embodied in the law written by the finger of God on the tables of stone which were given to Moses in the Holy Mount and the law written by the Spirit of God in the fleshy tablets of the heart on the day of the Christian Pentecost.

A well-known poet says—

"When I behold a factious band agree
To call it freedom when themselves are free,

Each wanton judge new penal statutes draw,
Laws grind the poor, and rich men rule the law;
Then, half a patriot half a coward grown,
I fly from petty tyrants to the throne."
—GOLDSMITH's *"Traveller."*

The false idea of liberty with which the old serpent never ceases to labour to deceive mankind is, that it consists in teaching each member of a society to consider himself independent of law. Liberty thus understood, according to the old serpent's doctrine, leads to the necessary and infallible consequence, as the lines above quoted suggest, of the extremes of tyranny on the one hand and of slavery on the other. If, for instance, as a member of society, I adopt the old serpent's doctrine as my rule, and place my freedom in being above law, I am above respecting the rights of my neighbour, which it is the duty of the law both to determine and to protect; and if he also entertains the same ideas with respect to his liberty, he is equally above paying any respect to my rights, and thus I and my neighbour are sure to quarrel with each other; each one in the just defence of his own right which the other deems himself at liberty to disregard. And it thus becomes easy to see how the old serpent, whose aim it is to destroy all society, succeeds in gaining his end wherever he is able in the heart of any society to establish his doctrine, that freedom consists in independence of law.

In opposition to the doctrine of the old serpent, St Augustine says, that a secure condition of civil society can only be made out of the "eternal living truths." "For a society is not a mere aggregate of any kind of living beings, but a multitude of rational creatures bound together by the social bond of one law" (Quæst. Evang. lib. ii. 46). It is self-evident that the laws which are to determine the respective rights of the members of the society must first themselves be just, which they cannot be except they are founded on eternal truths, and thus proceed from God, for unjust laws cannot constitute a society of rational creatures.

The Lawgiver, who is perfectly wise and perfectly just, and whose laws apportion equally the rights of each member of the society, can be none other than God Himself, and obedience to the laws of God can proceed only from two motives—from fear of the punishments annexed to breaking them, and from the assent of the understanding to their justice, together with the conformity of the will to their requirements. The first of these motives is the fear of the penal consequences of injustice, and the second is the inward love of justice.

The first of these motives is the basis of the covenant that was promulgated on Mount Sinai, and "that engendereth," as St Paul says, "unto bondage." The second is that of the new covenant, "which answereth," says St Paul, "to the Jerusalem that is above, the mother of us all."

"For all the people," says the scripture, "saw the lightnings and the mountain covered with smoke, and heard the words and the sound of the trumpet, and terror-stricken and overcome with fear, they stood at a distance, saying to Moses, Speak thou to us and we will hear, and let not the Lord speak to us, lest perhaps we die. And Moses said to the people, Fear not, for God is come to prove you, that His fear might be in you, and that you should not sin" (Exod. xx. 18).

The law of liberty of the new covenant was proclaimed, not from Mount Sinai, but from Calvary, and written not on tables of stone, but by the Spirit of God on the fleshy tablets of the heart (2 Cor. iii. 3). This expression St Paul more fully explains in the Epistle to the Hebrews. "But now," he writes, speaking of Christ, "He hath obtained a better ministry, by how much also He is a Mediator of a better Testament, which is established on better promises. For if that former had been faultless, there should not indeed a place have been sought for a second." For finding fault with them, he saith, "*Behold the days shall come, saith the Lord, and I will perfect unto the house of Israel and the house of Juda a New Testament. Not according to the Testament which I made with their fathers on the day when I took them by the hand to lead them out of the land of Egypt, because they continued not in My Testament, and I regarded them not, saith the Lord. For this is the Testament which I will make*

THE III. GLORIOUS MYSTERY.
The Sacrifice is consumed with fire.

LEGE · ET · IN · PROPHECIS

EUM · ET · FILIUM

THE DIVINE FIRE WHICH THE PROPHET CALLED DOWN
FROM HEAVEN.

THE OLD TESTAMENT TYPES OF
The Law given on the Holy Mount.

ROSA · MYSTICA · PASSIM · IN

SIBON · ET · ORE · PRO · NOBIS

ÆUMBRÆ

THE DIVINE LAW THAT IS TO BE MADE KNOWN TO MEN
BY A MAN LIKE TO THEMSELVES.

to the *house of Israel after those days, saith the Lord: I will give my laws into their mind, and in their heart will I write them: and I will be their God, and they shall be my people: and they shall not teach every man his neighbour, and every man his brother, saying, Know the Lord: for all shall know Me from the least to the greatest of them: because I will be merciful to their iniquities, and their sins will I remember no more*" (Jer. xxxi. 31). "Now in saying a new, He hath made the former old. And that which decayeth and groweth old, is near its end" (Heb. viii. 6–13).

"Where the Spirit of the Lord is, there is liberty," says the Apostle (2 Cor. iii. 17). By the grace of the Pentecostal gift of the Spirit of God, the law of Christ is written in the hearts of the faithful, and their obedience to it is no longer from fear, as in the former covenant: "That His fear might be in you that you should not sin." But from love of the law for its own sake, which love the Holy Ghost works in the heart; for "charity," says St Paul, "is the fulfilment of the law."

It is worth the remark also, as an evidence of multiplicity in the minute points of correspondence in which the covenant of Sinai serves, as St Paul says, "to the example and shadow of the heavenly things," that the delivery to Moses of the tables of the law, written on stone with the finger of God, took place on the fiftieth day after the date of Moses being called up for the first time into the mountain to speak with God respecting the covenant which He was about to make with the people. On receiving the first intelligence of the law that was to be proclaimed, the people were required to spend three days in sanctifying themselves, and in cleansing their garments; and on the third day, the glory of the Lord covered the mountain, and the law was proclaimed in solemn form. The mount continued covered with the glory of the Lord for six other days, and on the seventh day, or the tenth from the first proclamation of the covenant about to be made, Moses was called to ascend the mountain to confer with God. Here he continued forty days and forty nights, and at their expiration, that is, on the fiftieth day from the first proclamation to the people to prepare for the law, the law was written on the tables of stone with the finger of God. The parallel scarcely needs to be pointed out. The first notice to the fallen world to prepare for the new Christian law to be proclaimed to it is in the resurrection of Jesus Christ from the dead; and the new Christian law is written, as the Apostle says, on the fleshy tablets of the heart, on the day of Pentecost, fifty days afterwards.

2. *The type of the sacrifice consumed by the fire that fell from heaven at the prayer of Elias.*

To keep the laws of God in the midst of a fallen world, which is subject to every form of scandal, sin, and disorder, is plainly a very different thing from keeping the laws of God in a society where all is perfect order. The blessed spirits, who are confirmed in their election, conform themselves to the Divine order of their society with perfect gladness and joy of heart. This cannot be the case in the society of men, because the citizens of the city of God are mixed up with the citizens of the earthly city, as the clay was with the iron in the feet of the statue which Nabuchodonosor saw in his vision, and the order of the city of God is in perpetual clash and warfare with that of the city of confusion. The citizens of the city of God, in addition to the difficulties which the weakness of their flesh imposes upon the willingness of their spirit, are continually met with obstacles to keeping the laws of God, created by the contrary laws and maxims of the earthly city with which they are unavoidably mixed up. From whence it comes to pass, that they have frequently not only to keep the law of God, but to fly in the face, so to speak, and to despise, the contrary laws or customs of the city of confusion. A Catholic, for example, to have recourse to an instance taken from everyday life, finds himself at an entertainment where many strangers are present, and where he is hospitably pressed to partake of the refreshments that are provided, but the day is a fast-day according to the Church. Here it is plain that his obedience to the precept of the Church must inevitably have the effect of making him both singular and an object of remark, and perhaps derision, to the company in which he finds himself, and his observance of the precept, which, were he at home amongst a society where its binding force was acknowledged, might have been comparatively easy, now becomes a kind of profession of faith before the eyes of unbelievers, that is proportionably trying and difficult. As long, then, as the city of God, signed and sealed by the gifts of the Holy Ghost on the day of Pentecost, is in the midst of the Babel of the present world, obedience to the laws of the city of God will always demand an offering up of the heart and the mind in sacrifice to God, that they may become wholly His, and consecrated to Him to the perfect keeping of His law in the face of every obstacle that the contrary mind and spirit of the city of confusion may interpose in the way of perfect obedience. Thus St Paul says, "For whosoever are led by the Spirit of God, they are the sons of God; for you have not received the spirit of bondage again in fear, but you have received the Spirit of adoption of sons, whereby we cry, Abba Father. For the Spirit Himself giveth testimony to our spirit that we are the sons of God" (Rom. viii. 14). "As it is written," he continues, "for Thy sake we are put to death all the day long, we are accounted as sheep for the slaughter" (Ps. xliii. 22). Again St Paul writes to the Philippians, thus, "If I should be offered up as a victim in addition to the sacrifice and the obedience of your faith, I should rejoice and wish joy to you all; and do you in like manner rejoice and wish me joy" (Phil. ii. 17). Here the victim of sacrifice, who has offered himself up to God for the perfect keeping of His laws, expresses his joy, which nothing can diminish or repress, at the prospect of the speedy consummation of his own sacrifice, while he expressly calls the faith of those to whom he is writing a "sacrifice" as well as an "obedience." For the law of God written in the heart of man by the finger of God the Holy Ghost, makes him a victim that willingly offers himself to keep the law that has been written in his heart, come what may: "The Lord is become my light; I will not fear what man can do unto me."

"Many waters," says the bride in the Canticles, "cannot quench charity, neither can the floods drown it" (Cant. viii. 7). "Who then," exclaims St Paul, "shall separate us from the love of Christ? shall tribulation? or distress? or famine? or nakedness? or danger? or persecution? or the sword? But in all these we overcome, because of Him that loved us" (Rom. viii. 35). This character of victim consumed by the fire of the Holy Spirit which was poured out upon the Church at Pentecost, through the intercession of Jesus our High Priest, finds its type and parallel in the fire which God sent down from heaven at the prayer of Elias, to consume the sacrifice which he had prepared on the altar of God. "And Elias said: Fill four buckets with water, and pour it upon the burnt-offering: and when it was now time to offer the holocaust, Elias the prophet came near and said: O Lord God of Abraham, Isaac, and Israel, show this day that Thou art the God of Israel, and I am Thy servant, and that according to Thy commandment I have done all these things. Hear me, O Lord! hear me, O Lord! that this people may learn that Thou art the Lord God, and that Thou hast turned their heart again. Then the fire of the Lord fell, and consumed the holocaust, and the wood, and the stones, and the dust, and licked up the water that was in the trench. And when all the people saw this, they fell on their faces, and they said: The Lord He is God, the Lord He is God."

Elias hereupon took the prophets of Baal and killed them all at the brook Cison. So also when the company of the day of Pentecost was consumed by the fire of Divine charity which fell down from heaven, idols from that day began to be swept away from the face of the earth.

THE FOURTH GLORIOUS MYSTERY.

Ave ~ Maria ~ Gratia ~ Plena ~ Dominus ~ Tecum

Benedicta ~ Tu in mulieribus et Benedictus fructus ventris ~ tui Jesus.

Et concupiscet
Rex decorem
tuum, quoniam
Ipse est
Dominus Deus
tuus, et
adorabunt
eum.
(*Ps.* xliv. 11.)

Tu gloria
Jerusalem, tu
Laetitia Israel,
tu honorificentia populi
nostri. Ideo
eris benedicta
in aeternum.
(*Judith* xv. 10.)

THE ASSUMPTION.

And the king shall
desire thy beauty,
for He is the Lord
thy God, and they shall adore Him.
(*Psalm* xliv. 11.)

Thou art the glory
of Jerusalem, thou
art the joy of Israel,
thou art the honour of our people Therefore thou shalt be blessed for ever.
(*Judith* xv. 10.)

The Fourth Glorious Mystery of the Rosary.

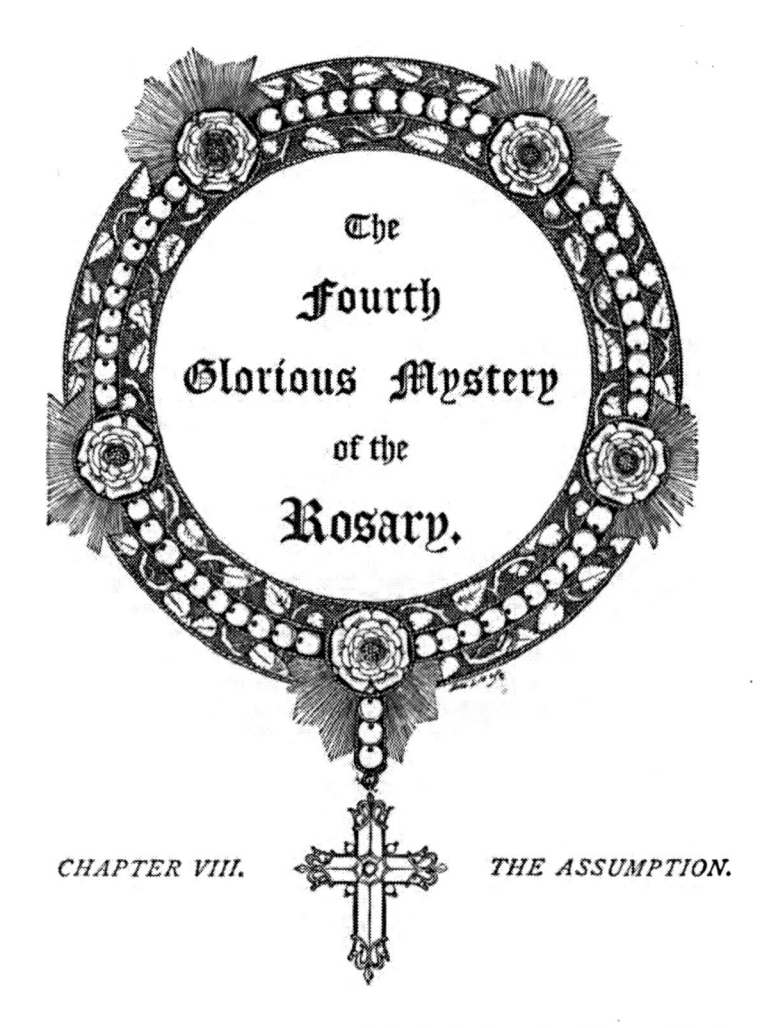

CHAPTER VIII. THE ASSUMPTION.

LESSON FROM THE ROMAN BREVIARY.

"To-day, the sacred and living ark of the God of life, which conceived the Creator of all in the womb, rests in the temple of the Lord, which is not built with hands. David, her father, rejoices, and with him the angels sing in choirs, the archangels praise her, the hosts of heaven glorify her, the principalities exult, the powers rejoice, the dominions wish her joy, the thrones keep high festival, the cherubim extol her, the seraphim proclaim her glory. To-day, Eden receives the living Paradise of the new Adam, in whom condemnation ends, in whom the tree of life hath been planted, and in whom our nakedness is covered" (St John Damascene II., Sermon on the Death of the Blessed Virgin).

The Assumption of the earthly Mother of Jesus into heaven may be easily seen, on a little reflection, to follow in the way of an event belonging to the fitting and beautiful order of the Divine plan of human redemption. Adam was created and placed in Paradise the sovereign lord over the whole of the work of God; but he was alone, and because it was not good for him to be alone, God said, "Let us make him a helpmate;" and thus creation received a sovereign lady, associated in power and dominion over all the works of God with its sovereign lord. The sovereign lady fell into transgression, and induced her lord to participate in her sin. Companions in the transgression, they remained companions in its penalties. Eve was not taken away from Adam, and no new companion was given to him in her place, but both were sent together to till the earth in toil and patience for their subsistence; for where it pleased God that Adam should be, there it was becoming that Eve should be found at his side; for even in fallen fortunes, where the bridegroom is there it is fitting that the bride be also. As, then, it was through Eve that the first Adam left the original Paradise and went to seek his fortunes in the rude world among its thorns and thistles, and as it was notwithstanding fitting that Eve, through whom he had been thrown upon the world, should find herself where Adam was, by his side, the inseparable companion of his toil and banishment, as she had been of his dignity and glory; so, in like manner, in the case of the second Adam, He came into the banishment of the first Adam to seek for and to espouse to Himself His Mystical Bride the Church; and it was undoubtedly becoming that she through whom He deigned to enter the first Adam's banishment,—she from whose virgin womb He vouchsafed to assume Adam's nature,— she whom He deigns to call by the name of Mother, should be ever near to Him at His side in the kingdom of His glory. If He Himself has said, "If any man minister to Me, let Him follow Me; and where I am, there also shall my minister be" (John xii. 26); and if it be thus becoming that the minister of the King should be where his Master is, in how much higher a degree is it becoming that where the Son is there also the Mother should be; and where the King and Mystical Bridegroom of the Church is, there also the Mystical Bride Herself, in the person of her Queen should also be? "Rise up, O Lord, into Thy rest," says the Holy Psalmist; but not in solitary dignity, "Thou and the Ark of Thy sanctification" (Ps. cxxxi. 8).

Where Jesus therefore is, now that He is ascended to sit at the right hand of the Father, what can be more becoming than that the Blessed Virgin Mary, the Mother of the human nature in which He has ascended, the Ark of His sanctification should be present with Him? Where can the poor exiled children of Eve find a more consoling pledge that it will be one day given to them to see the accomplishment of all the great and glorious promises that have been made to them in Jesus Christ than in the Assumption of Mary?

"Who is she who cometh up from the wilderness flowing with delights, leaning on her Beloved?" (Cant. viii. 5.) "This is she," writes St Peter Damian, "the Queen whom the daughters of Sion pronounced most blessed, and whom the princesses praised (Prov. xxxi. 28). She hath ascended to-day from the wilderness, that is, she has been raised from her lowliness in the world to the height of a royal throne, 'flowing with an abundance of delights;'—with an abundance of delights indeed, for 'many daughters have gathered together riches, but this one hath surpassed them all.' And, truly, her delights are without number, for as she receives the Holy Ghost, so she conceives the Son of God, gives birth to the King of glory, enters the heavens, and laden with riches and flowing with delights, she flees away to her eternal kingdom. 'Leaning upon her Beloved,' the Lord of hosts is the Father of her Beloved, in whom He was well-pleased. Upon Him, then, leans this most happy Mother, and reclining on the golden couch of the Divine Majesty, she reposes in the arms of her Spouse; yes, of her Son! Oh, how great the dignity, how special the power, to lean upon Him on whom the hosts of the angels reverently fix their gaze!" (St Peter Damian, Sermon on the Assumption).

"Rise up, O Lord, into Thy rest," says

the holy Psalmist, "Thou and the Ark of Thy Sanctification." "This Ark," writes Hesychius of Jerusalem, "can without doubt be no other than the Virgin Mother of God. For if Christ be the jewel, Mary is certainly its casket; if Jesus be the Sun, Mary is necessarily to be called the firmament; if He be the flower of immortality, the Blessed Virgin will of necessity be the stem which cannot wither, the garden that is ever-blooming" (Hesychius, Homily, § iii.)

But the Mystery of the Assumption, besides that it is one of the Glorious Mysteries of our faith, also contains a rich vein of consolation for our mortal pilgrimage, which it would be a sad want of gratitude and wisdom to fail in duly considering.

"It is appointed to all men," says St Paul, "once to die, and after that the judgment." Our mortal pilgrimage, be it long or be it short, terminates in death, from which there is no escape, as even all the heathen writers freely confess.

"O death!" says the son of Sirach, "how bitter is the remembrance of thee to a man that hath peace in his possessions, to a man that is at rest, and whose ways are prosperous in all things, and that is yet able to take meat!" (Ecclus. xli. 1); and then he goes on to say, "Fear not the sentence of death. Remember what things have been before thee, and what shall come after thee. This sentence is from the Lord upon all flesh." "Dust thou art, and unto dust shalt thou return," are the words in which God has conveyed His sentence; and by nature all men fear to die. "Charity, however," says the Canticle of Canticles, "is strong as death, and the blow which nature dreads, grace accepts, for death to the faithful Christian becomes the gate of an immortal life.

Thus St John Damascene writes, "Oh, wonder that truly surpasses the condition of nature! Oh thing full of marvel! Death, which once was hated and abhorred, is now a thing that is commended and pronounced blessed. That which once occasioned grief and mourning, tears and sorrow, is now a cause of gladness and joyful festivity. If it be asked how? Because that, to all the servants of God, whose death is said to be blessed, the termination of their life procures for them that they become fixed and confirmed in the favour of God; and for this reason their death is said to be happy and blest. For their death makes them perfected in bliss, gaining for them that their virtue is no longer subject to any change, according to the saying of Ecclesiasticus, 'Before death call no man blessed' (Ecclus. xi. 30); words, however, that are not to be understood of the Blessed Virgin. For thy blessedness, O Mary, came not to thee through death, neither was it thy passage from this world which fixed thy perfection nor placed thee in security; for the beginning of every good, its middle and end, thy perfect security and confirmation in truth was contained in thy miraculous conception, in the Divine indwelling, and thy immaculate childbirth; and hence, as thou hast thyself truly said, that all generations should call thee blessed, not from the moment of thy death, but from that of thy conception. Wherefore, it was not death which made thee happy, but it is thou who hast made death cheerful, inasmuch as thou hast taken away its bitterness, and hast changed it into a joy. For which reason thy sacred body was committed to religious burial, the angels partly surrounding and partly following in thy train, and omitting no kind of honour which it was befitting to show to the Mother of their Lord; the Apostles also, and the whole multitude of the Church, singing divinely-inspired hymns: 'He shall be filled with the good things of Thy house. Thy holy temple is wonderful in equity' (Ps. lxiv. 6.) And again, 'The Most High hath sanctified His tabernacle' (Ps. xlv. 5.) 'The mount of God is a fruitful mountain, a mountain in which it pleaseth Him to dwell' (Ps. lxvii. 17). The company of the Apostles taking thee up, the true Ark of God, as the priests formerly lifted up the typical ark, and laying thee in the tomb, brought thee, as it were, through another Jordan to the true land of promise, the Jerusalem that is above, the mother of all the faithful, whose maker and builder is

God. For thy soul did not go down to hell, neither did thy flesh see corruption. Neither was thy immaculate body, exempt as it had been from the least stain, left to remain in the earth, but thou wast translated to the royal throne of bliss in the heavens, — thou, their Queen, Lady, and Mistress, the true and very Mother of God" (St John Damascene, Sermon on the Assumption, § xii.)

CHAPTER IX.

SCRIPTURE TYPES OF THE FOURTH GLORIOUS MYSTERY.

I. THE VISIT OF THE QUEEN OF SABA TO KING SOLOMON.
II. THE RETURN OF JUDITH WITH THE HEAD OF HOLOFERNES.

1. *The Queen of Saba ascends to the Holy City to see the glory of Solomon, and to hear his wisdom.*

THE history of the coming of the Queen of Saba to Jerusalem is thus related in the Sacred Scripture :—" The Queen of Saba having heard of the fame of Solomon in the wisdom of the Lord, came to try him with hard questions. And entering into Jerusalem with a great train, and riches, and camels that carried spices, and an immense quantity of gold and precious stones, she came to King Solomon, and spoke to him all that she had in her heart. And Solomon informed her of all the things she proposed to him: there was not any word the king was ignorant of, and which he could not answer her. And when the Queen of Saba saw all the wisdom of Solomon, and the house which he had built, and the meat of his table, and the apartments of his servants, and the order of his ministers, and their apparel, and the cup-bearers, and the holocausts which he offered in the house of the Lord, she had no longer any spirit in her; and she said to the king: The report is true which I heard in my own country concerning thy words, and concerning thy wisdom. And I did not believe them that told me, till I came myself, and saw with my own eyes, and have found that the half hath not been told me; thy wisdom and thy works exceed the fame which I heard. Blessed are thy men, and blessed are thy servants, who stand before thee always and hear thy wisdom. Blessed be the Lord thy God, whom thou hast pleased, and who hath set thee upon the throne of Israel, because the Lord hath loved Israel for ever, and hath appointed thee king, to do judgment and justice. And she gave the king a hundred and twenty talents of gold, and of spices a very great store, and precious stones. There was brought no more such abundance of spices as these which the Queen of Saba gave to King Solomon" (3 Book of Kings x. 1).

"Ought it not to follow," writes St Bernard, "that in the same proportion as the heavenly city exults over the presence of Mary within it, in a like proportion this our lower world ought to deplore her absence. Yet, nevertheless, let all complaint on our part cease, for we have not here a continuing city, but we seek that one which the Blessed Mary has this day attained. In the which, if we are ourselves enrolled as citizens, it is doubtless fitting, even in our exile, and by the waters of Babylon, that we should recall it to memory, share in its joy, and participate in its gladness, and especially in that which, on this day, as it were, floods the city of God with so overflowing a stream of delight, that even we may feel the presence of the drops of joy distilling upon the earth. 'Our Queen has gone

The IV. Glorious Mystery.

The Old Testament Types of
Judith returns with the Head of Holofernes.
The Queen of Saba visits King Solomon.

LEGE · ES · IN · PROPHETIS
ECCE · ES · MATER · FILIUM · EIUS

THE WOMAN WHO CRUSHED THE HEAD OF THE ADVERSARY OF HER PEOPLE.

ROSA · MYSTICA · PASSIM · IN
AEDIFICATIO · ORA · PRO · NOBIS

THE VISIT TO BEHOLD THE WONDERS OF THE CITY AND TEMPLE OF GOD.

before us, she is gone before us, and has been so gloriously received, that her servants are able to follow courageously in the footsteps of their mistress, crying out: Draw us after thee, we will run after the sweet odour of thine ointments' (Cant. i. 3). Our land of sojourning has sent its Advocate before us, who, in the double character of Mother of the Judge and Mother of mercy, will suppliantly and yet effectively transact the business of our salvation" (St Bernard, Sermon i. on the Assumption, § 1).

The Blessed Mary, the sweet and gentle Advocate whom our land of sojourning has sent before us to the heavenly Jerusalem, affectionately calls all the banished children of Eve to lift up their eyes from the land of their exile to behold in spirit the glories of their true home. For she herself has been assumed thither, not merely to report and bear testimony to us of its glories, as the Queen of Saba bore testimony to the glories of the earthly Jerusalem, but by her prayers and intercession to aid us to accomplish our pilgrimage thither in safety. "Ye are not come," says St Paul, "to the mountain that might be touched, to a burning fire, a whirlwind, the darkness and storm. But you are come to Mount Sion, to the city of the living God, the heavenly Jerusalem, to the company of many thousands of angels, and to the Church of the First-born who are written in the heavens, and to God the judge of all, and to the spirits of the just made perfect, and to Jesus the Mediator of the New Testament, whose blood speaketh better things than the blood of Abel. See that you refuse not Him that speaketh" (Heb. xii. 18–22). "Blessed are thy men, and blessed are thy servants who stand before thee always and hear thy wisdom," is the report of the Queen of Saba of the earthly Jerusalem. And St Paul, who, had been also caught up into heaven, and who had seen the glories of the heavenly Jerusalem, bears testimony, "That eye hath not seen, neither hath the ear heard, nor hath it entered into the heart of man to conceive the good things that God has prepared for them that love Him" (1 Cor. ii. 9).

"There was brought no more such abundance of spices as these which the Queen of Saba gave to King Solomon." "O thou that dwellest in the gardens, make me to hear thy voice," says the Bridegroom in the Canticles, calling His beloved to himself; "and be like to the roe and to the young hart upon the mountains of aromatical spices" (Cant. viii. 14). From among the many who have been, equally with the Blessed Mary, citizens of the earthly Jerusalem, which now is in bondage with her children, and whom God has called to behold the glories of the heavenly Jerusalem, there is not one whose coming within the gates of the city has diffused around such an abundance of aromatical spices, as the triumphal entrance of the Virgin Mother of the King Himself. "For if," writes St Bernard, "the soul of the infant unborn melts within him as Mary speaks, what must have been the joy and exultation of the hosts of heaven, when they were first permitted to hear her voice, to behold her countenance, and to enjoy the happiness of her being present amongst them. Oh, who among us is able to picture to himself how gloriously the Queen of Heaven approached in procession the affectionate devotion with which the whole multitude of the hosts of heaven came forth to meet her, the canticles with which she was conducted to her throne, the calmness and serenity of countenance, the Divine embrace with which she was received by her Son, and by Him exalted above every creature, with the honour to which so august a Mother was entitled, and with the glory which became so great a Son! Of a truth, full of happiness as must have been the kisses which were impressed on the lips of the Infant as He lay in the virgin bosom of His Mother, yet must we not deem those happier still which she on this day received from the lips of Him who sitteth on the right hand of the Father, as she was ascending the throne of glory, singing her bridal hymn, and saying, 'Let Him kiss me with the kiss of His mouth?' Who is able to declare the generation of Christ, and the Assumption of Mary? For in the same manner as she was peerless while on earth in the graces which she received, so none can approach to the singular honour which is her portion in the heavens." Thus, "there were brought no more such abundance of spices as these which the Queen of Saba gave to King Solomon." "Behold," says the Blessed Mary, as she is assumed by the angels, "Behold, my Beloved speaketh to me, and saith, Arise, make haste, My love, My dove, My beautiful one, and come; the fig-tree hath put forth her green figs, the vines in flower yield their sweet smell. Arise, My love, My beautiful one, and come" (Cant. ii. 10).

2. *Judith ascends the mountain, and enters the gates of Bethulia, carrying the head of the enemy of her people in her hands, and as she shows it to them, she receives their praises and acclamations of joy.*

The following is the Scripture narrative describing Judith returning to her city with the head of Holofernes:—"And Judith from afar off cried to the watchmen upon the walls: Open the gates, for God is with us, who hath shown His power in Israel. And it came to pass, when the men had heard her voice, that they called the ancients of the city. And all ran to meet her, from the least to the greatest: for they now had no hopes that she would come. And lighting up lights, they gathered all round about her, and she went up to a higher place and commanded silence to be made. And when all had held their peace, Judith said: Praise ye the Lord our God, who hath not forsaken them that hope in Him. And by me, His handmaid, He hath fulfilled His mercy which He promised to the house of Israel, and He hath killed the enemy of His people by my hand this night. Then she brought forth the head of Holofernes out of the wallet, and showed it them, saying: Behold the head of Holofernes, the general of the army of the Assyrians, and behold the canopy where he lay in his drunkenness, where the Lord our God slew him by the hand of a woman" (Judith xiii. 13, &c.).

It was foretold by God in Paradise, "I will put enmities between thee and the woman, and thy seed and her seed; she shall crush thy head, and thou shalt lie in wait for her heel." And the victory which was there foretold as to be accomplished in the person of the Blessed Virgin Mother of Jesus Christ, is here prefigured in the person of Judith. "By thee He hath brought our enemies to nought," exclaimed all the citizens of Bethulia, as they beheld the head of Holofernes in the hands of Judith. "And when Vagao the chamberlain beheld the body of Holofernes lying upon the ground without the head, weltering in his blood, he cried out with a loud voice with weeping, and rent his garments; and going into the tent of Judith, and not finding her, he ran out to the people and said: One Hebrew woman hath wrought great confusion in the house of King Nabuchodonosor, for behold Holofernes lieth upon the ground, and his head is not upon him" (Judith xiv. 16). Judith in her victory is universally understood to be typical of the Blessed Virgin, and in the recent office of the Immaculate Conception in the Roman breviary, the words of the citizens of Bethulia and their acclamations in honour of her victory are applied to her in a figure. "This day the Lord hath so magnified thy name, that thy praise shall never depart from the mouth of men." As also those of the high priest Joachim, and the elders of the people who came from Jerusalem to greet her and said, "Thou art the glory of Jerusalem, thou art the joy of Israel, thou art the honour of our people."

Judith's work in behalf of her people, however, was not limited solely to crushing the head of their enemy; she also wisely directed the assault of her people upon the hosts of the discomfited chieftain, whose head had fallen by her hand. "Judith said to all the people: Hear me; hang ye up this head upon the walls, and rush down as if making an assault;

the watchmen must then needs run to awake their prince for the battle; and when the princes shall run to the tent of Holofernes, and shall find him wallowing in his blood, fear shall fall upon them, and when you shall know that they are fleeing, go after them securely, for the Lord will destroy them under your feet" (Judith xiv. 1–5).

"Who is this," says the Canticle of Canticles, "that cometh forth bright as the morning rising, fair as the moon, bright as the sun, terrible as an army set in battle array?" (Cant. vi. 9). Mary our Queen has not only crushed the head of our adversary the old serpent, but she is ever with the Church, marshalling and leading the hosts of Israel to the battle against his princes and the captains of his hosts. What is there of all that is done in the Church for destroying the works of the old serpent, and for building up the kingdom of God and His Christ, which Mary does not either direct by her counsel, or aid and sustain by her intercession? One branch indeed of the warfare against the kingdom of darkness, the destruction of heresies, is especially under her leadership; as the Church sings—

"Rejoice and be glad, O Virgin Mary!
For thou alone hast destroyed all heresies in the whole world."

The Fifth Glorious Mystery of the Rosary

CHAPTER X.

THE CORONATION OF THE BLESSED VIRGIN MARY, AND THE JOY OF ALL THE SAINTS.

A PASSAGE FROM THE APOCALYPSE OF ST JOHN.

"After these things I heard as it were the voice of much people in heaven, saying: Alleluia! Salvation and glory and power is to our God. And I heard as it were the voice of a great multitude, and as the voice of many waters, and as the voice of great thunders, saying, Alleluia! for the Lord our God the Almighty hath reigned. Let us be glad and rejoice and give glory to Him: for the marriage of the Lamb is come, and His wife hath prepared herself. And it is granted to her that she should clothe herself with fine linen, glittering and white. For the fine linen are the justifications of saints. And He said to me: Write: Blessed are they that are called to the marriage-supper of the Lamb. And He saith to me: These words of God are true" (Apoc. xix.)

The circle of the Fifteen Mysteries of the Rosary terminates in presenting to

The Fifth Glorious Mystery.

Ave Maria Gratia Plena Dominus Tecum

Si inveni gratiam in oculis tuis, O Rex, . . . dona mihi populum meum pro quo obsecro. (*Esther* vii. 3.)

If I have found grace in thine eyes, O king, ... give me my people for whom I intercede. (*Esther* vii. 3.)

Benedicta tu in mulieribus et Benedictus fructus ventris tui Jesus.

Habuit que gratiam et misericordiam coram eo super omnes mulieres, et posuit diadema regni in capite ejus. (*Esther* ii. 17.)

And she had grace and mercy in his sight before all women, and he set the diadem of the kingdom on her head. (*Esther* ii. 17.)

THE CORONATION OF THE BLESSED VIRGIN MARY

our minds a picture of the humble maiden of Israel who has been raised to the dignity of the Queen of Heaven, receiving an eternal diadem from the hands of her Divine Son, in the midst of the jubilee and acclamations of the whole assembled court of angels and saints; and in so doing, it displays before our thoughts a vision of the rest and glory which we are invited to share, by faithfully persevering in the true path of a Christian life unto the end.

"I am Alpha and Omega," says Jesus in the Apocalypse, " the first and the last, the beginning and the end. Blessed are they that wash their robes in the blood of the Lamb: that they may have a right to the tree of life, and may enter in by the gates into the city. Without are dogs, and sorcerers, and unchaste, and murderers, and servers of idols, and every one that loveth and maketh a lie. I, Jesus, have sent my angel, to testify to you these things in the Churches. I am the root and stock of David, the bright and morning Star. And the Spirit and the Bride say : Come. And he that heareth, let him say : Come. And he that thirsteth, let him come : and he that will, let him take of the water of life without price " (Apoc. xxii. 13).

"If in this life only we have hope in Christ," says St Paul, "we are of all men most miserable" (1 Cor. xv. 19). "For I think," as he says elsewhere, "that God has set forth us Apostles, the last as it were, men appointed to death; we are made a spectacle to the world, to angels and to men. We are fools for Christ's sake; we are weak, we are without honour. Even to this hour we both hunger and thirst, and are naked, are buffeted, and have no fixed abode. We labour, working with our own hands: we are reviled, and we bless ; we are persecuted, and we suffer it; we are blasphemed, and we entreat; we are made as the refuse of this world, the offscouring of all even until now" (1 Cor. iv. 9). St Paul here seeks no refuge whatever in any species of illusion as to the easiness of the course through which God has called him to earn for himself a share in the glory and blessedness which is shown, as it were, in a vision to the faithful, dispersed over the whole face of the earth, in the last Glorious Mystery of the Rosary. He diligently places before his own mind the true nature of the reward that is held out to him, and he leaves God Himself to determine the amount of labour and suffering which he must undergo in order to win his reward. Whether that which he is called to go through on earth be better entitled to the name of " easy" than of " difficult," never for a moment forms a question in the Apostle's mind; his course lies before him, and his mind harbours but one thought how to accomplish it. " Forgetting those things that are behind," he says, " and stretching forth myself to those things that are before, I press toward the goal, to the prize of the heavenly calling of God in Christ Jesus" (Phil. iii. 13). So said also the Lord Himself : " I have a baptism (that of His own blood) wherewith I am to be baptized, and how am I straitened until it be accomplished !" (Luke xii. 50.) St Paul, however, reveals to us the manner in which even the Lord Himself was sustained in bearing the burden with which He acknowledges Himself to be straitened : " Looking unto Jesus, the Author and Finisher of faith, who having joy set before Him, endured the Cross, despising the shame, and now sitteth at the right hand of God" (Heb. xii. 2).

So it had ever been from the ancient days. " For they that say these things," says St Paul, speaking of the Patriarchs, "do signify that they seek a country. And truly if they had been mindful of that from whence they came out, doubtless they had time to return. But now they desire a better, that is to say, a heavenly country; therefore God is not ashamed to be called their God, for He hath prepared for them a city. Moses, when he grew up, preferred to be afflicted with the people of God, rather than to have the pleasure of sin for a season, esteeming the reproach of Christ greater riches than the treasure of the Egyptians." His motive for this being, as St Paul states, that "he looked unto the reward." Again, Moses feared not the fierceness of the king, "for he endured," St Paul says, " as seeing the Invisible."

"And what shall I yet say?" continues St Paul; "for the time would fail me to tell of Gedeon, Barac, Samson, Jephthe, David, Samuel, and the prophets, who by faith conquered kingdoms, wrought justice, obtained promises, stopped the mouths of lions, quenched the violence of fire, escaped the edge of the sword, recovered strength from weakness, became valiant in battle, put to flight the armies of foreigners: women received their dead raised to life again. But others were racked, not accepting deliverance, that they might find a better resurrection. And others had trial of mockeries and stripes, moreover also of bands and prisons. They were stoned, they were cut asunder, they were tempted, they were put to death by the sword, they wandered about in sheepskins, in goat-skins, being in want, distressed, afflicted: of whom the world was not worthy; wandering in deserts, in mountains, and in dens, and in caves of the earth. And all these being approved by the testimony of faith, received not the promises; God providing some better thing for us, that they should not be perfected without us" (Heb. xi.)

According, then, to the inspired Apostle, not only all who were before Christ, and who saw the promises only by the testimony of faith, went through their appointed course, "looking unto the reward," but Christ Himself also set the same example in His own person for His Church for all ages, to the intent that each Christian soul should in this mortal pilgrimage learn to accept at the hands of God the appointed burden, and bear it, looking for the reward, following the pattern of the Lord of all, 'and turning his eyes to Him "who, having joy set before Him endured the Cross, despising the shame, and now sitteth for ever at the right hand of God." And that the Apostle himself fully understood it to be the wisdom and duty of the Christian in this mortal pilgrimage incessantly to set before his mind the example of his Master and the nature of the reward promised, is beyond all question plain from his words, and more plain than ever from his mode of life. "For I reckon," he says, "that the sufferings of this present time, are not worthy to be compared to the glory to come that shall be revealed in us" (Rom. viii. 18). And again, "For that which is at present momentary and light in our tribulation, worketh for us above measure exceedingly an eternal weight of glory, while we look not at the things which are seen, but at the things which are not seen; for the things which are seen are temporal, but the things which are not seen are eternal" (2 Cor. iv. 17, 18). And at the close of his life, which had been spent "in labours more abundantly than they all," in order to earn the reward for which he looked, the Apostle says, "I am even now ready to be sacrificed, and the time of my dissolution is at hand. I have fought a good fight, I have finished my course, I have kept the faith. As to the rest, there is laid up for me a crown of justice, which the Lord the just Judge will render me in that day: and not only to me, but to them also that love His coming" (2 Tim. iv. 6).

Thus, to sum up what has been said, the example of the servants of God, who saw the promises by faith afar off, the words and example of the Lord Himself, who died upon the Cross; the words and example of St Paul, and the other apostles; to which may be added the examples and the doctrine of the saints and martyrs of the Church, all conspire to impress upon the mind of the Christian this deeply important practical truth, that the Christian life upon earth is a pilgrimage and a service, in which for the present God measures both the duration and the amount of burden that each one is required to bear, and in which for the future, as the just Judge, He will apportion His reward according to the measure of faithfulness and perseverance which He may find in His servant.

The concluding Mystery of the Rosary, the Coronation of the Blessed Virgin and the joy of all the saints, then renders the Christian the invaluable service of bidding him contemplate and fix his mind upon the glory and the joy that is set before him. It stirs up the spirit of the Christian warrior within him to fight the good fight of faith, by forcibly turning his gaze to the "Mount Sion, the city of the living

God, the heavenly Jerusalem, the company of many thousands of angels, and to the Church of the first-born, who are written in the heavens." He has been called into the army of Christian warriors, that he may be found worthy to form one of this holy and blessed company. He has been marked in his forehead with the sign and seal of its King; he has commenced his pilgrimage and engaged in its service; but he finds that he cannot proceed in his course without fighting the good fight of faith. Surely, then, in the presence of the most glorious vision of the Coronation of the Queen, such an one cannot fail to say to himself: I am a soldier of Jesus Christ, and warfare is the life of a soldier. The city of the living God, the heavenly Jerusalem, an eternal place among the company of the many thousands of angels who have rejoiced to behold Mary the Mother of God crowned as their Queen, is clearly a prize worth a soldier's attempt to win, the unspeakable glory of the victory must be worth the fight to obtain it. Moreover, the joys of the glorious heavenly city cannot but be unspeakably great. " Eye hath not seen," says the Scripture, "ear hath not heard, neither hath it entered into the heart of man to conceive of the good things which God hath prepared for them that love Him" (1 Cor. ii. 9). As a Christian I bear the name of One who, having joy set before Him, endured the Cross, despising the shame, and now sitteth at the right hand of God. I will then strive to follow His example; I cannot do less. I will bear the burden that He is pleased to assign to me; and so having joy set before me, I will go forward on my way bearing indeed my burden, but nevertheless glorying and rejoicing in spirit, as remembering the words of the Holy Ghost speaking to me in the Psalm, and saying, " They that sow in tears shall reap in joy. They went forth on their way and wept, scattering their seed. But returning they shall come with joyfulness, carrying their sheaves with them" (Ps. cxxv. 6).

As it is but natural to suppose, the joys of the glorious "Coronation of the Blessed Virgin" form so constant a theme of praise in the writings of the Fathers of the Church, that there could be no difficulty in making a large selection from their writings. But where the well is so deep, and where the utmost extent of selection here practicable would unavoidably present only a mutilated and inadequate picture of what the Fathers have written, we may be pardoned for being satisfied with but a single extract, which may serve as a sample of the kind of treasures with which the sacred writings of the Church abound.

"Among the chief festivals of the Saints, my beloved brethren," writes St Ildephonsus of Toledo, " this day's great and glorious solemnity of Mary, the Mother of God, has dawned upon us, on which the ever Venerable and Blessed Virgin Mary was assumed to the courts of heaven, where, as we sing, "the King of kings, the Son of the Blessed Virgin Mary, sits upon His starry throne," where thousands of thousands of angels minister unto Him, and ten thousand times ten thousand stand around Him; in the midst of whose praises and acclamations the glorious Mother of God was on this day exalted from the earth, carried up in triumph and exultation, received into heaven, and placed in Paradise. This, my brethren, is that sacred and venerable solemnity, which was foreknown indeed, and foreordained before the formation of the world, but only on this day accomplished. To us, indeed, dearest brethren, it is an annual solemnity specially celebrated upon this day, while to the angels and the citizens of the heavenly city it is continuous and perpetual. For the very reason, however, that to us in our present condition the festival cannot be perpetual, it ought to be celebrated with so much the greater solemnity above all other festivals of the saints, inasmuch as to the Mother of the Lord belongs the gift of a perpetual virginity, and other ineffable privileges. For if, according to the Apostle, Christ the Lord, the just Judge, gives rewards to every one according to his works, in like manner, as that which was born from Her has nothing with which it can be compared, and as the gift which she has received is one that is unspeakable, how shall He not give to this most sacred Virgin, His own Mother, a glory and reward that knows no equal, and that is incapable of being estimated or comprehended. I do not say a reward among other sacred virgins, but such a reward as she alone has deserved, above the whole and entire universe of the saints. For she came blessed and glorious to the palace of heaven, where Christ the Bridegroom of the Church came forth to meet her, and placed her in the bridal chamber on the right hand of the Majesty on high. For thither hath He assumed her, the first in dignity among His elect, where, according to the words of David, the QUEEN stands at the right hand of God, in a vesture of gold girt about with divers colours.

"Without doubt, therefore, my dearest brethren, the Blessed Virgin now sits raised in glory upon her throne in virtue of her unspeakable grace and dignity as Mother of the King. For Daniel testifies that thrones were set in heaven, and that 'the Ancient of days sat' (Dan. vii. 9), without ever saying that their numbers were filled up. From which, as also from the number of assessors that are to sit with Him when the Son of this most sacred Virgin shall sit on the throne of His Majesty, it clearly appears that the throne of this most Blessed Virgin, which was prepared before the foundation of the world, must on this day have been raised higher in glory, and have become an object of veneration to all the Angels; and not without just reason, for she herself had been made the throne and resting-place of God, descending into whose sacred womb, the Wisdom of God the Father had been made flesh and had dwelt among us" (St Ildephonsus, Sermon on the Assumption).

As the proper fruit of meditating upon the glories of the heavenly kingdom, as we are taught to do in the Fifth Glorious Mystery, where the Blessed Mary sits as Queen at the right hand of Jesus Christ, her Divine Son, in the midst of rejoicing saints and angels, will be to fill the mind with a longing desire to taste the joys of that blessed company, we may conclude our volume with the following appropriate spiritual counsel of Thomas à Kempis: "Son, when thou perceivest the longing for eternal blessedness to be poured over thee from above, and thou desirest to go forth from the tabernacle of the body that thou mayest contemplate my brightness without shadow of changing, enlarge thine heart, and receive this holy inspiration with all the eagerness of thy soul. Render most ample thanks to the heavenly goodness which deals with thee after so princely a manner, visits thee so mercifully, inflames thee so lovingly, lifts thee up so powerfully, lest thou shouldst fall to the earth by thine own weight. Think not that it is by thought or endeavour of thine that thou comest to receive these things, but they come to thee solely through favour of the heavenly grace and the goodness of God, in order that thou mayest make greater advances in virtue and in humility, and prepare thyself for future trials, and that thou shouldst study to cleave to Me with the whole affection of thy heart, and to serve ME with a fervent mind.

"I know thy desire, and I have heard thy frequent sighs. Already thou wouldst wish to be in the liberty of the glory of the sons of God. The house of eternity and the heavenly country full of joy delights thee, but the hour is not as yet come. The present time is of another sort, a time of war, of labour, and of trial. Thou wouldst fain be filled with the highest good, but thou canst not have this now. I am He. Wait for Me, saith the Lord, until the kingdom of God shall come" (Book iii. ch. xlix.)

THE V. GLORIOUS MYSTERY.
Queen Esther intercedes for her people.

LEGE · E∴ · IN · PROPHETIS

EUM · FILIUM

THE INTERCESSION WHICH SAVES THE PEOPLE FROM DEATH.

THE OLD TESTAMENT TYPES OF
Queen Esther receives the Diadem of the Kingdom.

ROSA · MYSTICA · PASSIM · IN

SION · ORA · PRO · NOBIS

THE MAIDEN OF LOW ESTATE EXALTED TO THE CROWN OF THE KINGDOM.

CHAPTER XI.

SCRIPTURE TYPES OF THE FIFTH GLORIOUS MYSTERY.

I. THE ELEVATION OF THE HUMBLE VIRGIN ESTHER TO THE IMPERIAL THRONE OF THE PERSIAN EMPIRE.
II. ESTHER, RAISED TO THE THRONE, USES HER QUEENLY POWER TO SAVE HER PEOPLE BY HER INTERCESSION.

1. *The elevation of the Virgin Esther from a low estate to be Queen of the Persian Empire.*

THE especial charm of the beautiful figure with which we bring to a conclusion our series of types, taken from the former Covenant of God, as shadowing the mysteries of the New Christian Covenant, is by no means limited to the singular completeness of the parallel, in which, so far as things terrestrial can be compared with things celestial, the history of Esther appears almost an anticipation of that of Mary. It may much rather be taken to consist in the consoling light which it throws on the great characteristic of the Divine dealings with men, which we cannot understand too clearly—namely, that in every act of the Divine choice, whereby God exalts particular persons to high honour and dignity, there is contained the purpose, that the persons so chosen are to be ministers, in a corresponding degree, of great mercies and benefits to their fellows. The higher the dignity to which God raises any one of His intelligent creatures, the greater the service He requires the person so exalted to render to his or her compeers. And as God could raise no created intelligence, whether human or angelic, to a higher dignity than that which gives to Mary the indescribably marvellous right to say to one of the Divine Persons of the ever-blessed Trinity, Son, so God has intended Mary to become, in consequence of her exaltation, the minister in a corresponding degree of such great and wonderful mercies and benefits to all her fellow creatures, as would not have been otherwise given to them. The higher the dignity and the more signal the honour, the greater the mercies and the more wonderful the benefits which God has designed shall therein accrue to His creation through the person invested with them. To rejoice, therefore, in the glorious exaltation of the ever-blessed Virgin, Mother of God, as the Fifth Glorious Mystery of the Rosary teaches us to do, is thus, in another sense, to be taught to praise and bless God for the wonderful depth of the love and mercy which He has shown to us in it; there being, as we must ever be careful to bear in mind, an indefeasible connection between the supreme honour and exaltation which the humble Virgin of Juda has received, and the mercies and benefits which this very honour at once both enables and also pledges her to procure for us.

Thus St Bernard says, "Consider most deeply with what an affection of devotion God has willed that she should be honoured by us, when He has placed the fulness of every good in Mary, so that if there is in us any hope, any grace, anything of salvation, we may know that it flows to us from her, who herself 'came up flowing with delights,' a very garden of sweets, over which not only did the Divine south wind blow, but penetrated through and through, so that its sweet perfumes were made to flow and flow over on all sides; that is, her excellent gifts and graces. Take away the orb of the sun which gives light to this world, and where have you the day? Take away Mary, this Star of the sea, the great and mighty sea, and what have we left but clouds and thick darkness and the shadow of death" (Sermon on the Nativity).

It is precisely this beautiful truth, that

the exaltation of the Blessed Mary is for us and for our benefit, which shines throughout the type and figure of Queen Esther, and her singular providential exaltation to the imperial throne of the Persian Empire, and forms, as we may say, its pre-eminent charm and instructiveness. "Who knows," as Mardocheus pleaded with Esther, "that thou art not therefore come to the kingdom, that thou mightest be ready for such a time as this?" (Esther iv. 14). Who that believes will not exult in the inmost depths of his heart, and rejoice with all his might that it has pleased God to make choice of the lowly and humble Virgin of Nazareth, and to place her upon a throne at His own right hand, crowned with the crown of a kingdom of which there is no end, a kingdom that rules supreme and uncontested over angels and archangels, cherubim and seraphim, and the whole universe of the intelligent creatures of God, on the underderstanding that she is at all times to be ready to use all her marvellous power and dignity to plead with the better effect on behalf of the wants and sufferings of the exiled children of Eve?

The history of Queen Esther, as it may be briefly related from the Sacred Scripture, is as follows:—It happened in the empire of the Medes and Persians, in the reign of Assuerus (Artaxerxes Longimanus, of the Greek historians), that Vashti the queen gave such great offence to the king and his princes, that they all with one mind advised that she should be deposed. She accordingly was deposed, and a number of the most beautiful maidens were brought together from various parts of the empire, in order that from among them, the king might select his queen to take the place of Vashti. Among these maidens there was one Esther, a niece of Mardocheus, a Jewess of the captivity of Nabuchodonosor, and she was beautiful beyond all belief, and most gracious and amiable in the eyes of all. She was brought to the chamber of the king, on the tenth month which is called Tebeth, in the seventh year of his reign. And the king loved her above all the other women, and placed the diadem of the kingdom on her head, and caused her to reign in the place of Vashti. And on the occasion of the coronation of his queen, he gave rest to all the provinces of his kingdom, and distributed gifts with princely profusion.

2. Queen Esther uses her royal power of intercession to save her own people, and to crush the head of their adversary.

The circumstances which called Queen Esther's power of intercession into play, to save her own people and crush the head of their adversary, were as follows:—About the time of her coronation, one Aman an Amalekite was taken so highly into the king's favour, that all the princes and servants of the king bent their knees and did homage to Aman, for so the king had commanded them. Mardocheus alone did not bend the knee. Aman was so filled with indignation at this, that he counted it as nothing to lay hands on Mardocheus alone, but hearing that he was of the nation of the Jews, he chose to destroy all the Jews that were in the empire.

For this end he went to the king, and speaking against the Jews as a people that had laws different from all other people, and who were noted for being rebellious against kings, he obtained from the king a decree, authorising that on the thirteenth day of the twelfth month, the people of the empire should everywhere rise up and massacre the Jews, and make a spoil of their goods. Couriers were sent out with letters to this effect, and the decree was hung up in Susa, the king and Aman feasting together, and all the Jews that were in the city weeping.

Mardocheus at once bethought himself of their resource in Queen Esther's intercession, and sent to her intelligence of what had come to pass. Queen Esther answered, that he must know that it would be death to her to go into the inner palace to the king, except the king should hold out the golden sceptre in token of clemency; and that she had not been called to the king for thirty days. But Mardocheus insisted, and said, "Do not think that thou shalt save thine own life only because thou art in the king's house above all other Jews, for if thou shouldst keep silence, the Jews shall be delivered by some other way, and thou and the house of thy father shall perish. AND WHO KNOWS WHETHER THOU ART NOT THEREFORE COME TO THE KINGDOM THAT THOU MIGHTEST BE READY FOR SUCH A TIME AS THIS?" Queen Esther replied, that she would expose herself to danger and death for her people, but that Mardocheus must not fail to gather all the Jews of Susa together to offer up prayers for her for three days. On the third day, Esther having herself fasted and prayed, attired herself, and trembling as she went, presented herself to the king. The king seeing her pale with terror, extended the golden sceptre, saying, "What hast thou, Esther? I am thy brother, be not afraid, thou shalt not die. For not for thee, but for all others has this law been made. Come hither, and touch the sceptre." And kissing her, he said, "Why dost thou not speak to me?" Esther then asked the king to come with Aman to a banquet which she had prepared, to which he punctually came, bringing Aman with him.

In the meantime, other events were ripening. Aman had at the advice of his friends constructed a gibbet fifty cubits high, intending to obtain an order of the king that Mardocheus should be hanged upon it. But as he went into the king to obtain the order, he was to his dismay commanded to go before Mardocheus, arrayed in royal robes, leading his horse, and crying out, "Thus shall be honoured the man whom the king delighteth to honour." Aman did not dare to disobey, and when he had done as the king commanded, he went to his house mourning, and having his head covered. Now the Queen had not thought the time fully come to prefer her request at her first banquet, but had asked the king to come with Aman to a second banquet, and it was now time for Aman to go with the king to it. At this banquet, when the king, warm with wine, had asked the queen what was her petition, Esther said, "If I have found favour in thy sight, O king, and if it please thee, give me my life for which I ask, and my people for whom I request. For we are given up, I and my people, to be destroyed, to be slain, and to perish. And would God that we were sold for bondmen and bondwomen, the evil might be borne with, and I would have mourned in silence; but now we have an enemy whose cruelty redoundeth against the king." And the king said, "Who is this, and of what power that he should do these things?" And Esther said, "It is this Aman that is our adversary and most wicked enemy!"

In vain, after these words of the queen, did Aman fall on his knees before her to beg for mercy. The servants of the king covered his face and hurried him off to hang him on the gibbet which he had made ready for Mardocheus. Queen Esther, after this again, fell before the king, and implored that letters might be written and sent off, reversing the former letters against the Jews which Aman had obtained. Her intercession prevailed, and when the danger to the Jews was over, Mardocheus and Esther wrote letters to the Jews that the 14th and 15th of the month Adar should be kept with solemn honour, for a perpetual remembrance as holy days, for on those days the Lord had turned their sorrow into mirth and joy, through the prayer, that is, of Esther the queen, the type of the Blessed Mary, both in her exaltation and in her powerful intercession.

"O glorious Virgin!" is St Anselm's prayer, "who didst submit to death, but couldst not be bound by the bands of death, for thou, Virgin though thou art, wast the Mother of Him who was the Death of death and the Conqueror of the grave; aid me by thy death and the joys of thy Assumption into heaven, that I may spend the remainder of my life by thy help in faith unfeigned, and happily accomplish the end of my life, prostrate with tears to the earth in sackcloth and ashes, in the penitent confession of my sins, and, what is of still greater moment, in the confession of the name of Christ, in the receiving of His body and blood, and in the commends-tion of my spirit into the hands of His mercy. Pray for me, O holy Mother of God! that I who, conscious of a multitude of sins, look forward in fear and trembling to stand before the tribunal of Thy Son, may, through thy venerable intercession, rejoice, to be cleansed from all my transgressions by a true compunction of heart, and the grace of a devout confession obtained through thee. May my soul be never again stained with the stain of sin, but through the merits of thy most healing Nativity, Annunciation, thy most holy virgin maternity, most chaste purification, and most glorious Assumption, may I obtain to be presented with a clean heart and a chaste body in the lofty palace of heaven, where thou dost gloriously rejoice, Queen of angels and of men, and Mother of our Lord Jesus Christ. Help me in my transgressions, O Mother of mercy! by obtaining through thy Virgin prayers, the pardon of my sins from thy sweet Son Jesus Christ, who, with the Father and the Holy Spirit, liveth and reigneth, one God, blessed for ever, world without end" (St Anselm's Prayers, No. lx.)

"O Mother of my God, and my Lady Mary!" is the prayer of another holy saint and Doctor of the Universal Church, "as a beggar all wounded and sore presents himself before a great queen, so do I present myself before thee, who art the Queen of Heaven and Earth. From the lofty throne on which thou sittest, disdain not, I implore thee, to cast thine eyes upon me, a poor sinner. God has made thee so rich that thou mightest assist the poor, and has constituted thee Queen of mercy in order that thou mightest relieve the miserable. Behold me, then, and pity me! behold me, and abandon me not until thou seest me changed from a sinner into a saint. I know well that I merit nothing; nay, more, that I deserve on account of my ingratitude to be deprived of the graces which through thy means I have already received from God. But thou, who art the Queen of mercy, seekest not merits but miseries, in order to help the needy. Now, who is more needy than I?" (St Alphonsus Liguori, Glories of Mary, ch. i. § 1.)

Printed in the United States
135770LV00006B/109/A